CW01190635

That Greece Might Yet be Free

The mountains look on Marathon—
And Marathon looks on the sea;
And musing there an hour alone,
I dream'd that Greece might yet be free
For, standing on the Persians' grave,
I could not deem myself a slave.

Must we but weep o'er days more blest?
Must we but blush?—Our fathers bled.
Earth! render back from out thy breast
A remnant of our Spartan dead!
Of the three hundred grant but three,
To make a new Thermopylae.

Byron, *The Isles of Greece*

That Greece Might Yet be Free
The Struggle for Greek Independence from the
Ottoman Turks
ILLUSTRATED

The War of Greek Independence
1821 to 1833

W. Alison Phillips

With a Short Historical Record of the
Battle of Navarino
by Herbert Russell

LEONAUR

That Greece Might Yet be Free
The Struggle for Greek Independence from the Ottoman Turks
ILLUSTRATED
The War of Greek Independence 1821 to 1833
by W. Alison Phillips
With a Short Historical Record of the Battle of *Navarino*
by Herbert Russell

FIRST EDITION

Leonaur is an imprint of Oakpast Ltd
Copyright in this form © 2017 Oakpast Ltd

ISBN: 978-1-78282-592-0 (hardcover)
ISBN: 978-1-78282-593-7 (softcover)

http://www.leonaur.com

Publisher's Notes

The views expressed in this book are not necessarily those of the publisher.

Contents

Preface	7
Effect of the Ottoman Conquest	9
Hope of Russian Support	18
Massacres at Galatz and Yassy	24
The Beginning of Hostilities	31
Anarchy in Greece	49
Fall of the Acropolis	56
First Civil War	72
The Second Civil War	86
Insurrection in Crete	96
Siege of Navarino	106
The Siege of Missolonghi	114
Defeat of the Greeks Before Athens	126
Successes of the Greeks	138
Treaty of London	145
The Battle of Navarino	153
Policy of Wellington	162
Piracy in the Ægean	169
Greek Naval Operations	177

Indignation of the Greeks	184
Anglo-Austrian Entente	191
Intervention of the Russian Admiral	201
The Approach of the Crisis	210
Civil War	218
Conclusion	229
Navarino *By Herbert Russell*	238

Preface

This little book makes no pretence to be the result of original research, nor does it aspire to compete with the more elaborate works which have already appeared on the same subject. In offering it to the public, my aim has been to make more generally accessible a chapter of modern history which recent events have invested with a new interest; and I am not without hope that the following pages may be of some use in helping those, who have no time or opportunity for an extended study of the Greek question, to form a clearer judgment upon the matters at issue.

For the materials on which this volume is based I am mainly indebted to Mendelssohn-Bartholdy's *Geschichte Griechenlands*, &c. (vols. xv. and xx. of C. Biedermann's *Staatengeschichte der neuesten Zeit*), Finlay's *History of the Greek Revolution* (2 vols. 1861), Gordon's *History of the Greek Revolution* (2 vols. 1832), and Prokesch-Osten's *Geschichte des Abfalls der Griechen vom Türkischen Reich*. Baron von Prokesch-Osten's work is interesting as an elaborate and able apology for Prince Metternich's Eastern policy. It is especially valuable for its detailed account of the diplomatic developments of the Eastern Question during the ten years of the War of Independence; and, of its six volumes, four are devoted to the publication of the full texts of the treaties, protocols, and diplomatic correspondence on which the work is based. The more important of the treaties and protocols will also be found in full in Professor Holland's *The European Concert and the Eastern Question*.

Of the other books which I have used, I will only refer here to M. Alfred Lemaître's *Musulmans et Chrétiens: Notes sur la Guerre de l'Independance Grecque* (Paris, 1895), from which I have occasionally quoted. This little book was issued by its author as a counterblast to the Armenian agitation, and is intended as an apology for the Turk, and an indictment of the Oriental Christian. M. Lemaïtre, however, damages a strong case by his extreme partisanship. The facts he gives are true enough; but he carefully omits all those that would tell against his case. This is perhaps only repaying the more fanatical Philhellenes in their own coin; but it is a method of controversy for which it is impossible to feel much sympathy.

My hope is that, whatever fault may be justly found with the following pages, the charge of partisanship at least may not be proved against their author.

W. Alison Phillips.

September 1897.

Chapter 1
Effect of the Ottoman Conquest

Once more the Greek has measured his strength with the Turk, and once more the passionate cry of the Hellenes for the fulfilment of their national aspirations has, in spite of the unfriendly attitude of the Governments and of the warnings of experienced statesmen, awakened sympathetic echoes throughout Europe. This Philhellenic enthusiasm is an instinct rather than a deliberate conviction. Europe, educated for centuries in an almost religious reverence for antique culture, cannot forget the debt which she owes to the land which was the birthplace of her sciences and the cradle of her arts. In vain it is pointed out that, after the changes and chances of twenty centuries, the modern Greeks have little in common with the race of Pericles and Plato. In vain has grievous disillusion followed the high hopes which greeted the foundation of the Hellenic kingdom.

The mountains look on Marathon,
And Marathon looks on the sea,

.... and the imagination of Europe is still fired with Byron's dream of a Hellas on whose soil, freed from the blighting rule of the barbarian, the arts and sciences shall once more flourish in their ancient glory. An idle dream, perhaps, which should have no place in serious politics. Yet a wide-spread sentiment, however empty, is not a factor which the statesman can neglect with impunity. Metternich did so, and the whole fabric of his policy, laboriously built up on the most approved lines of Machiavellian state-craft, collapsed at the first strong breath of the *pathos* he affected to despise.

The question of the historical continuity of the Hellenic race is, then, of more than mere academic interest, and enters to no slight degree into the domain of practical politics. It played an important, even an exaggerated, part in the history of the first Greek revolt, and even now, when the Hellenic cause is more commonly associated in the public mind with that of the oppressed oriental Christian races in general, it has no small influence upon opinion. What then is the truth?

On the one hand it is urged that the conquest and reconquest of Greece, the manifold migrations of the northern nations during the middle ages, must have completely obliterated the pure Hellenic race, and that the so-called Hellenes of today are, in fact, a mixed breed of Albanian, Slavonic, and Latin origin, with but a slight tincture of Greek blood. On the other hand, it is urged that no nation, if we except the Jews, has ever been so tenacious of its individuality. Conquered again and again, Hellenism, vanquished in arms, ever retaliated by a bloodless victory over its conquerors. Macedonians and Romans in turn, while placing Greece under their political yoke, themselves submitted to the empire of Hellenic culture; and though, with the decay of the ancient civilisation, this culture gradually faded away, all the evidence tends to prove that the Greeks, more than any other nation of modern Europe, have succeeded in assimilating those numerous foreign elements which must, in the confusion of troubled centuries, have become intermingled with them.

The capture of Constantinople, in 1453, by Mahomed the Second would indeed seem to have crushed the last remnant of Greek nationality. Already the barbarian invasions had, for centuries, been gradually driving what survived of Hellenic culture within the walls of the capital. But now the collapse of the last bulwark of the ancient civilisation produced a result far other than had been expected; for it was the dispersal of the Greek scholars, which followed the fall of Constantinople, that led directly to the great revival of Hellenism which is known to us as the Renaissance: a movement itself destined, in modern times, to react, through their literary leaders, on the Hellenes.

For the time indeed, among the Greeks themselves, the last frayed cord that bound them to the classical tradition was snapped. They survived as a people: but the tie which united them was not the memory of their ancient greatness, but that of their common religion, an influence all the stronger and more effective because their conquerors were of an alien faith. In most of the other parts of Europe the barbarian invaders had been converted to the faith of the nations they conquered, and had gradually intermingled with the subject populations to produce nationalities of an entirely new type. The Mohammedan conquerors, disdaining to mix with the *rayahs*, the subject races, have by their very exclusiveness served to maintain the national characteristics of the Christian peoples they subdued, except, of course, in those instances where they succeeded in imposing their own faith upon the conquered.

The tie then which, after 1453, bound together the scattered Greek communities was the organisation of the Orthodox Church. The *sultans* were indeed glad to employ an instrument of government which they found ready made to their hand, and it was by their authority that the Patriarch of Constantinople displaced the Byzantine Caesars as official head of the Greek Christian subjects of the Porte. Himself, by the very exigencies of his position, the mere creature of the *Sultan*, dependent as he was on the whims and caprices of court favourites, and bound to acquire and maintain his position by lavish bribes, he nevertheless exercised over the Christian subjects of the Porte an immense influence, and was invested by the policy of the sultans with great temporal as well as spiritual powers.

As the Patriarch over the whole Greek world, so, in each diocese, the bishop became the embodiment at once of spiritual and temporal authority. To him were brought suits between Christians for settlement; and even Mussulmans would occasionally, in disputes with. Christians, prefer episcopal arbitration to the dilatory processes of the cadi's court. It was, however, through the lower clergy that the organisation of the Orthodox Church was most intimately bound up with the life of the people; for, as married men, the parish priests shared to the full in the feelings and aspirations of their flocks, from whom, though set apart by the sanctity of their office, they were hardly distinguished by culture or attainments.

Just then as, in the West, the idea of imperial unity had been preserved, all through the troubled period of the barbarian invasions, by the Church of Rome, so, throughout the Ottoman dominions, the theocratic basis of Greek unity had been deliberately maintained by the policy of the Ottoman conquerors. The creation or toleration of such *an imperium in imperio* might from the first have seemed of doubtful wisdom. As a matter of fact, it worked, from the point of view of the Sultan, well enough, as long as the Patriarch remained completely at his mercy. The danger of the system became apparent only when, with the decay of the Ottoman Empire, the Christian subjects of the sultans began to look abroad for support, and the Patriarch of Constantinople could reckon upon the assistance of a foreign power.

The Greek then became attached to his religion by a double tie of faith and national sentiment. To his religion and to the head of his religion alone does he owe allegiance; and no element of loyalty has ever entered into his relations to the *Sultan*, who ruled him, and rules him, by force alone. As soon then as the rigour of the Turkish tyranny relaxed, no obligation lay upon the *rayah* to obey a government which could no longer enforce its claims. It is a mistake to suppose that it was the intolerable tyranny of the Turk which forced the Greeks into rebellion. All history and experience indeed prove that a people will bear without murmuring the most crushing burdens; and it is only when the cords have been relaxed, and the load lightened, that the oppressed will feel the energy to turn upon the oppressor. It was the conscientious efforts at reform of the government of Louis XVI. which directly produced the French Revolution. It was the lessening pressure of Turkish rule, and the growing prosperity of the Greek population, that rendered the Hellenic revolt possible and inevitable.

******

Cf. De Tocqueville, *L'Ancien Régime et La Révolution:* 'L'expérience apprend que le moment le plus dangereux pour un mauvais gouvernement est d'ordinaire celui où il commence à se réformer. . . . Le mal qu'on souffrait patiemment comme inévitable semble insupportable dès qu'on conçoit l'idée de s'y soustraire . . . le mal est devenu moindre, il est vrai, mais la sensibilité est plus Vive.'

******

The rule of the Ottoman is indeed harmful rather for what it leaves undone than for what it does; it is intolerable rather for what it implies than for what it is. The Christian subject of the *Sultan*, even before modern capitulations, was free to exercise his religion, to accumulate wealth, to educate himself as he pleased; he could even rise to high office in Church or State, become Dragoman to the Porte, or governor of a province. The status of the peasantry under Ottoman rule was, in the eighteenth century, far more tolerable than in most parts of Europe. Serfdom, still almost universal throughout Christendom, had disappeared; and, in many parts of the Turkish dominions, the cultivators of the soil enjoyed a prosperity unknown to the peasantry of some nations accounted more civilised. It was the capricious and uncertain character of the Ottoman Government, rather than any conscious oppression, that provoked misery and discontent.

The custom of farming the taxes and of taking these in kind, though in theory workable enough, became, in fact, too often an engine of ruinous exactions; for, where the crops could not be cut until the tax-assessor had made his rounds, there were obviously endless openings for bribery and extortion. The evils of this system fell indeed on Christian and Moslem alike. Far more intolerable was that pride of religion and of race which gave to the Christian, in relation to his Mohammedan conqueror, the status of a slave, whom any good Mussulman might insult or outrage with impunity, and who, for the mere right to exist, was compelled to pay an annual poll-tax. All men will more readily forgive an injury than a slight; and the most intolerable of all tyrannies is that which expresses itself, not in isolated acts of violence, but in a consistently applied system of contemptuous toleration.

In dealing with a conquered people, Machiavelli had said, one must either crush or conciliate. The Turks had done neither. They had made their rule as galling as possible to the pride of the subject race, while they had neither destroyed its organisation nor even, in some cases, deprived it of its weapons. Under the Byzantine Caesars, certain of the wild hillsmen of the Thessalian border country had been enrolled in a sort of irregular militia, called *armatoli*, for the defence of the passes and the protection of the roads. This system was continued and extended by the sultans; and the Greek mountaineers were thus, by the deliberate policy of the Porte, accustomed for generations to the use of arms, and trained in all the arts of mountain warfare.

From *armatole* to brigand was but a short step; and when, toward the end of the last century, the *sultans* began to diminish the numbers of the Christian militia, and to curtail the power of the captains, these became the enemies of the order they were no longer paid to defend; and, from this time, the brigands, or *klephts*, grew into social and political importance as a permanent class. (Finlay, i. Fyffe, *Modern Europe*, i.). Where the government shows no respect for justice, lawless men are often supported by the lower orders as a means for securing revenge, or for redressing intolerable social evils. There was as yet no organised effort to throw off the Ottoman yoke; but the bolder and more reckless spirits among the peasantry, weary of a galling subservience, hurried to the mountains, and turned brigand.

To be a *klepht* was, in the popular view, a glory rather than a disgrace; and for whole decades before the war of independence the *klephts* were, in the eyes of their countrymen, the defenders of faith and fatherland against the Turk; though, to tell the truth, they plundered Christian and Mussulman with a commendable impartiality. Owning 'no *pasha* save the naked sword, no *vizier* save the gun,' they looked down upon the Ottomans and their 'slaves' with equal contempt. A thousand tales were current of their reckless courage, their cruelty, or their generosity; their deeds of valour against the Turk were sung in countless ballads, and the names of their celebrated leaders repeated from mouth to mouth in awe-struck tones. And indeed, though of schooling they knew nothing beyond their wild war-chaunts, in courage and physical endurance they in no wise fell short of the heroes of antiquity. One thing alone they feared: to fall alive into the hands of the Turks; and their accustomed toast was '*καλὸν μολύβι*'—the welcome bullet which should save them from this fate. Yet, if it should befall them, it was easier to crush their body than their spirit. The following story is characteristic.

The chief Katsantonis and his brother George had been betrayed into the hands of their mortal enemy Ali Pasha, and were by him condemned to have their limbs broken piecemeal with heavy hammers. Katsantonis was operated on first. Weakened by illness, he was unable to bear the agony, and, when the hammer fell upon his knee, uttered a sigh. George turned to him in surprise. 'What, Katsantonis, are you howling like a woman?' When his own turn came, he lay without a sound or look of suffering, while both his legs, from the hips to the ankles, were shattered to pieces.

The following story is delightfully reminiscent of our own Robin Hood and Friar Tuck. The *klephts* of the Pindus had a priest attached to the band, whose cell was a huge hollow oak. When they made a captive they would lead him up to the tree, and the chief would say; 'Speak, holy oak, which our fathers reverenced, what shall we do with our prisoner?'

'Is he a Christian,' asked the tree, 'or an unbelieving heathen?'

'Thou knowest, sacred tree, that he is a Christian!'

'Then let our brother go on his way rejoicing, after receiving the kiss of fraternal peace, and dedicating his purse for the relief of the needs of his poor brethren!'

If the prisoner was a Mussulman the answer was simply 'Hang the *infidel* on my holy boughs, and confiscate all he has for the use of the true Church and her faithful children.'

A religious sanction, then, was not lacking to this patriotic brigandage. The Orthodox Church gladly forgave crimes committed in the cause of faith and fatherland; and the *klepht* could pray, in all sincerity of heart, to '*Panagia Klephtrina*,' the Mother of God, who protects all robbery by sea and land.

Such were the *klephts* who played so important a part, for good and evil, in the war of Greek independence. (Gordon, i., says 'the Greeks had cause to repent their early predilection for the *klephts* or predatory chiefs, who were almost all infamous for the sordid perversity of their dispositions'. Certainly the wretched peasants suffered, during the war, far more from them than from the Turks).

Another and even more potent weapon, forged by the policy of the Porte, and to be used in the same cause, was the maritime power of the Greek islands. Long anterior to the Hellenic revolt many of these islands had, by one means or another, gained a large measure of independence. Some were practically autonomous, their subservience to the *Sultan* being evidenced only by the obligation to pay a small annual tribute, and to supply a certain number of sailors to the Ottoman navy. The islanders, accustomed from earliest infancy to face the perils and chances of the sea, were magnificent seamen; and, favoured by their political circumstances, they speedily built up a very considerable maritime trade.

To the development of this a great impetus was given in 1774 by the treaty of Kainardji, by which Russia obtained certain privileges in the navigation of the Bosphorus and the Dardanelles, and a somewhat vague and shadowy right of protection over the *Sultan's* Christian subjects. Greek merchants now began to trade under the Russian flag. Their vessels, hitherto mainly small coasting brigs, increased in size; and their voyages, at first adventured timidly from island to island, began to extend from Cherson to Gibraltar, and even beyond. The danger from Algerine pirates necessitated the ships being armed; and the crews were trained to fight as well as to navigate the vessel. Thus, under the eyes of the Ottoman Government, was gradually built up that naval power which, during the war of liberation, was to win such signal successes for the cause of Hellenic freedom.

On the mainland, as well as in the islands, the Turks had permitted a considerable measure of local self-government. In the *pashalik* of the Morea, while the taxes were usually farmed by the *beys* of the twenty-three provinces into which it was divided, the village communities were allowed to elect their own officers, the *demogeronts*, or village elders, who, besides collecting the taxes and managing the affairs of their own villages, met in a district assembly, with the representatives of the towns, to elect the *proestoi*, whose duty it was to determine what share of the district taxation each community should bear, and who, in their turn, chose one Greek officer, called *primate*, and one Mohammedan, called *ayan*, to represent the province, and to take part in the council of the *Pasha* of the Morea, who resided at Tripolitza. Though of but small service in preserving any liberty for their countrymen, and indeed themselves more often than not the instruments of oppression, the *primates* became a sort of Greek aristocracy, who, at the outbreak of the revolt, formed the natural leaders of the people, and whose financial experience was especially useful during the first years of the war. Moreover, it was the communal organisation alone which, in the absence of any other order, preserved the Greeks from, destruction during the anarchy of the civil wars.

Yet another class of Greeks, who played a very important part in the revolt, remains to be mentioned. The Phanariots were so named from the Phanar, or lighthouse, quarter of Constantinople, where the palace of the patriarch was situated, which, with its numerous offices and law courts, had gathered about it a considerable Greek colony. From this class were mainly drawn the officials of the Porte, as well as those of the patriarchate; and, though their general character was by no means high, they had produced, from time to time, men of distinguished ability and genuine devotion to the Hellenic cause. To this class belonged those Phanariot leaders in the revolt, like Alexander Mavrocordatos and Demetrius Hypsilanti, whose European culture and wider experience of affairs served, in some measure, as a check upon the frank barbarism of the Greek native chiefs.

Before closing this sketch of the Hellenic race under the Ottoman dominion, a few words must be added about that remarkable literary movement which produced so profound an effect on the development of modern Greece. In the course of ages, the ancient language of Hellas, the tongue of Plato and Demosthenes, had become for all practical purposes extinct. It was indeed still the language of the Church and of the learned; but learning itself had become confined to barren theological discussions, and, to the modern Greeks, the masterpieces of the ancient literature were quite unknown. For centuries education had been either wholly neglected, or consisted only in such schooling as could be obtained from monks hardly less ignorant than those they taught.

To restore to the Hellenes their language and literature became the self-imposed task of several enthusiastic spirits, among whom Adamantios Korais stands preeminent. Already indeed numerous schools, in which the classic writers were taught, had been founded in various parts of Hellas and the islands, mainly by the generosity of wealthy

Phanariots. But as long as the language of ancient Greece remained, to all intents and purposes, a dead tongue, it was impossible to restore to the Hellenes the intellectual heritage of their greater past, and to make it a real power among the people.

Korais then set himself the deliberate task of reconstructing for his countrymen a literary language which should combine, as far as possible, the best elements of both the ancient and modern tongues. He opposed equally those who, despising the idiom in common use, wished to preserve classical Greek as the language of the learned, and those who desired to raise the vulgar patois to the dignity of a literary language. His plan was to base his language on the common tongue, but to remove from it all foreign accretions, and as far as possible restore all such ancient and pure forms as had not become wholly obsolete. What Luther's Bible had done for Germany, Korais's editions of the classics, with their prefaces in modern Greek, were to do for Greece.

His efforts were crowned with remarkable success. The mixed *patois* is still the language of common life; but, in the press and the schools, a Greek is used which differs, not in kind, but in degree only, from the tongue of Homer; and the magnificent literary monuments of Greece have thus been preserved as the common property of the whole people.

★★★★★★

One of the most essential differences between modern and classical Greek: the pronunciation according to accent instead of quantity, is apparent comparatively early in the Christian era. Nonnus, an Egyptian-Greek poet, in the fourth century *A.D.*, is the first writer to reckon with accent. See Prof. Murray's *Ancient Greek Literature.*

★★★★★★

By this revival of the tradition of the dead glories of Hellas a new motive and a new force were added to the growing national consciousness of the Greeks. To the dream of the restoration of the Greek Empire of the East was added that of the re-birth of the Hellas of antiquity; the Greeks, ceasing to call themselves, as they had done for centuries, Romaioi, or Romans, resumed their ancient name of Hellenes; and the sea captains of Psara and Hydra, while continuing to pay their vows to the Mother of God, began to call their vessels by the names of the pagan heroes of old.

CHAPTER 2

Hope of Russian Support

With the consciousness of their past greatness and their present unity astir within them, it needed but the impulse and the occasion to make the Greeks rise against the hated rule of their Ottoman masters; and neither the impulse nor the occasion were long lacking. Ever since the Venetians had been finally expelled from the Morea, at the beginning of the eighteenth century, the eyes of the oppressed Greeks had turned eastward to the rising star of Russia. From the Church of the West, divided from their sympathies by the double barrier of the Papal supremacy and the 'Procession of the Holy Ghost,' the Greek Christians had met with little save cruelty and persecution.

With the growth of the power of the *Czars*, their eyes turned naturally to an empire united with them by the bonds of the orthodox faith, and which seemed destined to restore in the East the supremacy of the Cross. Catherine II., pondering in her mind vast designs of aggression, was nothing loath to encourage the hopes of the Greeks. At war with the Porte, she did not scruple to send a Russian fleet and Russian agents to rouse the Greeks of the Morea and Archipelago against the Turk, only to abandon them, as soon as the immediate ends of her policy were secured, to the frightful vengeance of their oppressors. Even this terrible object lesson in the methods of Russian state-craft could not destroy the hopes which the Hellenes based on the great Orthodox Power.

The Treaty of Kainardji, indeed, distinctly conceded to the Russians some shadowy protectorate over the Christian subjects of the Porte, a weapon which she was prepared to use or lay aside as suited her policy. Yet, baseless as this trust in Russia's disinterestedness really was, it was this more than anything else which gave such tremendous weight to the propaganda of the great secret society which, in the early years of the present century, prepared the way for, and gave the impulse to, the uprising of the Greeks.

The '*Hetairia Philike*' was founded in 1814, at Odessa, by three Greek merchants named Skuphas, Athanasios Tsakaloff, and E. Xanthos. It had for its object the uniting of all the Hellenes in an armed organisation, for the purpose of throwing off the Ottoman yoke and restoring the Greek Empire of the East. Childishly fantastic in its constitution, with its elaborate hierarchy, its masonic ritual, and blood-curdling oaths, it was nevertheless inspired by a determination of purpose which scrupled at no methods for the attainment of its ends. Its success was immediate and universal.

Nothing, indeed, displays the inferiority of the despotic methods of Turkey to those of Russia so clearly, as the ease with which a conspiracy so elaborate and so ill-disguised was developed and spread. In the course of a year or two the society had extended its operations over all the Greek world, drawing its recruits from all classes. Heartwhole devotion to the cause of Greece was the condition of membership; the most important rule, that which compelled every member to provide himself with arms and ammunition. The propaganda was extended even beyond the limits of the Hellenic nation; Servians and Roumanians were invited to attach themselves to the cause of the Cross, and restore, under the hegemony of Greece, the supremacy of the Church in the East.

And behind all the agitation loomed the shadow of Russia. It was the assumed support of Russia that formed the guarantee of the triumph of the cause of freedom; and this at a time when Alexander I. had surrendered himself, heart and soul, to the policy of Metternich and the Holy Alliance, and the whole weight of the Muscovite power was being used, in favour of the forces of reaction and despotism, in the attempt to crush out the liberties which the French Revolution had won for the peoples of Western Europe!

This, then, was the situation at the end of the second decade of the nineteenth century: at Laibach. Metternich with cynical satisfaction putting the finishing touches to the edifice which his diplomacy had raised to that Concert of Europe, united upon the basis of the *status quo*, which was to stamp out any symptoms of 'Revolution' wherever found, and make 'sentiment' in politics henceforward impossible: throughout the length and breadth of the Ottoman Empire a vast ramification of conspiracy, owing but little to the revolutionary forces of the West, but none the less a very magazine of inflammable sentiment, which needed but a spark to explode, and blow into the air with it all that elaborate diplomatic edifice which Metternich had raised with so much skill and labour.

For six years the Hetairia had developed and expanded without any definite plan or policy. Governed by a directorate of a dozen or more self-constituted leaders, it necessarily lacked the clearness of view and unity of purpose which could alone insure success; and it became necessary to seek a reliable leader, who could be placed at the head of the whole enterprise. One man alone seemed, by his position and great reputation, to be marked out for the post. Count Capodistrias, (Capo d'Istria), a Greek of Corfu, had, after the peace of Tilsit, which surrendered the Island to Napoleon, been taken into the service of the Czar Alexander, and had rapidly gained the entire confidence of his master. In 1820 he held, as Foreign Minister of Russia, an immense ascendency over the *Czar's* mind.

A Greek who had openly expressed his sympathy with Hellenic aspirations, and at the same time the trusted minister of the power from which so much was expected, seemed the most ideal of all possible leaders of the revolt. A deputation from the Morea, headed by Xanthos, accordingly proceeded to Moscow, and formally offered to Capodistrias, in the name of the Hetairia, the leadership of the Greeks. But, however much he might sympathise with the objects of the league, Capodistrias was too intimately acquainted with the secret counsels of the *Czar* to allow him for one moment to place any reliance on Russian help in such a cause, or to barter his own splendid position for a career fraught with such perilous chances. The offer was refused with sympathetic regret, and the Greeks advised to exercise their souls in patience.

It now became necessary to look round for another leader; and the choice fell on Prince Alexander Hypsilanti, the *scion* of an ancient Phanariot family which boasted its descent from the Byzantine Caesars, who was at the same time a general in the Russian service, and reputed to enjoy the special favour of the *Czar*. Hypsilanti, moved perhaps by a genuine enthusiasm for the Greek cause, and perhaps still more by wild dreams of ambition, accepted the call, not doubting that he would have the moral, if not the material, support of Russia. The Greeks were now provided with a leader; and nothing remained but to decide whether the blow for freedom was to be struck in the South, in reliance on Greek power alone, or in the North, in the certain hope of Russian assistance. The opportunity for the rising had already been given by the revolt from the. Ottoman, allegiance of Ali, Pasha of Janina, whose extraordinary career exercised so direct an influence on the fortunes of the Hellenic insurrection, that it will be necessary to devote a few words to it before proceeding.

The story of this remarkable man reads like a lurid romance of the Middle Ages rather than a chapter in modern history. Born at Tepeleni in Epirus, in the year 1741, of Albanian parents, the boy's surroundings impressed on him from the first the untamed and savage character of his race. His father had died, whilst he was still an infant, and his mother, Khamko, a woman of extraordinary character, had, on pretext of securing the rights of her children, exchanged the veil for the sword, and, gathering about her a band of fierce warriors, terrorised the surrounding country.

At last, betrayed into an ambuscade, she and her daughter had been imprisoned and insulted by the men of Gardiki and Kormovo. Released through the generosity of a Greek merchant, Khamko had, after this, nurtured in the breast of her son a lust for vengeance, none the less fierce that it was content to bide its time; and to revenge his mother's dishonour became the supreme object of Ali's life. It was this passion of hate, no less than his devouring ambition and inexhaustible avarice, that caused him to embark on a career which ultimately led him to measure his strength against the Ottoman power, and so compassed his downfall; not, however, before his vengeance had been satisfied and, after thirty years, the wrong suffered by his family atoned for by a holocaust of innocent victims.

At the outset a mere cattle stealer and brigand chief, Ali took the first step in his upward course by making himself master of his native town of Tepeleni; and the method used was highly characteristic of the man, and of the social condition of the country. Dressing up a goat in his cloak and fez, he gagged the animal to prevent its bleating, and laid it under a tree, at a place he had been accustomed to frequent. He then despatched a trusty messenger to Tepeleni, who was to act the traitor, and tell his enemies that the hated Ali was close at hand, asleep and unsuspecting.

The chance was not to be neglected. Seizing their guns, they hurried out and, from a safe distance, poured a volley into the sleeping body of the supposed Ali. Having watched with exultation the death quiver of the unhappy goat, they returned to the town, and proceeded to celebrate their prowess with feasting and revelry. In the midst of their merriment, and while they were completely off their guard,

Ali, with his trusty followers, suddenly fell upon them, and massacred them all. Thus he became lord of his native place. (Pouqueville, *Régénération de la Grèce*, i.)

Starting from this beginning, by violence, by fraud, by intrigue, he gradually acquired a dominion which extended from the Adriatic to the Ægean, and threatened at once the hopes of Greece and the authority of the *Sultan*. Restrained by no motives of religion or humanity, his cruelties revolted even the hardened sensibilities of a people accustomed to deeds of blood. But he knew well how to turn to his own advantage the mutual hates of the races under his rule. When the soldiers of his Mussulman regiments refused to massacre in cold blood the Mohammedan Gardikiots, whom he had lured into his power by a promise of amnesty, he found his Greek mercenaries willing enough to become the instruments of his revenge. The drowning of eighteen Greek ladies of Janina, accused justly or unjustly of immorality, sent a thrill of horror through the country, and witnessed at once to his cruelty and his hypocrisy; for he was himself an abandoned libertine.

Yet, in spite of his monstrous crimes, the rule of Ali Pasha was by no means altogether a curse to the country he governed; for, like many other tyrants, he would suffer no tyranny but his own, and crushed out with impartial cruelty the feudal anarchy of the Albanian chiefs, the lawlessness of the *klephts*, and the peculations of the Turkish officials. Recognising too, though himself a mere savage, the value of learning as an instrument of government, his court at Janina became the centre of whatever culture existed in the north of Greece; and under his patronage Mohammedan poets composed Greek odes in celebration of his unspeakable cruelties! (Religious intolerance could not be reckoned among his faults. When he wished to conciliate the Greeks, he would hold out hopes of his conversion, and drink to the health of the Mother of God!)

The ambitious views of Ali were notorious, and the Hetairists had from the first reckoned upon the Pasha of Janina as a possible ally against the Porte. Nor did he scruple to enter into relations with the Hellenic leaders.

******

The Greek Paparigopulos went to Russia, shortly before Ali's breach with the Porte, as the representative at once of the *pasha* and of the Hetairia, to try and induce the *Czar's* Government to declare war against Turkey. See Mendelssohn, i.

******

It had indeed been his policy throughout to conciliate and betray every interest in turn; and it was, in the end, to the advantage of the Greek cause that Ali was in no sense its protector. Before the outbreak of the Hellenic revolt, an attempt of Ali to compass the murder of his enemy Pacho Bey, chamberlain to the *Sultan*, at last moved the Porte, long since alarmed at the growth of his power, to effect his overthrow. Ali embarked on the struggle without misgiving; but he was soon to learn the hollowness of that Machiavellian maxim which he had adopted as his own '*That it is better for a prince to be feared than loved;*' for, at the first opportunity, his own sons deserted him, his generals went over with their armies to the Turks, and the wild tribes, whom he had governed by terror alone, threw off the hated allegiance. Ali found himself shut up with some four thousand men, in the fortress of Janina; and, besieged by the whole forces of the Ottoman empire, his fall was only a question of months.

There can be no doubt that the triumph of Ali would have been fatal to the Greek cause, and, in place of a Hellenic, an Albanian kingdom have been its result. As it was, the service which the Pasha of Janina rendered to the Greeks was, firstly, in distracting the attention of the Porte from the plots of the Hetairists, and secondly, in keeping, during the first months of the rebellion, the main body of the Ottoman troops, under their most able general, Khurshid Pasha, locked up before Janina.

CHAPTER 3

Massacres at Galatz and Yassy

If the revolt was not to be indefinitely postponed, the war between Ali Pasha and the *Sultan* presented too favourable an opportunity to be neglected. On the 6th of March, then, Prince Alexander Hypsilanti, accompanied by a few Greek and Russian officers, began the rising by crossing the Pruth from Russia into Moldavia. From the first the enterprise was hampered by the vanity, incapacity, and weakness of its leader, by his over-confidence and complete misunderstanding of the conditions of the struggle. Secure in the fancied support of Russia, and in the assumed sympathy of the Roumanian people, he believed he had but to show himself in the principalities to be at once welcomed as a deliverer, and carried in triumphal procession to the throne of the East. In high sounding proclamations, addressed to the Moldavians and the Greeks, he announced himself as the champion of the Cross and herald of the dawn of freedom, and, lastly, and most important of all, declared that his enterprise had the support of a *Great Power*. (Prokesch. i.)

To the Roumanian peasants, however, the appearance of a band of Phanariot Greeks in the disguise of deliverers seemed but a mockery and a snare. The Greeks had hitherto only been known to them through their own Hospodar and other subordinate agents of extortion, under whose rule their lot was far more wretched than that of the peasantry under the immediate government of the *Sultan*. Nor was the name of Russia a grateful sound to a people who, during the Muscovite occupation of the principalities from 1808 to 1812, had been reduced to the last stages of misery by the extortion of the invaders, and had seen their homes and fields devastated by the cruel policy of the *Czar*.

Had Hypsilanti appeared as the champion of the Roumanian people against the tyranny of the Hospodar and the *boyards* (as the great landowners were called), he might have received a different welcome; and even a Roumanian national rising against foreign tyranny might have had some prospect of success. But the Hospodar was his active ally, having made over to him all the fiscal and military machinery of the province, and with him he could not afford to quarrel; and a Greek rising on Roumanian soil was from the first doomed to failure. To the mass of the people he appeared merely as the leader of a band of mercenaries, plotting to transfer the sovereignty of the principalities from the *Sultan* to the *Czar*, and they received his advances with a sullen indifference which, as his difficulties increased, was changed into active hostility.

The history of Hypsilanti's enterprise is a record of incredible folly, of sordid intrigues, and revolting crimes; the sombre picture being only here and there lighted up by gleams of heroic fortitude or self-devotion. On the night before the prince crossed the border, a deed of blood was perpetrated which was the first of many that cast indelible disgrace on the Greek cause. Galatz is the principal port of Moldavia. Several Ottoman trading-vessels lay at anchor in the harbour, and some Turkish merchants resided in the town, where also a small guard of Turkish troops was maintained, in accordance with the laws of the Ottoman Empire, to act as police to insure the obedience of the Mussulman inhabitants to the fiscal laws of the principality.

The Christian troops of the Hospodar stationed at Galatz were commanded by a Greek named Karavia; and this man, who had joined the Hetairia, thought the present an excellent opportunity for enriching himself, in the name of patriotism, at the expense of the Turks. He accordingly assembled the Hetairists and his own mercenaries, and, informing them of the revolution that was about to break out, led them to the attack of the Turkish guard. Of these a few, taken by surprise, were slain at once. The rest held out for some time; but their resistance was at last broken, and Karavia then ordered his men to seize and murder all the Turkish merchants in the town, to take possession of the goods in the warehouses and seize all the vessels in the port. In obedience to these orders, Turks of every rank, merchants, sailors, soldiers, were surprised and massacred in cold blood. (Gordon, i.; Finlay, i).

The bloody example thus set was followed in many places. At Yassy had been left a body of fifty Ottoman troops to act as a guard of honour to the Hospodar. Before Hypsilanti entered the city, Michael

Soutzos, the Hospodar, had persuaded the commander to order his men to lay down their arms, under promise that their persons and property should be protected. The Turks, believing the Hetairists to be but the vanguard of a Russian army, obeyed; and Soutzos ordered them to remain in their quarters, and the Turkish merchants to be imprisoned, under the pretext that this measure was necessary to insure their safety. Yet, as soon as the news of the massacre of Galatz reached the capital, both soldiers and merchants were murdered in cold blood, under the eyes of the Hospodar and of Hypsilanti, without either of these princes making the slightest effort to save their lives. Hypsilanti even set the seal of his approval on the massacres by making Karavia a general.

The weakness and wickedness which made the Greek leader connive at these horrors was not counterbalanced by any skill in forming a plan of campaign, or energy in carrying out what he had planned. Had he advanced on Ibraila, and there concentrated his power, holding from this base the line of the Danube, it is possible that he might have prevented the Turks from entering the principalities, and forced Russia to recognise a *fait accompli*. As it was, he preferred to linger at Yassy, playing the prince, conferring titles, and alienating his own supporters and the proud *boyards* by his absurd affectation of royal exclusiveness. Several weeks he wasted in these congenial trivialities, while the Turks, thoroughly alarmed at last, made vigorous preparations for crushing the revolt.

At length he marched southward, and, on the 9th of April, fixed his headquarters at Bucharest. The forces of the insurrection were of the most motley description. Hypsilanti himself, though nominally commander-in-chief, had at his personal orders only a band of some two thousand undisciplined ruffians, more skilled in the art of plundering defenceless peasants than in that of war. The so-called 'Sacred Legion,' a regiment of five hundred Greek youths, whose courage was greater than their experience or physical powers, formed a nobler element; and besides these he could also depend upon a small but well-trained force of cavalry, under Georgaki of Olympus, the only one of the Greek leaders who displayed courage, skill, and disinterestedness.

The garrison of Bucharest consisted of a thousand veteran troops, under the practically independent command of the Greek Savas; and Theodore Vladimiresco, a Roumanian *boyard*, who had joined the Hetairists for his own ends, attached himself to Hypsilanti's fortunes with a force of some two thousand *pandours*, or Wallach cavalry. To weld these heterogeneous elements into an effective force needed a stronger hand than that of Prince Alexander Hypsilanti.

Already ominous signs were not lacking. Vladimiresco, at the outset of the rebellion, issued a manifesto to his countrymen, calling on them to support him in presenting to the *Sultan* a list of grievances against the Phanariot misrule! This was hardly reassuring from the point of view of the Greek leaders; but Hypsilanti could not afford to quarrel with any of his allies, and Vladimiresco continued to follow him, though their relations were naturally a little strained.

At Bucharest, Hypsilanti pursued the same fatuous course as at Yassy. Surrounded by crowds of adventurers and sycophants, he could find no more important business to transact than the engagement of a comedy company, and the fitting up of a theatre; to pay for which princely necessaries he plundered the monastery of Maryeni. (Gordon, i.) Of military activity the only signs were the ceaseless depredations of his ruffianly soldiers in the country round, and, in the town, the running to and fro, from morning till night, of a numerous staff of gorgeously uniformed officers, apparently intent on business, but in reality doing nothing in particular.

The course of this childish comedy, laughable enough had its *dénouement* been less tragic for the actors, was suddenly interrupted by news which should have at once brought it to an end. The Patriarch of Constantinople issued his anathema against the Hetairia, and denounced the curse of the Church on the rebels. Henceforward Hypsilanti became, not the leader of an orthodox crusade, but the head of a band of ambitious and turbulent conspirators. But a still more serious blow was impending. Hypsilanti had himself believed, and had suffered it to be generally understood, that he had the support of Russia in his enterprise; but now there came letters from Laibach in which the Emperor Alexander denounced the revolt, upbraided the prince for his perfidy in misusing the *Czar's* name, struck his name from the Russian army list, and called on him at once to lay down his arms. (Prokesch. iii. The letter is signed by Count Capodistrias).

The right and reasonable course would have been to obey; for the whole enterprise had been initiated and supported on the confident assumption that it had the sanction of the *Czar*. Deprived of this sanction it was foredoomed to failure; and all that remained was, by a speedy submission, to obtain the best possible terms for its deluded supporters. But Hypsilanti was too foolish, or too blinded by vanity, to take a just view of the situation; he preferred to continue his course, and to cover its fatuity from the eyes of his followers, and perhaps from his own, by a fabric of lies. Alexander, he told the assembled leaders, had denounced the revolution publicly in order to preserve the peace of Europe, whilst privately commanding him to persevere, and promising support. The revolutionary leaders were but half deceived; Savas and Vladimiresco opened negotiations with the Porte; and many *boyards*, protesting their devotion to the Ottoman rule, fled for safety over the Austrian frontier.

Hypsilanti now at last took the field at the head of a small and irregular force, lacking artillery, and almost destitute of ammunition. Instead, however, of marching towards the Danube to cover Bucharest, he crept away northward towards the Austrian frontier. Savas and Vladimiresco, though suspecting some sinister design on the part of the prince, still followed him with their troops; but the treachery of Vladimiresco being suspected, Georgaki arrested him in his own camp, and brought him before Hypsilanti, who amnestied him, and then allowed him to be assassinated. Savas thereupon deserted to the Turks, but, in place of the reward he had counted on receiving, was promptly beheaded.

The Hetairists were now in danger of being surrounded by three divisions of Ottoman troops advancing from Widin, Giourgevo, and Bucharest. On the 8th of June there was a skirmish at Tergovisht, and though both sides claimed the victory, Hypsilanti retreated in haste to Rimnik. After remaining here three days, he decided to attack a body of Turkish cavalry which had advanced from Kraïova, and taken post at the village of Dragashan, about thirty miles from his camp.

The force at his disposal numbered four thousand infantry, two thousand five hundred cavalry, and four guns. The Turks were in all eight hundred horsemen; and the issue of the fight seemed beyond doubt. On June 19, 1821, Prince Nicholas Hypsilanti, at the head of the Sacred Battalion, supported by Karavia with five hundred horse, took up a position opposite Dragashan; while Georgaki sent forward a strong body of Wallach infantry to hold the road to Kraïova, strengthening them with some cavalry to cut off the Ottoman retreat. As the troops were exhausted after a long and wet march, Georgaki, who was now the senior officer in command, decided to postpone the attack till the next morning, meanwhile dispatching an orderly to Prince Alexander Hypsilanti, who was with the rear-guard some nine miles behind, to bid him hasten forward and secure the glory of the expected victory. He then retired to his quarters.

In his absence, however, Karavia, envious of the Olympian's reputation, and thinking to snatch an easy victory, persuaded the weak Prince Nicholas Hypsilanti to disregard the orders of his superior officer, and advance at once to the attack. Unsupported, the Sacred Battalion advanced upon the village held by the Ottomans. These at once saw their chance of destroying the enemy piecemeal, and, with wild cries and brandished swords, charged from behind their cover on the advancing infantry, breaking their ranks before they had time to form square. The weary and inexperienced boys of the Greek regiment, though they fought and fell with the utmost gallantry, were unable to withstand the fierce onslaught of veteran troops. The butcher Karavia, brave enough against defenceless men, no sooner saw the infantry show signs of yielding, than he set spurs to his horse and fled with all his men, spreading panic among the troops in the rear. Georgaki, hearing the firing, hurried up, but was unable to do more than save the standard and a poor remnant of the Sacred Battalion. The day, and with it the last hope of the Greeks, was lost.

Hypsilanti, with a scared remnant of his followers, escaped to Rimnik, where he spent some days in negotiating with the Austrian authorities for permission to cross the frontier. In terror lest his confederates should buy their own safety by surrendering him to the Turk, he invented a last lie to secure his retreat. Pretending that Austria had just declared war on Turkey, he caused a *Te Deum* to be sung in the church of Kosia to celebrate the event; and, on pretext of arranging co-operative measures with the Austrian commander-in-chief, crossed the frontier. (Pouqueville, *Régéneration de la Grèce*, ii.)

His fate could hardly have been worse had he fallen into the hands of the Turks; for Austria, under the rule of Metternich, had little sympathy with leaders of revolts. For upwards of seven years Hypsilanti was kept in close confinement; and when, at the instance of the Czar Nicholas, he was at last released, it was only to die shortly afterwards of a broken heart.

The fate of the remaining leaders is better worth following, and throws a halo of glory over the end of an enterprise which had begun in such pitiful disgrace. Georgaki, who was joined by the Albanian chief Pharmaki and some two hundred and fifty men, made a bold attempt to fight his way through to the frontier of Russia. Their fate was accelerated by the hostility of the justly enraged peasantry. Hemmed in by the Ottoman forces, their whereabouts was always betrayed to the enemy, while they themselves could obtain neither guides nor information. At last they found themselves surrounded in the monastery of Seko. Georgaki, determined not to fall alive into the hands of the Turks, held the campanile of the church until it was no longer tenable, then fired his pistol into the store of powder, and perished in the explosion. Pharmaki defended the main buildings of the monastery for a fortnight longer, and at last, deceived by the promises of the Turks, surrendered on condition of amnesty and the honours of war. Thirty-three of his men, distrusting their enemies, escaped the night before the capitulation was carried out. The rest, about twenty in number, were shot in cold blood. Pharmaki himself was taken to Constantinople, tortured, and beheaded.

In Moldavia, meanwhile, the insurrection had been suppressed without difficulty. As soon as it was certain that no Russian aid was to be expected, the *boyards* deposed Michael Soutzos, who fled to Russia. (He went, later on, to Paris, where he acted as Greek Minister during the presidency of Count Capodistrias). A Greek named Pentedekas, however, collected some troops, and, in defiance of the *boyards*, seized the government. His rule was not of long duration. Prince George Cantacuzenos, his lieutenant, had stationed himself with the Greek troops near the Russian frontier; and when the Turks entered Yassy, on the 25th of June, he crossed the Pruth. His officers and soldiers, however, pleading their military honour, refused to retire without fighting; and, entrenching themselves as best they could at Skuleni, they awaited the onset of the Turks.

The result could not be doubtful. Advancing with enormous superiority of numbers, the Turks first bombarded and then stormed the camp, losing, however, in the engagement a thousand men. Of the Greeks some few survivors escaped by swimming the Pruth. This gallant affair of Skuleni terminated the Hellenic rising in the North, with the collapse of which ended also all idea of restoring the Greek Empire of the East.

CHAPTER 4

The Beginning of Hostilities

The attempt of Hypsilanti in the principalities had never met with the united support of the Hetairists. To the directors of the conspiracy it had seemed more promising to raise the standard of Hellenic freedom upon Greek soil; and the movement in the north was not allowed to interfere with the preparations for the revolt in the Morea. Here, indeed, where the Mohammedans, sparsely scattered in agricultural settlements, formed but a small proportion of the population, a feeling of unrest and foreboding had for some time been abroad, and among the superstitious population this had been intensified, in the autumn of 1820, by a terrific earthquake which convulsed the Peloponnese.

Yet, though the Mussulmans were well aware of the rising which the *rayahs* had in contemplation, they neglected, with their usual impassiveness, even the most ordinary precautions. The impregnable towers and fortresses, with which the country was studded, would have afforded, had they taken the trouble to arm and provision them, irresistible barriers to the progress of irregular and ill-armed forces. As it was, the storm, when at last it broke, found them utterly unprepared, and swept them away in the first outburst of its fury, before they had time to concert measures of resistance.

The supineness of the Ottomans was paralleled by the unpractical character of the Greek preparations; for of a consistent and well-pondered scheme there was no question. Emissaries of the Hetairia, so-called apostles—too often unscrupulous agitators who embezzled the money subscribed for the cause—travelled about the country, everywhere inflaming the passions of the people against their Turkish masters, and calling on them to take up arms for the cause of religion and liberty. Of these agitators the best known and most influential was the Archimandrite Dikaios, popularly known as Pappa Phlesas, a priest whose morals were a scandal to the church, as his peculations were to the national cause, yet, for all that, a brave man, as he proved by his heroic death on the field of battle.

To the violent counsels of Phlesas and his like were opposed the views of a more moderate party, comprising the wealthier and official element of the movement. At the head of this stood the Archbishop Germanos of Patras, and it included those of the primates who had as yet committed themselves to the Greek cause. In the autumn of 1820, the directorate of the Hetairia had made an attempt to organise the movement in the Morea, and seven *ephorates* or district governments were created under the leadership of Germanos; but the scheme was only partially successful. Moderate counsels, in times of great popular excitement, are apt to produce results opposite to those intended. Lashed to madness by the eloquence of the agitators, the common people suspected the motives of the official leaders of the Hetairia, disregarded their advice, and by acts of violence and cruelty precipitated the crisis which these had been anxious to postpone.

The disquieting news from the Morea had determined the Porte to place the province under the command of Khurshid Pasha, an officer of tried honesty and capacity. On his arrival, however, he found the country to all appearance peaceful and settled; and, when the Sultan ordered him to take over from the hands of the incompetent Ismael the task of blockading Ali Pasha in Janina, he left the government, without misgiving, in the hands of the *kaimakam* Salik Aga. His absence, however, was the signal for renewed activity on the part of the conspirators; and, at last, the Turkish governor, alarmed at the increasing agitation, issued a proclamation ordering the Christians to surrender their arms, and summoning the bishops and primates to Tripolitza. By some the invitation was obeyed, though with misgiving; others, and among them the Archbishop Germanos, started on the journey, but made one excuse or another for arresting it half way.

The proclamation of the *kaimakani* had, indeed, only hastened the crisis it had been intended to avert; and the leaders of the revolt seemed on the brink of a decision, when it was taken out of their hands by the furious impatience of the common people. The War of Greek Independence was, in fact, from the first a people's war, a revolt of peasants and *klephts* against an intolerable subjection; and it succeeded only because of this irresistible popular impulse, and in spite of the general corruption and incapacity of its so-called leaders. It began, characteristically enough, with isolated acts of violence which could hardly be distinguished from brigandage. A Turkish tax-gatherer and his retinue were fallen upon and murdered. A band of sixty Albanian mercenaries were surprised and butchered by three hundred Greek *klephts*. This was in March, 1821; and in April the insurrection was general. Everywhere, as though at a preconcerted signal, the peasantry rose, and massacred all the Turks men, women, and children on whom they could lay hands.

In the Morea shall no Turk be left,
Nor in the whole wide world.

Thus rang the song which, from mouth to mouth, announced the beginning of a war of extermination. The Mussulman population of the Morea had been reckoned at twenty-five thousand souls. Within three weeks of the outbreak of the revolt, not a Moslem was left, save those who had succeeded in escaping into the towns.

Meanwhile the national uprising had found leaders. On the 2nd of April Archbishop Germanos raised the standard of the cross, and occupied Kalavryta; and four days later, accompanied by the primates Londos, Zaimis, Sotiri, and Papadiamantopulos, and by a wild rabble of peasantry armed with scythes, clubs, and slings, he marched to Patras. The Turks had been warned two days earlier of the occurrences at Kalavryta, and had occupied the citadel, whence for forty-eight hours they had bombarded the town; while, among the burning ruins, fanatical bands of Christians and Moslems massacred each other without mercy. The arrival of Germanos and the primates was hailed with delight by the Greeks; and it was hoped that the citadel would now be speedily reduced.

With an imposing religious ceremonial, a crucifix was erected in the central square of the town, and a proclamation issued in the name of the Greek leaders, containing merely these emphatic words, 'Peace to the Christians! Respect to the consuls! Death to the Turks.' (Gordon, i.) The sole immediate result, however, of the rising at Patras was the destruction of a once flourishing town. The Greeks, a mere undisciplined rabble, commanded by leaders of no experience, and divided by mutual jealousies, could not reduce the citadel; and when this was relieved, on the 15th of April, by Yussuf Pasha, Germanos and his followers were forced to retire into the mountains. Many subsequent attempts were made to reduce Patras, but with no better success; and the place remained in the hands of the Turks till after the retirement of Ibrahim from the Morea in 1828.

While the bishops and primates were thus raising the banner of revolt in the north of the Peloponnese, the southern districts were flying to arms under leaders of a different stamp. In Messenia Petros Mavromichales, generally known as Petrobey, Prince or Bey of the Maina, a wild and mountainous district in the southern spur of Laconia, inhabited by warlike robber tribes who boasted their descent from the ancient Spartans, took the field at the head of his clan. (For an account of the Mainotes, see chapter 22). Niketas, Anagnostaras, and other well-known chiefs of *banditti* joined the revolt; and, above all, Kolokotrones, a celebrated *klepht* of the Morea, who for some time had been an officer in a Greek regiment in English service, crossed over from Zante to share in the liberation of his country. His courage, personal strength, and proved skill in the conduct of irregular warfare made Kolokotrones a fitting leader of wild warriors; and on his arrival he was recognised as the chief of the insurrection, a position to which Petrobey's hereditary dignity and patriarchal power, though not his easy-going and somewhat weak nature, would seem to have entitled him.

★★★★★★

Cf. Gordon, i. Kolokotrones had in full measure the vices as well as the virtues of a robber chief. 'His military talents as a partisan were unparalleled in Greece; at the same time . . . his sordid avarice, and mean ambition, . . . severely scourged his country.'

★★★★★★

The war was, from the beginning, conducted without organisation or plan. All the open country was speedily in the hands of the insurgents; the Turks found themselves surrounded in the towns by fierce hordes of peasants and hillsmen; and, as no preparations either of arms or provisions had been made, their reduction was, in most cases, but a question of days. Kalamata, besieged by Petrobey and his Mainotes, had fallen even before the arrival of Kolokotrones. Of the Ottoman inhabitants, the men were massacred, the women and children enslaved; and on the banks of the wild mountain torrent that rushed past the town twenty-four gorgeously vested priests, surrounded by an army of five thousand warriors, sang a solemn *Te Deum*, in celebration of the first victory of the war.

The career of Kolokotrones opened less auspiciously. His great reputation had gathered about him a force of some six thousand men, with which he proceeded to lay siege to Karytaena. The appearance of five hundred Turkish cavalry was, however, sufficient to raise the

KOLOKOTRONES

siege, and put his untried levies to rout. The check was only a temporary one; for Kolokotrones, encouraged by a vision of the Virgin, soon gathered another army; and, before long, nearly every town of the Morea had fallen into the hands of the insurgents, the Mussulman prisoners being everywhere mercilessly put to the sword.

The conflagration now spread to the north of the Gulf of Corinth. At the beginning of April, the Albanian Christians of Dervenakhoria, (the ancient Megaris), rose; and the whole of Attica and Boeotia speedily followed suit. Salona, instigated by the Klepht Panourias, threw off the Ottoman yoke; and, in Levadia, the Mussulmans found themselves besieged by the Christian population under the heroic Diakos. At the beginning of May, the Mussulmans of Athens were surrounded in the Acropolis. Missolonghi, a name afterwards so famous in the history of the rising, did not declare itself till June.

In the Morea meanwhile, at the beginning of April, only a few of the Ottoman fortresses still held out; and these were closely invested by hordes of savage warriors. Two thousand were blockading Coron; three thousand others besieged Modon and Navarino; four thousand had collected before Patras, and ten thousand on the heights round Tripolitza. Acrocorinthos was beset by eight thousand insurgents, while three thousand of the wild tribesmen of the Maina surrounded Monemvasia.

The last-named fortress was the first to fall. Perched on an inaccessible rock, it could not be taken by storm; but the place was insufficiently provisioned, and the hope of relief from the sea was cut off by the arrival of a Greek squadron. The garrison were soon reduced to the most desperate straits; but a practical hint of what they might expect, if they surrendered, had been given them by the besiegers, and they were determined to resist to the uttermost. For the Greeks, thinking to intimidate them, had brought ashore some wretched prisoners, men and women, whom they had captured on the high seas, had led them before the walls, and there butchered them in cold blood.

After this object lesson in the methods of their enemies, famine alone could persuade the Mussulmans to surrender. Soon their food stores were all exhausted; and for a while they subsisted on vermin and the seaweed scraped from the rocks; but soon this, too, was no more to be obtained; and now, from time to time, gaunt and fierce-eyed bands of warriors would issue from the fortress in furious sorties, drive back the besiegers, and drag in the bodies of their slain enemies, the last ghastly sustenance suggested by their despair.

At this point, Prince Demetrius Hypsilanti, who had recently been appointed commander-in-chief in the Morea, interposed. Prince Demetrius, whose arrival in Greece had been greeted with unbounded delight, was the brother of Alexander Hypsilanti, whose failure in the Principalities has already been recorded; and, in spite of the collapse of the northern rising, he proclaimed himself the lieutenant of his brother, and persisted in looking upon himself as acting under the authority of the Hetairia. He was no more remarkable for capacity than his brother, but he was superior to him in character; and there is no reason to suppose that he was otherwise than an honourable, brave, and upright man, or that he would not have done all in his power to prevent the ghastly and shameful scenes which he was too soon to witness.

★★★★★★

M. Lemaître, whose bias is obvious, maintains the contrary; he accuses Hypsilanti of having foreseen what would take place after the capitulation, 'though he none the less displayed a lively indignation against his men, which gained him the momentary esteem of our officers.' Since, even by M. Lemaître's admission, he had the esteem of the French officers on the spot, it should require more than the bare assertion of a prejudiced partisan to make us believe him guilty of a base and senseless crime. Cf. Gordon, *History of the Greek Revolution*, i. 'Even his enemies were forced to confess that, to ardent patriotism, he united courage, integrity, and humanity.'

★★★★★★

Hypsilanti now proposed, by the mouth of Prince Gregorios Cantacuzenos, terms to the besieged. He promised that, if they would cease to prolong a useless resistance and peaceably submit, their homes would be respected and they would have nothing to fear for their lives; or, in case they should prefer to leave the country, that he would place two Spezziot brigs at their disposal, with orders to land them on any part of the coast of Asia Minor they might select. It is impossible to believe that these promises were made in bad faith; but Hypsilanti was a vain man, he had but recently been placed in a position of unaccustomed command, and he probably quite misjudged the amount of authority he was likely to have over the undisciplined brigands who formed the bulk of his army. This is most probably the measure of his responsibility in the awful scenes that followed.

The Turks, weakened by famine, and rendered desperate, whether they trusted the promises or not, grasped at the last straw of hope that was held out to them. They opened the gates of their citadel, and laid down their arms. The greater number of them now elected to go into exile and the work of embarkation began. Six hundred had already gone on board the brigs, when, suddenly, the Mainotes burst into the town, murdering and outraging all those who had not as yet succeeded in reaching the shore, or who, trusting in the promise of Prince Demetrius that their homes and lives would be spared, had chosen to remain in the town. Those on the ships were meanwhile carried out to sea, and, after a voyage of some hours, were landed, not on the coast of Asia Minor, but on a desolate rock in the Ægean; where, after being stripped of their clothes, insulted, and beaten, they were left, without food or covering, to perish. (*Archives du Ministère de la Marine*, 1821; Lemaître).

A few were saved by the exertions of a French merchant, M. Bonfort, who, hearing of their case, chartered an Austrian ship, and took off those who survived. It has been very usual, in speaking of atrocities committed by the Greeks, to condone them by talking of 'the cruel reprisals of a wild people for cruel wrongs.' Let us then see what manner of men the Mussulmans of Monemvasia were. Admiral Haglan, commanding the French squadron in the Levant, in a report sent home to his government, in 1821, says:

> In the fortress of Malvoise (Monemvasia) were found three hundred Greeks, who had not been molested in any way by the Turks. On the contrary, these had treated them, during the famine, like brothers, and had always respected their churches; but the Mainotes and the Greeks of the Morea did not repay them in kind when they took the town; they committed all sorts of infamies in the mosques of the Turks.

******

Lemaître; I should not have ventured to tell this story on the authority of so fierce a Mussulman as M. Lemaître, had he not substantiated it by citing unimpeachable authorities. The account in Finlay i. is slightly less horrible; that in Gordon i. differs, to the advantage of the Greeks; but the authorities quoted by M. Lemaître were not accessible to the author.

******

Everywhere, indeed, the conduct of the insurrection was characterised by the same treachery and unbounded cruelty. It may perhaps be permissible to make allowances for the excesses of a wild people, whose passionate hatred, suppressed for centuries, had at last found vent. But nothing can excuse the callous treachery which too often preceded deeds of blood; and since Europe passed a heavy judgment on the cruel reprisals of the Turk, historical justice does not allow us to hide the crimes by which they were instigated. Let two more examples suffice.

Vrachori was the most important town of Western Hellas. It contained, besides the Christian population, some five hundred Mussulman families and about two hundred Jews, people for the most part of some wealth and consideration. The Ottoman garrison consisted of six hundred Albanian mercenaries. On the 9th of June the town was attacked by about two thousand *armatoli*, who were afterwards increased to four thousand. The Albanians, seeing themselves outnumbered, and having, through their chief Nourka, relations with the *armatoli*, opened negotiations with the Greeks, and were allowed to march out with arms and goods.

Before leaving, however—thinking, doubtless, that it was a pity all the spoil should fall into the hands of the Greeks—they plundered the Turks, and forced the Jews to give up to them all the money and jewellery in their possession. With the wealth of which they were thus deprived these poor wretches had hoped to purchase the protection of the captains of the *armatoli*; and as soon as they could do so, they informed the Greeks of Nourka's treachery, and laid down their arms on promise of personal safety. That promise was immediately violated. The massacre commenced with the Jews. Men, women, and children were murdered without mercy, after being tortured to make them reveal their supposed hidden treasures. The poorer Mussulmans shared the same fate; and only a few of the wealthier families were spared by the Greek leaders, who hoped to hold them to ransom.

The horrors that followed the surrender of Navarino on August 19, 1821, were only less revolting because they were perpetrated against the will of the leaders, who had made preparations for transporting the Turkish prisoners to Egypt.

✶✶✶✶✶✶

Cf., however, Gordon, i. He adds, in a footnote, that one of the negotiators of the capitulation boasted to him that he had succeeded in purloining and destroying the copy given to the Turks, that no proof might remain of any such transaction having been concluded.

✶✶✶✶✶✶

While the confiscated valuables of the Turks were being carried on board a Greek ship in the harbour, a dispute arose as to the way in which the women were being searched. (Lemaître is more explicit). A general massacre ensued. Phrantzes, (Finlay, i.), a Greek ecclesiastic who was present, describes the scene with horror and indignation:

> Women, wounded with musket balls, rushed into the sea, seeking to escape, and were deliberately shot. Mothers, robbed of their clothes, with infants in their arms, plunged in the water to conceal themselves from shame, and were then made a mark for inhuman riflemen. Greeks seized infants from their mothers' breasts, and dashed them against the rocks. Children, three or four years old, were hurled living into the sea, and left to drown.

Let us be just. The awful massacre of Chios, which roused the public opinion of Europe against Turkey, and made the independence of Greece a possibility, was a great crime, as it was a great mistake; but it was not without its motive, or its justification, according to the wild code of barbarous peoples.

The other atrocities of the Greeks, however, paled before the awful scenes which followed the storming of Tripolitza. Throughout the summer and early autumn of 1821, the town had held out against the besiegers. A force had been sent by Khurshid Pasha to its relief, but this had been defeated by Kolokotrones at Valtetsi, and the place, which had waited in vain for the arrival of the Ottoman fleet with supplies, was reduced to the last stage of starvation. At the end of September, it was obvious that the fall of the town could not be postponed for many days.

At this time the command-in-chief of the army was held by Prince Demetrius Hypsilanti; and had he remained before Tripolitza, it is possible that the horrors which followed might have been avoided, and the Greek cause saved from an indelible disgrace. Unfortunately, however, the Greek leaders, for their own purposes, wanted him out of the way; and he allowed himself to be persuaded to go to the north of the Morea, to prevent the Turks landing troops from the Gulf of Corinth. The insurgent chiefs took advantage of his absence to prepare for the surrender of the town by selling promises of protection to the richer inhabitants, and by opening, during the negotiations, a brisk trade in provisions, at exorbitant prices, with the starving townspeople.

Meanwhile, also, Elmas Bey, who commanded the Albanian garrison, was arranging special terms with Kolokotrones for himself and his men. The cupidity of the chiefs dragged on the negotiations, till the soldiers, suspecting that they were being cheated of their prey, took the matter into their own hands, and stormed the town. For three days the miserable inhabitants were given over to the lust and cruelty of a mob of savages. Neither sex nor age was spared. Women and children were tortured before being put to death. So great was the slaughter that Kolokotrones himself says that, when he entered the town, from the gate to the citadel his horse's hoofs never touched the ground. His path of triumph was carpeted with corpses. At the end of two days, the wretched remnant of the Mussulmans were deliberately collected, to the number of some two thousand souls, of every age and sex, but principally women and children, were led out to a ravine in the neighbouring mountains, and there butchered like cattle.

The fall of Tripolitza completed the first phase of the Greek rising. Nauplia, Patras, and one or two other fortresses still held out; but, within six months of the beginning of the revolt, the Greeks were practically masters of all the country to the south of the Isthmus of Corinth.

In Northern Greece, meanwhile, the fortune of the war had been more varied, and the first successes of the Greeks had been followed speedily by a series of reverses. Diakos and the Bishop of Salona, who, after the capture of Levadia, had advanced to Thermopylae, were here defeated, on the 5th of May, by Khurshid's lieutenants, Omer Vrioni and Mehemet. Diakos and the bishop were both captured and executed; and the victorious pashas pressed on across the defiles of Mount Oeta.

At the Khan of Gravia they were intercepted by the famous captain of Armatoli, Odysseus, who was compelled to retire, after a stubborn resistance. The Ottomans now recaptured Levadia, burnt it to the ground, and inflicted another defeat on Odysseus at Scripu. Instead, however, of advancing at once to the relief of the Acropolis, they wasted a month in inaction, and allowed time for the Greeks to recover. All the attempts of the insurgents to capture the Acropolis had hitherto failed; and, save for the scarcity of water, the fortress would have been impregnable. As it was, it held out until the rumour of the Ottoman advance spread a panic among the besiegers, who rapidly melted away; and on the 30th of June, Omer Vrioni, at the head of some two thousand troops, relieved the garrison, after a blockade of eighty-three days.

Meanwhile Mehemet Pasha had been awaiting at Thebes the arrival of strong reinforcements before beginning a regular advance into the Morea, for the purpose of raising the siege of Tripolitza. The supineness of the Turks allowed the Greeks to form their plans without interruption; and the passes of Oeta and Parnassus were occupied by Odysseus and other Rumeliot captains of renown. At the end of August an Ottoman army of some five thousand men, under the three *pashas*, Bayram, Memish, and Shahin Ali, advanced through the pass of Thermopylae, and on the 4th of September attacked the Greeks at Vasilika, on the road to Levadia. The latter waited until the Turks had entered a defile of Mount Oeta, when they fell upon them on either flank, pouring a hail of bullets into their ranks, embarrassed as they were with cavalry, baggage, and a train of artillery. The victory of the Greeks was complete. Encouraged by a rumour of the arrival of Odysseus, the Armatoli charged the broken ranks of the Ottomans, sword in hand, and routed them, with the loss of eight hundred men. (Gordon, i.)

After this defeat, and the news of the fall of Tripolitza, Omer Vrioni commenced his retreat from Attica; and the Turks withdrew across the mountains into Thessaly.

In West Hellas and Epirus, during the same period, the interest of the war had centred round the last stand of Ali Pasha in Janina, and the activity of the Suliots. Here the struggle had not yet assumed the aspect of a purely Greek and Christian revolt; and the Suliots under the brave Marko Botzares had formed an alliance against the Ottomans, not only with the Greek captains of *armatoli*, but with those of the Albanian Mussulman chiefs who were devoted to the cause of Ali Pasha. Together they had made considerable headway against the Turks, and had all but conquered the important town of Arta, when rumours of the massacre of Mussulmans at Vrachori reached the Albanian chiefs, who, realising now the true nature of the revolt, threw in their lot with their co-religionists. Although this rendered any active policy against the Turks impossible, West Hellas remained, pending the fall of Ali Pasha and the reduction of the Suliots, in the hands of the Greeks.

By the end of the year 1821, then, the Hellenic cause was everywhere triumphant. The Turks, it is true, still occupied the important island of Euboea, and, on the mainland, held the Acropolis and the fortress of Lepanto; while, in the Peloponnese, Nauplia, Patras, Coron, and Modon still defied all the efforts of the Greeks to take them, and the castles commanding the entrance to the Gulf of Corinth remained in Ottoman hands. With these exceptions, however, all Greece to the south of the Thessalian frontier had been freed from the Mussulman yoke.

In achieving this result, the activity of the Greeks at sea had played no inconsiderable part. As early as the 7th of April, the important island of Spezzia had declared for the Hellenic cause, and a squadron of eight brigs was at once fitted out for a cruise along the coast of the Peloponnese. Off Milos they surprised and captured a Turkish corvette and brig. The Mussulmans on board were taken to Spezzia, publicly tortured and executed. (Finlay i.) This was the first episode in the naval struggle which reproduced at sea the heroism and the cruelty of the war on land. On the 23rd of April Psara followed the example of Spezzia; an event of great strategical importance to the Greeks, because the Psariot sea force was enough to prevent the Turks of Asia Minor sending reinforcements to their compatriots in the Morea.

Hitherto Hydra, the most important of the 'naval' islands, had held back, owing to the timidity of the ruling oligarchy. On the 28th of April, however, the people rose, under the demagogue Oeconomos, ousted the oligarchy, and hoisted the Greek flag. The islands now combined their forces in a single fleet, under Jakonaki Tombazes, a worthy and honourable man, though a poor admiral.

Not even a Nelson, however, could have kept discipline in a fleet of which each ship was a democratic community in whose management every common seaman had a voice. The Greek war vessels were in fact little better than pirates; and the war at sea became, in its want of plan and in its incidents of horror, a counterpart of that on land. A single instance may suffice. Two Hydriot brigs, commanded by Sachtouris and Pinotzi, captured a Turkish ship laden with a valuable cargo, and carrying a number of passengers. Among these was a recently deposed Sheik-ul-Islam, or patriarch of the Orthodox Mussulmans, who was said to be going on pilgrimage to Mecca, accompanied by all his family. He was known to have belonged to the tolerant party in the Ottoman Government; and, indeed, it was his efforts to prevent the cruel reprisals which, at Constantinople, followed the news of the massacres at Galatz, Yassy, and in the Morea, which had brought him into disfavour, and caused his exile. There were also several other Turkish families on board.

The Hydriots murdered all in cold blood; helpless old men, ladies of rank, beautiful slaves, and little children were butchered on deck like cattle. The venerable old man, whose crime had been an excess of zeal on behalf of the Greeks, was forced to see his family outraged and murdered before his eyes, for, with a refinement of cruelty, he was spared to the last.

An attempt was afterwards made to extenuate this unmerciful conduct, by asserting that it was an act of revenge. This assertion is false. Those who perpetrated these cruelties did not hear of the execution of their Orthodox patriarch until after they had murdered the Orthodox patriarch of their enemies. The truth is that, both by land and sea, the war commenced as a war of extermination. Fanatical pedants talked of reviving the glories and the cruelties of classic times as inseparable consequences of Greek liberty. They told how the Athenians had exterminated the inhabitants of Melos, and how the Spartans had put all their Athenian prisoners to death after their victory at Aegospotamos.—Finlay i.

The capture of this valuable prize was of little service to the Greek cause which the cruelty that attended it had sullied; for the sailors refused, on their return to Hydra, to share the booty in accordance with the national rules, and insisted on keeping it all to themselves. This provoked such bitterness of feeling that the fleet was for the time broken up, and no united action against the Turks was possible.

Meanwhile the Ottoman Government had been thrown into the greatest difficulties by the revolt of the islands, and the necessity of fitting out a fleet against the very people from whom it had hitherto drawn its naval recruits. The Turks themselves were no sailors, and, invincible as warriors on land, were helpless at sea. They were now forced to man their ships with untrained fishermen and boatmen, and a motley crowd of Algerine pirates and Maltese and Genoese adventurers. Under these untoward circumstances, though the revolt of Samos on the 30th of April had impressed upon them again the necessity for action, it was not till the 3rd of June that the Ottoman fleet left the Dardanelles. It consisted even now of only two line-of-battle ships, three frigates, and three sloops of war, and these were undermanned, and sailed by crews who had but a rudimentary knowledge of seamanship.

The Greek fleet had meanwhile divided into two squadrons, of which the larger, consisting of thirty-seven sail, under Admiral Tombazes, cruised in the Archipelago, with a view to intercepting the Ottoman fleet. The other, which sailed to blockade Patras, and watch the coasts of Epirus, was commanded by Andreas Miaoulis, a name destined to become famous in the annals of the war.

The character of this remarkable man raises him high above the crowd of self-seeking ruffians by whom he was, for the most part, surrounded. He was the Kallikratidas of modern Greece; and to him apply perfectly the words in which Grote paints the character of the noble Spartan:

> Besides perfect courage, energy, and incorruptibility, he was distinguished for two qualities, both of them very rare among eminent Greeks; entire straightforwardness of dealing, and a Pan-Hellenic patriotism alike comprehensive, exalted, and merciful.—*History of Greece.*

While most of the other leaders of the revolt were thinking only how they could best attain to wealth and power, he devoted the whole of his private fortune to the cause of Greece; and even when all his efforts to inspire his colleagues and his crews with some of his own disinterested patriotism failed, his unshaken firmness might well have earned for him a guerdon similar to that once bestowed by the Roman Senate on the consul who had shared in the crushing defeat of Cannae and yet 'had not despaired of Rome.' Even by the bitterest critics of the Greeks he is excepted from the condemnation which is the lot of all the rest. By one of these a story characteristic of him is told by the French Captain Peyronnet. He adds:

> *L'admiration dont j'étais rempli pour cet homme-là s'est sauvée du naufrage de mon enthousiasme pour ses compatriotes, et même pour la cause des Grecs.*—Lemaître.

The men of his squadron had been pillaging on shore, without his having the power to stop them. On complaint being made to him, he deplored that he was powerless to prevent the outrages, but asked at how much the damage was reckoned. The reply was: 'Six hundred *piasters*,' and Miaoulis thereupon paid the money out of his own pocket. Amid the sordid chicanery and lurid horrors of the war, it may perhaps be excusable to have lingered awhile over this brighter picture.

The squadron under Tombazes had fallen in with the Ottoman fleet; but though superior in numbers, the Greeks were very inferior in size and in weight of ordnance, and they did not venture to come to close quarters. Taking advantage of their more easily managed craft, they manoeuvred just outside the range of the Ottoman guns, waiting for an opportunity to strike. This soon presented itself. In the early morning of the 5th of June, one of the Turkish battle-ships, which had been separated from its companions during the night, was observed to the north of Chios, making all sail in the direction of Samos. The Greeks immediately gave chase; and it did not take long for their light vessels to overhaul the slow-sailing Ottoman.

The Turkish captain, seeing that he had no chance of regaining the squadron, now changed his course, and made for the Bay of Eresos on the North-West coast of Mitylene, where he cast anchor and cleared for action. He had scarcely finished his preparations when the Greeks attacked him. Sailing under the stern of the Ottoman, so as to avoid his broadside, they poured in a hail of shot; but their guns were of small calibre, and the bullets for the most part buried themselves harmlessly in the solid timbers of the Turkish battle-ship.

Tombazes, recognising after a while the futility of this method of attack, gave the order to cease fire, and summoned a council of war to meet on his flag-ship. It was now determined to have recourse to fire-ships, which it was remembered had been employed with such signal success by the Russians against the Ottoman fleet at the Battle of Tchesmé in 1770. A Psariot captain consented, for a sum of 40,000 *piastres*, to sacrifice his brig for the purpose; and this was now hastily prepared, and, manned by a crew of twenty men, who had been secured by the promise of a bounty of a hundred dollars each, it was despatched during the night against the enemy. It was, however, timidly manoeuvred, was ignited too soon, and drifted, magnificently ablaze, out to sea, without coming anywhere near the Ottoman ship.

Soon after this failure, two more fire-ships having arrived from Psara, another attempt was made, but with no better success. At last, however, a Psariot named Pappanikolo succeeded in steering his *brûlot* into the Turkish ship, and jamming its bowsprit under the prow of the Ottoman. Setting light to the fuse, he jumped with his crew into a boat, and rowed away while the fire-ship burst into a blaze. The flames, driven by the stiff breeze over the Turkish ship, soon enveloped it in a mass of fire. A couple of boatloads of the Ottoman sailors succeeded in getting clear of the burning vessel; and many of the crew who could swim leaped overboard and made their way ashore. But between three and four hundred souls are supposed to have perished on board the doomed ship. (Cf. account from MS. journal of Admiral Tombazes. Gordon, i. Appendix.) The 'secret of the war' had been discovered; and this conflagration was 'the naval beacon of Greek liberty.'

The disasters of the Ottomans at sea were somewhat compensated for by the destruction, shortly before the fall of Tripolitza, of Galaxidi, a flourishing seaport in the Gulf of Corinth. This was attacked on the

1st of October by a Turkish squadron under Ismail Djebel Akhdar, who took advantage of the longer range of the Ottoman ordnance to silence the Galaxidiot battery and cannonade the town, without himself coming within gunshot of the Greeks. Under these circumstances, no effective resistance was possible; and the victory of the Turks was complete. The town, the boats on the beach, and the vessels which were aground, were burnt. The whole of the remainder of the Galaxidiot navy, which chanced unfortunately to be all in the harbour at the time of the attack, fell into the hands of the Ottomans, who carried off no less than thirty-four brigs and schooners. (Finlay, i., following Gordon, i., who, however, calls Ismail, Ismail *Gibraltar*. Cf. Lem.)

Hypsilanti, who was at the head of a considerable force on the opposite shore, was compelled to witness the fate of Galaxidi, without being able to do anything to prevent it.

★★★★★★

Note:—The Greek seamen have been accused of cowardice as well as cruelty. It is pointed out that they seldom ventured to approach boldly within range of the Ottoman guns, and stand up to their enemy in fair fight, and never so much as dreamed of laying their vessels alongside even a disabled enemy and taking it by the board. To the first of these criticisms the answer is provided by the action in the Bay of Eresos; for this proved the weak ordnance of the Greeks to be powerless against the heavy Turkish ships. When the combatants met on more equal terms, the Greeks proved themselves not deficient in courage; as is shown by their gallant attack, under Captain Hastings, on the Ottoman squadron in the Bay of Salona, later on in the war. As for boarding, to make this possible some proportion is necessary between the size of the combatants; and for the Greeks to have laid their little brigs and sloops alongside the great battleships of the Turks might have been magnificent, but it would not have been war. The object of war is not to exhibit one's prowess, but to disable the enemy as speedily as possible, with the least amount of damage to oneself. This fact explains and justifies the use of fire-ships, which the Greeks were accused of using only because they were too cowardly to employ other means of attack. As to the amount of courage needed for their effective employment, this surely could hardly be exaggerated. *Brûlots* were to the wooden navies what torpedo-boats are in our own day; and no naval officer would deny that, for the effective handling of torpedo craft in time of war, nerves of steel and a swift and unerring judgment are absolutely essential. It is true that the crews of the fire-ships almost invariably escaped; but this was due, not to the inevitable condition s of this method of warfare, but to the bad watch kept on board the Ottoman ships, and the panic which the approach of a *brûlot* generally created.

CHAPTER 5

Anarchy in Greece

The crimes by which, at the outbreak of the rebellion, the Greeks disgraced themselves and their cause were not without their expiation. The massacre of Tripolitza was followed by a pestilence, due to the masses of unburied corpses, which swept off thousands of the Greeks; and the vengeance of Sultan Mahmoud completed what the pestilence had left undone.

When the news of the Greek atrocities in the Morea reached Constantinople, the slumbering embers of Mohammedan fanaticism burst into flame, and raged with uncontrollable fury. The perpetrators of the outrages might be beyond their reach, but throughout the Ottoman empire was scattered a large Greek population, on whom the Turks might execute a justice not accustomed to discriminate between the innocent and the guilty. Sultan Mahmoud himself proved both his energy of character and the terrible intensity of his wrath. Not content with ordering the arrest of members of the Hetairia wherever he could lay hands on them, he determined by a signal act of vengeance to strike terror into the whole Greek world. According to the Ottoman theory of government, the higher State officials are personally responsible for the conduct of those they rule.

Already, on the 16th of April, Musuri, the Greek *dragoman* to the Porte, had been led forth in his official robes to execution. A more terrible example was to follow. The Patriarch of Constantinople was, as has been already explained, at once the civil and religious head of the Greek Nation. As the civil head, he was responsible to the Ottoman Government for the conduct of the Greeks; as the religious head, he was the centre of all that was to them most venerable and sacred. The war had been proclaimed from the first as a crusade and a war of extermination. Sultan Mahmoud now wished to prove by a signal example that he took up the challenge.

In the early morning of the 22nd of April the Patriarch Gregorios celebrated solemn mass, as usual, surrounded by his *prelates*. After the service a *synod* was assembled, and a messenger from the palace read a *firman* of the *Sultan* deposing Gregorios, and ordering the assembled bishops to proceed at once to the election of a new patriarch. The terrified *prelates*, with tears and trembling, had no choice but to obey; and, while the new Head of the Orthodox Church was receiving the investiture of his office, the venerable Gregorios, still in his sacred robes, was led forth and hung before the gate of the patriarchal palace. The body, after being suspended for a day or two, was cut down and handed over to the Jews, to be dragged through the streets and thrown into the sea. Picked up by a Greek ship, it was recognised and carried to Odessa, where it was buried by the Russian authorities with the honours of a martyr.

★★★★★★

It is characteristic of the theological amenities for which Constantinople has in all ages been distinguished, that the Greek 'Catholics' are said to have sung a solemn *Te Deum* to celebrate the death of the heretical patriarch. Mendelssohn, i.

★★★★★★

For a moment it seemed as though this act of barbarous vengeance would defeat its own ends, by breaking up the concert of the powers and provoking an anti-Turkish war. A thrill of horror and indignation ran through all Christendom. To the Emperor Francis it was almost as though the Pope himself had been murdered. In Russia especially, the whole population was deeply stirred, and, at the slightest word, would have risen as one man to revenge the death of the Orthodox Patriarch. Had Alexander I. been guided by the sentiment of his subjects, had he even been in Russia at the time, war could hardly have been delayed. As it was, he was too deeply committed to the policy of Metternich; and, after wavering awhile, he contented himself with ordering his ambassador, Stroganoff, to present a vigorous protest to the *Sultan*, and withdraw from Constantinople.

To Metternich a massacre more or less beyond the eastern borders of Austria was a matter of little moment compared with the peace of Europe and the policy of reaction of which he was the director. To Castlereagh, too, a period of repose seemed absolutely essential to Europe, after the exhaustion of the Napoleonic wars; and a proposal for a joint demonstration of the powers at Constantinople, for the protection of the Christians, failed owing to the strenuous opposition of Lord Strangford, the British ambassador. For the time Turkey was freed from all fear of European intervention between her and her rebellious vassal.

Meanwhile the course of the struggle itself was once more demonstrating the wisdom of the Machiavellian maxim, '*No half measures.*' Outside Greece proper and the Archipelago, the ruthless severity of the *Sultan* had produced its effect, and, by the beginning of 1822, such isolated risings as had occurred were all suppressed, and the country to the north of Janina and of Mount Pelion restored to the Ottoman allegiance. To the south of this line, the no less 'thorough' policy of the Greeks had been similarly crowned with success. All the Morea, except the fortresses of Nauplia, Coron, Modon, and Patras, was now in their hands; and to the north of the Gulf of Corinth, they were masters of the country as far as the Gulf of Arta and the pass of Thermopylae. From a people of slaves, the Greeks had become a nation.

The problem that now presented itself to them was to evolve out of the anarchy of the insurrection a system of national government: a problem which, unfortunately for them, they were far less capable of solving than they were of carrying on a guerilla war. That sectional patriotism, with its local feuds and jealousies, which had proved the ruin of the ancient civilisation of Hellas, was quite as characteristic of the modern Greeks; while the sweeping away of the Ottoman power removed the only paramount authority, and gave full play to all centrifugal forces. The communal organisation, untouched by the revolt, served indeed still to preserve order among the people; but the confiscation of Turkish property to the public use had placed vast sums in the hands of the rebels, and as there was as yet no centralised fiscal system, this fell into the hands of the primates and military leaders, who too often used it to further the ends of their own private pleasure or ambition.

The result was a complete anarchy, which nothing but the habits of obedience of the people to their local authorities, and the bond of union which they had in their common religious enthusiasm and hatred of the Turk, could have prevented from ending in the ruin of the Greek cause. Every primate, or bishop, or military chief assumed himself to have succeeded, in his own locality, to the *Sultan's* prerogative. Under them was the whole military, fiscal, and criminal government of the various districts, and as yet they owed no allegiance to any higher authority. Nor had there been the slightest effort to reform the most crying abuses of the Ottoman system.

Nothing proves more clearly that the revolt of the peasantry was motived by religion rather than political grievances than that, after their success, no improvement was made in the financial arrangements of the country, or in the method of collecting taxes; that nothing was done for the security of property, to establish law-courts, or to arrange for a publication of accounts. (Finlay, i.)

In the local centres, indeed, public opinion put some check on the worst abuses; but, in the wider sphere of which a patriotism purely local could take no account, corruption and knavery reigned supreme. The political history of this period is a disgusting record of petty jealousies, intrigues, shameless peculations and contemptible incompetence; and only the heroic patience and indomitable fortitude of the people at large can relieve the sordidness of the picture. No one seems to have had any idea of the right way to set about constructing a constitution. That of England had been in its origin a 'concentration of local machinery,' and had the Greek constitutions similarly been based on the existing communal system, they would have had more chance of success. As it was, the attempts at constitution-making of the successive National Assemblies, when they did meet, were but plausible schemes evolved by pedantic doctrinaires out of their own inner consciousness, and were for the most part still-born.

Meanwhile the demand of the people for some sort of central executive could not be neglected; and on June 7, 1821, there was formed the *Gerousia*, or Senate of the Peloponnese, a purely oligarchical committee based upon no popular suffrage, of which the authority was to last till the fall of Tripolitza. This derived especial power from the co-operation of Archbishop Germanos, whose eloquence, assumed sanctity, and energy at the beginning of the revolt had given him great popularity. The subsequent career of this prelate, however, did little to fulfil the hopes excited by its commencement; and his popularity soon waned, when it was seen that his religious zeal was but a mask to hide unbounded pride, ambition, and love of pleasure. He soon cast aside his pretended sanctity, and assumed the airs and gorgeous attire of a barbarian prince. This role he had not the qualities necessary to maintain; and he was soon pushed aside by others, no less unscrupulous, but more able than himself. (Gordon, i.)

The arrival, on the 22nd of June, of Prince Demetrius Hypsilanti introduced a new factor into the situation. Holding that his brother Alexander, as chief of the Hetairia, was thereby *ipso facto* Prince of Greece, he believed himself entitled to act as his viceroy, and announced himself as empowered to act as lieutenant-governor of the country on his brother's behalf. In view of the already notorious ill-success of Prince Alexander in the principalities, the pretension was foolish; but Demetrius was understood to be supported by Russia, and received, therefore, an enthusiastic welcome from the soldiers and common people. By the oligarchs, headed by Germanos, on the other hand, who were jealous of outside interference, he was bitterly opposed; and his arrival was followed by a war of intrigues and recriminations.

At last, he made a bold move to induce the people to declare actively in his favour. He suddenly left the camp before Tripolitza, and issued a proclamation stating that all his efforts on behalf of Greece had been rendered nugatory by the selfish opposition of the primates and senators. The stratagem was successful. On the news of his departure, the soldiers rose in arms; and for a while the lives of some of the oligarchs were in danger. Order was only restored by their promising to submit to the authority of Prince Demetrius, who was now brought back in triumph from Leondari, and established in undisputed power.

Had he possessed the ability, he was now in the position to have become 'the Washington of Greece;' but he was, in fact, too incompetent to retain the authority he had won. Bit by bit this was usurped by his lieutenants, or resumed by the primates; and since he was in the eyes of the common people supreme, the misdeeds of his supposed agents were laid at his door, and so, with the gradual decline of his power, his popularity also waned.

In the midst of the confusion caused by these quarrels and intrigues, on the 3rd of August, another Phanariot Greek, Alexander Mavrocordatos, also arrived in Greece. He had already acquired at the court of Karadja, Hospodar of Wallachia, a considerable reputation for political ability, which, however, his long career in the service of Greece did little to justify. He was known, moreover, as an honourable man and a sincere patriot. But neither his reputation nor his honesty availed to reduce the chaos which he found to order; and after struggling awhile unsuccessfully with the confusion, he caused himself to be nominated administrator of West Hellas, and left for Missolonghi. Here, without further authority from the central government, he proceeded to summon a meeting of deputies from the provinces of Acarnania, Ætolia, Western Locris, and the part of Epirus which had joined the Greek cause. Theodore Negris, who was acting as administrator in East Hellas, convoked a similar meeting at Salona, of deputies from Attica, Boeotia, Megaris, Phocis, and Eastern Locris. At Missolonghi a senate was appointed to conduct the executive government; and a corresponding body at Salona took the high-sounding title of the Areopagus.

Meanwhile Hypsilanti had made another bid for popularity, and summoned the National Convention to Argos, where it met in December. From the outset it was violently opposed by the oligarchy of primates and military chiefs; and since, in Argos, these had, through their armed followers, complete control, the Assembly was moved to Piada, not far from the ancient Epidaurus. The oligarchs, in the meantime, remained in Argos, and proceeded to revive the Peloponnesian Senate, claiming for it such complete supremacy in the Morea, that the central government remained practically powerless.

Greece was thus, at the end of the year 1821, divided into three sections, each under its own senate, and all nominally dependent on the central government. But the Constitution published by the Assembly at Piada, known as that of Epidaurus, remained a dead letter; and the provincial senates only exercised any power in so far as they were governed by the faction which chanced to have command of most men and money. For the most part their pedantic discussions were treated by the wild chiefs of the revolt with the contempt they deserved.

The new constitution was proclaimed on January 22, 1822, and Alexander Mavrocordatos was elected President of Greece. He had few of the qualities necessary to maintain so difficult a position. It is true that in culture and experience, as in probity of motive, he was superior to the mass of the leaders of the revolt; but he lacked strength and firmness, and the breadth of view which enables a statesman to look beyond the details of administration and to understand the wider issues involved in the government of men. To him, moreover, applied with double force a remark which Goethe, in a conversation with Eckermann, afterwards made with reference to Count Capodistrias.

> Capodistrias will in the long run not be able to maintain himself at the head of Greek affairs; for he lacks a quality which is essential to such a position. He is no soldier. Now we have no example of any mere diplomat being able to organise a revolutionary State, or secure the obedience of soldiers and military chiefs.

This proved profoundly true of Capodistrias; it was no less profoundly true of Mavrocordatos. Moreover, whereas Capodistrias, a man of dignified and imposing presence, never affected to be a soldier, Mavrocordatos, in spite of his spectacles and his plump little figure, more than once made himself ridiculous by attempts to play the general, with disastrous results both for himself and Greece. Thus it came about that he entered on his office under inauspicious omens. Thinking to strengthen his position by adding military glory to his diplomatic prestige, he attempted, on his way from Missolonghi, to reduce the Turkish garrison of Patras. But he only proved that nature had not intended him for a general. The Ottomans overwhelmed him in a sortie; and, defeated, and stripped of all save the clothes on his back, he arrived ignominiously at the seat of government.

It may be doubted whether, at that time, the strongest and wisest of rulers could have reduced the chaos of Greek affairs to order. It needed the awful lesson which was about to be given them, to make the Hellenes forget, for a while, their selfish ambitions and jealousies, under the compulsion of a common fear and a common passion of revenge.

CHAPTER 6

Fall of the Acropolis

The year 1822, which was to prove on the whole so full of glory and of hope for Greece, began with a series of disasters. The rumour that Sultan Mahmoud was preparing a great expedition to crush out the revolt in the Morea determined the Greek Government to forestall him by pressing the war in Eastern Hellas. The Acropolis of Athens was still held by a Turkish garrison, and Elias Mavromichales, the eldest son of Petrobey, had been invited by the Areopagus to aid in its reduction.

At Athens, however, he was met by an invitation from the Euboeans to help them in an attack on Karystos; and as this seemed to promise more adventure than was likely to be found in blockading the Acropolis, he responded to the appeal. Before his arrival at the camp of the Euboeans, the men of Kumi had already elected a Montenegrin named Vassos as their captain, and Elias Mavromichales, with a rare generosity, consented to share his authority with this comparatively inexperienced soldier. Together they determined to attack the Turkish post at the village of Stura, where a considerable quantity of grain for the use of the garrison at Karystos had been collected.

Unfortunately, owing to the neglect of the Greeks to secure in time the pass of Diakophti, and so cut off the possibility of relief from Karystos, the attack failed. The small Ottoman garrison held out until Omer Bey arrived with reinforcements. The Greeks were routed; and Elias Mavromichales himself was surrounded in an old mill, where for some time he defended himself with great bravery. At last, seeing no chance of relief, he tried to cut his way out, but was killed in the attempt. His death was the first blow to the Greek cause during the year, and created great sorrow; for to the bravery which was usual among the chiefs of the insurrection, he added a disinterested patriotism which was far from being so common.

Shortly after his death, Odysseus of Ithaka, whose authority, since the death of Diakos, had been paramount in East Hellas, arrived from Attica with a force of seven hundred men. The Greeks now advanced once more upon Stura, but found it evacuated and cleared of its stores. Karystos itself was then besieged; but suddenly Odysseus, without giving any warning of his intention, marched away with all his men. This action, in one who was suspected of playing at all times a double game, so alarmed the rest of the besiegers that they raised the siege.

Odysseus, one of the most celebrated leaders of the war, was as Homeric in his personality as in his name, and his feats of physical strength and endurance rivalled those of the mythical hero from whom he pretended to trace his descent. It was said that he could leap clear over the backs of seven horses placed side by side, and that, after his defeat by Mehmet at Gravia on November 13, 1822, he ran for eight leagues through the rough and mountainous country occupied by the enemy, with scarce a pause, and with no signs of exhaustion or distress. (Mendelssohn, i.) Such feats would have been enough to make him a hero among the wild and barbarous mountaineers, even without that courage and cunning which seemed the ordinary qualifications for a captain of Armatoli.

Strength and courage were indeed his sole apparent virtues. For the rest, he had been, like so many other leaders of the revolt, trained at the court of Ali Pasha of Janina, and had there learned to combine the worst vices of Albanians and Greeks. He was false as the most deceitful Greek and vindictive as the most bloodthirsty Albanian. (Finlay, i.; Gordon, i.) His object in joining the Greek revolt was not to liberate Greece from the Ottoman rule, but, if possible, to establish his own authority permanently in Eastern Hellas; and, if he could achieve this better by attaching himself to the Turks, it was certain that he would not hesitate to betray the Hellenic cause.

Odysseus himself asserted that he had been compelled to retire from Karystos owing to want of food; but this did not explain his leaving without informing his colleagues of his intention; and the Greeks believed that he had been in treasonable communication with Omer Bey. Possibly the true explanation was that he knew that his enemies, and especially the Minister of War, Kolettes, were endeavouring to break his power in Attica, and that he suspected them of hatching some sinister plot against him in his absence.

Meanwhile, however, there had arrived from the Archipelago the news of a disaster which threw the other misfortunes of the Greeks into the shade, and for the time made the factions lay aside their quarrels under the influence of a common horror and thirst for vengeance. Of all the island communities of the Ægean none was more prosperous or more inoffensive than that of Chios. Among their more turbulent neighbours, the well-to-do and peace-loving Chiots had a reputation for stolid simplicity. *'Easier to find a green horse,'* ran the saying, *'than a clever Chiot.'* One attempt to rouse the island had failed; but its wealth and general importance made it desirable to secure its adhesion to the national cause; and Hypsilanti allowed himself to be persuaded to authorise a Chiot adventurer named Ralli, and a certain Lycourgos Logothetes of Smyrna, to make a descent upon it.

In March, Lycourgos, with some 2,500 men, landed at Koutari, and, calling on the unwilling Chiots for aid, proceeded to lay siege to the Turkish garrison. From the first he proved himself totally incompetent. Not only did he mismanage the operations on shore in every possible way, but he neglected utterly the all-important precaution of keeping the command of the sea.

The news of the attack on Chios roused Sultan Mahmoud once more to fury; the ladies of his *harem*, too, indignant at the devastations committed in their mastic gardens by the insurgents, clamoured for the suppression of the revolt; and preparations for this were pressed on with unwonted vigour. On the 11th of April, without any resistance on the part of the Greeks, the *Capitan Pasha*, Kara Ali, landed 7,000 troops on the island. Lycourgos and his rabble had proved their courage by murdering in cold blood the crew of a Turkish *felucca* which had run ashore, and in general by massacring all the Mussulman captives who fell into their hands. They now, at the approach of the Ottoman force, took to their boats and fled, leaving the wretched Chiots to their fate.

The 'blood bath' that followed is the most horrible episode in a history of horrors. The Turkish commander, aided by the local Mussulman authorities, made some effort to curb the excesses of the troops, less, perhaps, in the interests of humanity, than in those of the imperial revenue. But the Ottoman soldiery had been reinforced by hordes of fanatics, who had crowded over from the mainland to share in the holy war; and these it was impossible to control. A few of the islanders succeeded in escaping in Greek vessels; and even these poor wretches were usually robbed of everything they had saved from the wreck of their homes by the boatmen, who made the surrender of all

Death of a General Markos Botsaris

they possessed the price of safety. (Cf. Gordon, i. The Philhellene Jourdain himself saw, on the island of Psara, many victims of this 'atrocious speculation.' *Mémoires historiques, &c.* i.).

Of the rest of the inhabitants, some 27,000 are said to have been put to the sword, while 43,000 were collected and sold into slavery; and of a once flourishing community of a hundred thousand souls, barely two thousand remained to people the island.

The unhappy Chiots were not long unavenged. On the 10th of April the Greek fleet put to sea under Admiral Miaoulis; and on the 31st, a naval engagement was fought off Chios, but without result. The Greeks then determined to have resort to their favourite device of fire-ships. On the 18th of June, the principal officers of the Turkish fleet assembled on board the flagship, to celebrate the feast of *Bairam* with the *Capitan Pasha*. The night was pitch dark; but the admiral's vessel, decorated from masthead to waterline with coloured lanterns, was a blaze of light. On board, some three thousand men were celebrating the great Mohammedan festival with laughter and music; and, in the universal jollity, but a poor watch was kept.

Suddenly, through the lines of the Turkish vessels, glided, like dark shadows, two Greek fire-ships. One of these, steered with admirable precision by Kanaris, made straight for the flagship of the *Capitan Pasha*; and, unobserved, the cool-headed Greek ran his bowsprit into an open port of the Turkish vessel, fixed his grappling irons, fired the train, and, quietly slipping with his men into a boat, rowed off, while the fire-ship burst into flame. In an instant, sails and cordage being soaked in turpentine, the fire ran up the rigging, and, carried by the wind over the Ottoman ship, rapidly enveloped it in a mass of flame.

An awful scene followed. Completely taken by surprise, the Turks had no time to save themselves. The few boats that were launched were, for the most part, swamped by the panic-stricken crowds that leaped into them. The other ships of the fleet sheered off, to avoid sharing the fate of the admiral, or to escape the hail of bullets from her exploding guns. Of the whole 3,000 men on board, but very few survived. Kara Ali himself was struck by a falling yard, and carried dying ashore. The second Greek fire-ship, less fortunate, or less skilfully steered, did not effect anything. This episode, when:

> *Twice twenty self-devoted Greeks assailed*
> *The naval host of Asia, at one blow*
> *Scattered it into air—and Greece was free,*   Savage Landor.

....earned for Kanaris a fame which spread far beyond the limits of the Greek world, and which, among the Hellenes themselves, will endure as long as there is a Greek Nation to cherish the memory of its heroes.

The frantic delight with which the news of this exploit was hailed at the time was possibly not shared by the surviving Chiots. Several hundred of them, captive on board the Turkish ship, had perished with it. The miserable island, too, was now exposed again, by way of reprisals, to a second devastation, which completed what the first had left undone; and even the mastic villages, whose industry was so indispensable to the ladies of the *Sultan's harem,* were this time not spared. Their vengeance sated, the Turks sailed away to take refuge, from Kanaris and his fireships, under the guns of the Dardanelles.

The news of the massacre of Chios awoke the Greeks to some sense of the seriousness of their position. But, in the meantime, while they had been wrangling and intriguing, Sultan Mahmoud had been making preparations for a first great effort to reconquer Greece. The troubles with Russia, in which the execution of the patriarch had threatened to involve him, had been smoothed over; and, above all, the destruction of the power of Ali Pasha had set free the army of Khurshid for the suppression of the Hellenic revolt. Mahmoud, deceived by the ease with which the insurrection had been suppressed in Thessaly, Macedonia, and Epirus, believed that his troops would experience little difficulty in the task of reducing the whole of Greece. The plan of campaign which he devised was a good one, and, if properly carried out, promised to be successful.

Nauplia, the most important fortress in the Morea, with its two impregnable citadels of Palamidi and Itsh-Kalé, had now for months been blockaded by the Greeks, and its relief was the first object of the Ottoman campaign. So far, the place had resisted all the efforts of the Greeks to capture it; and an attempt made by Hypsilanti, in December, 1821, to carry the castle of Palamidi by storm, had ignominiously failed. But the garrison, now reduced to the last stages of starvation, could not expect to hold out much longer; and on the 30th of June a capitulation was actually signed, by which the Turks agreed to surrender, if not relieved within twenty-five days. If, then, the Ottoman campaign was to attain its object, there was little time to lose.

At Larissa, Khurshid, now appointed *Seraskier,* or Governor-General, of Rumelia, had collected a large body of troops; and another army, under Omer Vrioni, was assembled in Epirus. It was arranged that, while the latter advanced by Western Hellas on Missolonghi, with a view to capturing this, and crossing thence to Patras, the main army under Khurshid's direction should force the Isthmus, advance to the relief of Nauplia, where it was to be met by the Ottoman fleet, and march thence on Tripolitza. Here it was to establish its headquarters, in the very centre of the Arcadian plain; and it was judged that if the fleet threw supplies into the fortresses of Coron, Modon, and Patras, communications with these could be easily established, and that the Morea being thus cut up into several sections, the population, deprived of mutual support, would be reduced to submit before the winter.

As the spring advanced, Dramali, (Mohamet Ali Pasha of Drama), to whom the command of the expedition was given, was ordered by Khurshid to push on into the valley of the Spercheios, and there review his troops. Before this was effected, an attempt was made, under the leadership of Odysseus, to destroy the Turkish troops in Zeituni. The plan had been devised by the Areopagus, and its failure, due to various causes, led to the relations between that body and the masterful *Klepht* becoming somewhat strained. An attempt was made to remove Odysseus from his command in East Hellas; whereupon he immediately resigned his commission in the Greek Army, and remained at the head of his troops as an independent chieftain!

It now became the first object of the central executive to destroy the power of Odysseus in East Hellas; and Alexis Noutzas and Christos Palaskas, partisans and friends of Kolettes, were sent, the former to act as civil governor, the latter to supersede Odysseus in the supreme command of the forces. Their appointment to these posts had been kept secret; but Odysseus knew perfectly well the object of their coming. His suspicious nature, moreover, led him to believe that they had been commissioned by Kolettes to assassinate him, a task for which their previous reputations seemed to point them out as very suitable agents. He determined to frustrate the plot. He received them with all the polished courtesy of which he was capable, and gave them a hearty welcome. After entertaining them at supper, he conducted them to the small wayside chapel which was to serve them for bedroom, wished them goodnight, and left them. In the morning they were found murdered.

The horror which this crime excited, and the anarchy which was its immediate result, were soon afterwards overshadowed in the public mind by the news of the fall of the Acropolis, an event of great importance to the Greek cause, but which was again sullied by the treachery and cruelty by which it was accompanied. On the 21st of June, the Turkish garrison, driven by want of water to surrender, agreed to a capitulation, by virtue of which they were to be removed to Asia Minor in neutral ships. They were to lay down their arms, but were to be allowed to retain one-half of the valuables in their possession. The Bishop of Athens, a man of honourable character, and president of the Areopagus, made the Greek leaders swear on the Holy Mysteries to observe the terms of the capitulation.

Eleven hundred and fifty Mussulmans, of whom only one hundred and eighty were capable of bearing arms, surrendered on these terms, and were lodged, pending the completion of the arrangements for their removal, in the extensive buildings contained within the ruins of the Stoa of Hadrian, formerly occupied by the *voivode*. Meanwhile news reached the town that the army of Dramali had passed Thermopylae. An Albanian savage named Nikkas now incited the people, as a pledge that they would never yield to the Turk, to slaughter the defenceless prisoners; and the *klephts* and *armatoli*, joined by the rabble of Athens, ever ready to make mock-heroics the excuse for satisfying their native lust for cruelty, set willingly to work.

A scene of horror followed which has only too many parallels during the course of this horrible war. For a whole day the streets of Athens resounded with the shrieks and cries of tortured women and children. The leaders, who had sworn, by all they held most sacred, to see the capitulation carried out, did not care, or were afraid, to interfere. The foreign consuls did what they could; but the mob had tasted blood, and their interference all but proved fatal to themselves. At last the arrival of two French ships of war in the Piraeus put a stop to the slaughter. Under a strong escort of marines, some three hundred and ninety of the Mussulmans, who had sought refuge in the French, Austrian, and Dutch consulates, were conducted to the harbour through a mob of wild tribesmen and Athenian citizens, who brandished their weapons, and yelled like demoniacs at the sight of their escaping prey.

★★★★★★

The account given by Finlay i. of this horrible affair differs from that of M. Lemaître. The former gives the Greeks credit for having been ashamed of themselves. After the departure of the refugees in the French Consulate, 'shame operated, and all the Turks who remained in the Austrian and Dutch consulates were allowed to depart unmolested.' But M. de Reverseaux, commanding the *Active* (quoted *verbatim* by M. Lemaître), states that he only succeeded in rescuing the latter with the utmost difficulty from the 'mob of assassins'; '*Je criai que c'était sur moi qu'ils devaient tirer, et non sur les restes infortunes d'une population désarmée; mais que s'ils avaient l'audace, je trouverais promtement des vengeurs . . . ! Mon mouvement les déconcerta,*' &c. Cf. also Gordon, i.

✯✯✯✯✯✯

Vengeance in this case followed hard upon the footsteps of crime. The advance of Dramali was facilitated by the quarrels among the Greek chiefs; and at the head of twenty-four thousand infantry and six thousand cavalry he marched through Boeotia and Attica, without encountering serious opposition. Athens and the Acropolis next fell into his hands, and the Ottomans wreaked their vengeance for the slaughter of their co-religionists.

Rumour exaggerated the numbers of the Turkish host; no such display of military pomp had been seen since, in 1715, Ali Kummargee had crossed the Spercheios to reconquer the Morea from the Venetians; and at the terror of its approach all opposition vanished. The Isthmus was passed; and the impregnable rock of Acrocorinthos fell, abandoned by its cowardly garrison without a blow. Had Dramali proceeded with ordinary caution, the Greek revolt would have been at an end; and already Metternich and his allies were beginning to rejoice at the prospect of its speedy collapse.

But his undisturbed march led the Turkish commander, very naturally but no less fatally, to underrate his enemy. He expected to meet everywhere with as little opposition as he had hitherto experienced, and that the whole of the Morea would submit on the mere rumour of his arrival. Advised to make the Acrocorinthos his base, and, from this centre, subdue the country methodically and piece by piece, he rejected the cautious counsel with scorn. Instead, he decided to advance with his whole force to the relief of Nauplia.

Fortune seemed to smile upon the enterprise. The direct road to Nauplia lay over the difficult pass of Devernaki, and this the Greeks had neglected to occupy. Full of contempt for so despicable a foe, the Turks pushed on over the mountains, and descended into the plain of Argolis, without even thinking it worthwhile to secure their communications, by occupying the defiles in their rear. At the rumour of their approach, panic terror seized the eloquent legislators of Greece, assembled at Argos. Ministers and deputies, officials, and place-hunters, fled in all directions, leaving the town to be plundered by the wild

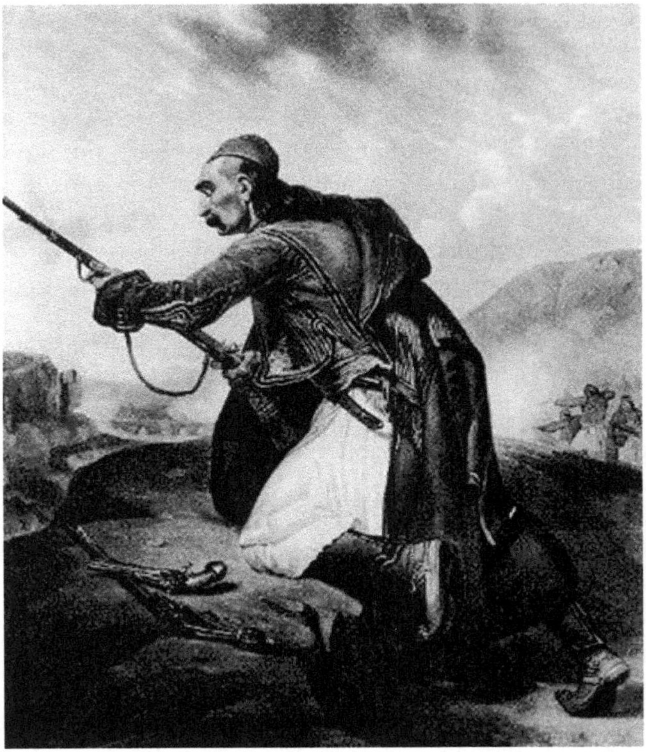

klephts and *armatoli*. Only a few, and notably Kolokotrones and Demetrius Hypsilanti, refused to join in the stampede.

✶✶✶✶✶✶

Those of the wretched fugitives who escaped the attentions of the Mainotes, by whom they were stripped without compunction, and who sought refuge on board Hydriot and Spezziot boats at Lerna, were robbed by the sailors of the last fragments of their property, and left to starve in out-of-the-way points of the Morea and Archipelago. Gordon, i.

✶✶✶✶✶✶

A small band of Greeks, under the Mainote Kariyanni, had seized Larissa, the mediaeval castle which crowns the Acropolis of ancient Argos; and here they were joined by Hypsilanti, who, with a band of seven hundred men, threw himself into the fortress. Ill-provisioned and insufficiently supplied with arms, they could not hope to hold out long; but they achieved their purpose of holding the Turks in check until Kolokotrones had had time to collect an army. Their desperate courage placed Dramali in an awkward position; for he was unable to advance to Nauplia, leaving an unreduced fortress in his rear; and his neglect of the question of supplies and communications now began to tell.

The Ottoman fleet, under Mehmet Pasha, was to have kept pace with him along the coast, and served as his base of supplies. But Mehmet, with true Turkish inconsequence, had preferred to cruise on his own account round the Peloponnese; and the army of Dramali was, therefore, left without a base, and without supplies. The very folly of the Greeks had turned to their advantage; for, between the mountains and the sea, the Ottomans were now fairly caught in a trap, and it seemed almost as though the Greeks had purposely left the door open in order to lure them to destruction.

Dramali was soon persuaded of the necessity of falling back by the way he had come, before his supplies were utterly exhausted, and on the 6th of August began his retreat. But in the meantime Kolokotrones had realised the situation, and hurried with a small force to occupy the defile of Devernaki; and, when the Turkish Army reached the pass, they found it already in the possession of the Greeks. The vanguard, consisting of some thousand Albanian mountaineers, succeeded in evading the Greeks by following difficult and circuitous paths; but the main body of the Ottomans attempted to force their way through the narrow defile; and here they were overwhelmed by a murderous fire, which soon choked the road with the bodies of men and horses, and made it impossible for them to advance. It was a massacre rather than a battle; and nothing but the plundering instincts of the Greeks saved the Ottoman Army from absolute annihilation. A few of the better mounted *delhis* succeeded in spurring over the heaps of dead and dying, and cutting their way through to Corinth; but the rest of the army, with the loss of some four thousand men, and of all its baggage, was forced to return into the plain of Argolis, with less chance than ever of being able to force its way out.

Dramali seemed as though stunned by this blow; and a whole day passed in inaction. Then the absolute impossibility of remaining longer in the barren plain of Argolis forced him to move, and he determined this time to attempt to force his way out by the pass of Agionori. Once more the indiscipline and greed of the Greeks proved the salvation of the Turks. Kolokotrones had arranged, with Niketas and several other chiefs, a plan for cutting off the Ottoman retreat; but this broke down, owing to the Armatoli waiting to plunder the Turkish camp, while those who reached the pass in time to intercept the Turks devoted more attention to the Ottoman baggage than to the Ottomans. With the loss of about a thousand men and all his train, Dramali, breathless, footsore, and bedraggled, at last reached Corinth.

Even at Corinth, however, the Ottomans were not in safety; for the Greeks, encouraged by their unhoped-for success, were hard on their heels. With the aid of Odysseus, Kolokotrones closed all the passes, and shut up the beaten army in Corinth. Starvation and disease did the rest. Dramali himself died on the 9th of November, and only a miserable remnant of his great host were at length taken off by a Turkish fleet.

The collapse of Dramali's invasion decided the fate of Nauplia. The advance of the Turkish Army had encouraged the defenders, already reduced to the last most desperate straits, to persevere; and the appearance off the harbour of Mehmet's fleet had given them an instant's hope. This, however, had been dashed by the cowardice and incapacity of the Ottoman admiral, who sailed away without attempting anything; and when, therefore, they heard the tidings of Dramali's defeat, the Turkish garrison lost all hope of succour, and at last, weakened by hunger and disease, consented to surrender. Already, on the night of the 12th of December, the castle of Palamidi, which the Turks were too weak to hold any longer, had been occupied by the Greeks; and, under these circumstances, the conditions granted by Kolokotrones to

THEODOROS KOLOKOTRONES COMMANDER OF THE GREEK FORCES IN THE MOREA

the garrison were far less favourable than those agreed to by the treaty of the 30th of June; but, such as they were, the presence of an English frigate in the harbour ensured the terms of the capitulation being observed; and the Turks were removed by sea to Asia Minor. Only Ali Pasha, the governor, who refused to sign the capitulation, was held a prisoner.

While the Greeks were thus successful on land, the courage of Kanaris had secured them another victory at sea. He had succeeded in destroying with a *brûlot* the flagship of the Turkish vice-admiral, as it lay at anchor in the midst of the Ottoman fleet between Tenedos and Troas; and this exploit so alarmed the *Capitan Pasha,* that he retired with the Ottoman Navy under the guns of the Dardanelles, leaving the Greeks masters of the open sea.

In West Hellas, meanwhile, the other half of Khurshid's plan of campaign had likewise started with success, and ended in disaster. Before marching southward to effect his junction with Dramali in the Morea, it was necessary for the Ottoman commander to reduce the Suliots, that bravest and most celebrated of the Albanian hill tribes, whose desperate resistance to Ali Pasha of Janina had once roused the sympathy and admiration of Europe, and who were now in arms against the Ottoman power. Though they had not as yet formally thrown in their lot with the Greeks, Mavrocordatos, whose fiasco before Patras had not cured him of his belief in his military capacity, determined to march to their relief. At the head of a considerable force, comprising the only disciplined troops in the Greek Army—the regiment commanded by Colonel Tarella, and the corps of Philhellenes, consisting entirely of foreign officers, commanded by Colonel Dania—he crossed to Missolonghi, and advanced upon Arta.

The Ottoman forces in Arta were commanded by Reshid Pasha, known to the Greeks and Albanians as Kiutayeh, an officer as experienced and capable as Mavrocordatos was the reverse. (He had been Pasha of Kiutayeh in Asia Minor. His father had been a Georgian priest, and he himself was a convert to Islam). The latter made his headquarters at Kombotti, where he remained, while the Greek Army advanced some fifteen miles further, and took up a position at Peta. Here, disadvantageously posted and without having entrenched themselves, they were attacked, on the 16th of July, by the Turks in overwhelming force.

In the absence of the commander-in-chief, no one possessed sufficient authority to produce unity of action among the heterogeneous elements forming the Greek Army. The Philhellenes, indeed, fought with desperate courage; but the treachery of the chief Gogos, who had been entrusted with the defence of the key of the position, suffered the Turks to attack them both in front and rear, and only some twenty-five succeeded in forcing their way through at the point of the bayonet. At the same time Colonel Tarella fell, and his regiment was annihilated. (Detailed account of this battle, Gordon, i.)

This battle had several important effects, apart from its leaving the Turks free to reduce the Suliots; for it destroyed the prestige of Mavrocordatos, and all hope of forming a strong central government under his leadership. It inspired, too, the wild Greek warriors with an intense conviction of the superiority of their own irregular methods of warfare over those of European discipline, a conviction all the more fatal as, just at this time, Sultan Mahmoud was planning the reorganisation of his army on Western models.

The defeat of the Greeks at Peta, and another at Splanga, rendered the position of the Suliots hopeless. Even in these straits, however, their reputation for dauntless courage made the Ottoman commander unwilling to drive them to desperation, and obtained them favourable terms. Once more they evacuated their impregnable mountain fastnesses, and, receiving in compensation a sum of 200,000 *piastres*, crossed over into the Ionian Islands. Henceforward they cast in their lot with the Greeks, and became, for better or for worse, a conspicuous element in the War of Liberation.

Meanwhile the Greeks had spent the short period of respite, due to the Suliot defence, as usual, in internecine feuds. The difficult pass of Makrynoros, through which any force advancing into West Hellas from Epirus would have to make its way, they left undefended; and when Omer Vrioni, Khurshid's lieutenant, at last marched southward, he had no difficulty in pushing as far as Missolonghi.

This insignificant little town, which lies on the shore of a shallow lagoon, between the mouths of the Aspropotamos and the Phidari, did not look as though it would present any serious obstacle to his further advance. Garrisoned only by some six hundred men, its sole fortifications were a low earth wall and a shallow but muddy ditch, its only armament some antiquated guns. Had the Turks advanced at once to the assault, the place must have fallen. As it was, Omer preferred to commence a regular siege, and on the 16th of November sat down before the town.

The Ottoman Army had been joined by crowds of Albanian Armatoli eager to share in the expected booty. The defenders, under Mavrocordatos, were full of courage and enthusiasm; and nothing occurred to damp their ardour. A fleet of Turkish ships, sent by Yussuf Pasha from Patras to blockade the town by sea, was dispersed by a Hydriot squadron; and a thousand men from the Morea, under Petrobey, crossed the Gulf as a welcome reinforcement to the sparse garrison. The Turkish bombardment produced no effect; for the cannon balls sped away over the roofs of the low houses, and the shells from the Ottoman mortars sank in the filth of the unpaved streets and courts without exploding.

At last Omer decided to assault; and chose the night of January 6, 1823, the Greek Christmas Day, for the enterprise, with the idea that the Greeks would be all at church. But the garrison had received information of the move; and, when the assault commenced, it was the besiegers, and not the besieged, who were surprised. A murderous fire greeted the Albanian brigands as they floundered in the muddy ditch. They broke and fled, leaving two hundred dead behind; while the victorious Greeks lost no more than four men. Omer now decided to raise the siege, and retired, in some confusion, back through the pass of Makrynoros, leaving part of his siege train and ammunition behind. The aged Khurshid, on receiving the news, poisoned himself, anticipating by only three days the order for his execution which had been despatched from Constantinople.

Chapter 7

First Civil War

The campaign of 1822 had resulted altogether favourably for the Greeks; and from the diplomatic standpoint, also, the new year opened under promising auspices. The news of the massacre of Chios had dealt a severe blow at Metternich's efforts to counteract the growing influence of Philhellenic sentiment in Europe; and there were not wanting signs of a change in the attitude of the Powers. Alexander, it is true, still remained faithful to the Holy Alliance, refused to receive the Greek envoys sent to him at Verona, and dismissed his Greek Minister, Capodistrias. Thus far the diplomacy of Metternich had triumphed.

For a moment, however, it seemed as though the war between Russia and Turkey which he dreaded was on the point of breaking out. Certain Hydriot brigs, sailing under the Russian flag, had been seized in the Dardanelles by order of the Porte; and the Ottoman Government, thinking it intolerable that hostile vessels should, under cover of a neutral flag, defy it at its very doors, thereupon claimed and exercised the right to stop and search all ships passing through the straits. This action still further increased the tension already existing between the two governments.

To the protests of Russia, the Porte replied by a polite but firm insistence on what it considered to be its rights; and for some time the situation appeared extremely critical. But Metternich was anxious, at all hazards, to prevent Russo-Turkish complications; and, above all, to prevent the Greek question from becoming entangled with those that were purely Russian. (Mendelssohn, i.) He now moved heaven and earth to persuade the Porte to concede the Russian demands; and in this he was vigorously seconded by Lord Strangford, the English Ambassador at Constantinople, whose policy at all times was but a reflection of that of the Austrian Chancellor. (*Ibid.*)

Their united efforts, at last, succeeded in overcoming the stubborn opposition of the Porte, and prevailing on it to sign an agreement which, for the time being, postponed the danger of a Russo-Turkish war. By this treaty the free navigation of the Dardanelles was conceded to the ships of all nations, only the Americans being excepted from its terms, 'because the *Sultan* did not like Republicans!' (Prokesch, i.)

The *Czar* now consented to reopen relations with the Ottoman Government, though only, for the present, informally. M. de Munciaky was sent, as the agent of Russia, to Constantinople, and charged to watch over the execution of the treaty, and to clear up certain other outstanding questions with regard to navigation. At the same time, the Russian Minister, Count Nesselrode, while thanking the Porte for the concessions it had made, hinted darkly at certain claims for which as yet no satisfaction had been received. (*Ibid.* i.) The breach was merely patched up, not completely healed, and the danger of a Russo-Turkish conflict was only postponed.

Meanwhile the Holy Alliance itself was threatened with disruption. The death of Castlereagh had removed one of Metternich's most faithful henchmen, and Canning, who succeeded him as Foreign Secretary, was heartily favourable to the Greek cause. As early as February 1823 his dispatches to Lord Strangford show a complete reversal of British policy; and England now appears, for the first time, as the advocate of the cause of the oppressed Christian subjects of the Porte.

✶✶✶✶✶✶

Prokesch, i.: 'Canning approached the subject from the religious point of view, which had been, for a hundred years, entirely subordinate in English politics; and he laid thereby special stress on the very aspect of the question which made a peaceful settlement most difficult of attainment. It was the danger of Alexander taking this view which had, two years before, most disquieted the Cabinets; and England had successfully united with the other powers to draw him away from it.'

✶✶✶✶✶✶

On the 25th of March England recognised the Greeks as belligerents; and the struggle was henceforward invested with a new significance. (Mendelssohn, i.)

From this time it became impossible for even the most reactionary Powers of the Holy Alliance to deal with the Hellenic rising as they had dealt with the popular movements in Spain or Naples. The diplomatic game began once more on a new basis: the recognition of the Greek claims.

In October 1823 the *Czar* and the Austrian emperor met at Czernowitz, to prepare for the interference of the Powers, in the interests of Europe. (Prokesch, i.) A divergence of views became at once apparent. Russia then, as now, unwilling to see any really powerful State established on the ruins of the Ottoman Empire, or to encourage a Pan-Hellenic as opposed to a Pan-Slavonic movement—proposed the opening of conferences on the basis of the division of Greece and the islands into three principalities, under Ottoman *suzerainty*, and guaranteed by the European Powers. (Prokesch, i.). In view, however, of the aggressive policy of Russia in the Danubian principalities, her motive in making this suggestion was too apparent. Austria could not afford to see Russian influence paramount over the whole Balkan peninsula; and Metternich began to suspect that the true interest of Austria lay in the erection of Greece into an independent State.

Meanwhile the Greeks had profited little by the lessons of the war. No sooner was the immediate danger removed than the old anarchy once more broke out. The lamentable failure of the attempts of Mavrocordatos at generalship, as well as the cowardice displayed by the government on the occasion of Dramali's advance on Argos, had filled the fierce Armatoli and their captains with contempt for the civilian leaders, and still further accentuated the already deeply-marked line between the parties. Apart from numberless motives of personal ambition or jealousy, these were divided also by sharply contrasted principles of policy, which were sure, sooner or later, to produce a conflict between them.

On the one side were the Phanariots, and such of the Greeks as had received a European training, and who desired to see Greece established as a constitutional State on the European model. These were supported also by the islanders, whose commercial enterprise had brought them into contact with European ideas. On the other side were the bishops, primates, and military chiefs, whose sole idea was to sit in the seat from which they had expelled the Turks; to wear fine weapons and gorgeous clothes, to play the *pasha*, to pay nobody and take from all; and, finally, to live on terms of good fellowship with the common people, sharing their pleasures, their customs, their superstitions, and their faith. (Prokesch, i.).

For the present, indeed, at the beginning of the year 1823, the party of the primates made common cause with that of the islanders and Constitutionalists against the military chiefs, whose power now

EXPEDITION AT ARGOS OF MAHMUD DRAMALI PASHA

overshadowed every other authority in Greece. West Hellas, it is true, was still held for the government by Mavrocordatos, though with a weak hand; but, in East Hellas, Odysseus now reigned with undisputed authority; and, in the Morea, Kolokotrones was supreme.

During the summer of 1822, Attica had been given up to anarchy; until, at last, some of those Athenian citizens who had most to lose begged Prince Demetrius Hypsilanti to come and take over the command of the country. On his arrival, however, the garrison of the Acropolis had refused to admit him, and elected Odysseus as their general, Hypsilanti had no choice but to give up his enterprise; and Odysseus, seizing eagerly at the chance presented to him, proceeded to consolidate his power. He sold the booty captured from the Turks in order to pay his troops, strengthened the defences of the Acropolis, and, dissolving the Areopagus, summoned another Assembly entirely devoted to his interests. A serious mischance had, however, nearly destroyed his newly acquired power.

After the defeat of Dramali, Khurshid Pasha had sent Mehemet, with eight thousand men, to hold the line of the Spercheios; and the Ottoman commander had made a rapid dash with some of his troops, by way of the pass of Gravia, on Salona. After burning part of the town, he had returned by the same road, and on the 13th of November, was intercepted by a Greek force, under Odysseus, at the inn of Gravia.

After a sharp fight, the Greeks were routed, and Odysseus himself only with difficulty escaped. In terror lest the Ottomans should now advance into Attica, and lest, in the presence of this danger, the Athenians should elect a new commander-in-chief, he concluded an armistice with the Turks, at the same time offering to make his submission to the Porte, and to secure that of the other captains of East Hellas, on condition of his being continued in his position as a chief of *Armatoli*. Though the Turks did not believe in his offers of submission, they accepted the armistice, for their own purposes, and retired to Zeituni for the winter. The peasants of Boeotia and Attica, relieved from immediate danger, and able now to sow their fields in peace, gave Odysseus all the credit for saving them from the Turks, and, knowing nothing of the terms of the armistice, began to regard him as an ideal hero.

It was, however, the power of Kolokotrones that most excited the jealous apprehensions of the other parties. In the Morea, the possession of Nauplia, which, since its surrender by the Turks, had been held for him by his son-in-law Koliopulos, rendered him supreme; and

Battle of Dervenakia

to break his power became the main object of primates and islanders alike. The government in vain demanded admission into Nauplia; and, when it became plain that Kolokotrones had no intention of surrendering his vantage ground, it retired to Astros. Here, in December 1822, the new National Assembly, for which writs had already been issued, proceeded to collect. Deputies streamed in from all sides, representatives being present even from Crete. Members of the former conventions seemed to think they had a prescriptive right to sit in the new one, without any fresh election; and many deputies appeared who could pretend to represent none but themselves. Among the more prominent leaders present were Petrobey, Londos, Zaimis, and many other primates of distinction. Mavrocordatos and Hypsilanti also attended; and even Odysseus condescended to appear.

Among this motley assemblage there was, of course, little question of useful legislation. The Greeks from of old have loved oratory and the game of debate, and the making of laws better than the observance of them; and the new-born liberties of Greece seemed now in danger of being drowned in a flood of talk, or strangled in a network of intrigues. There was, indeed, some attempt made to establish a criminal code, and to discuss the publication of a budget; and, above all, the necessity was universally recognised of raising money by means of foreign loans. But by far the most important business of the Assembly was in connection with the formation of the new government, and the attempt to oust Kolokotrones from his dangerous predominance.

It was, indeed, the feud between the military and the civilian elements which had rendered all efforts at legislation impossible. The soldiers, less skilled with the tongue than with the sword, withdrew in dudgeon from the war of words, and formed a sort of Upper Chamber of their own. The measures which survived the strife of tongues in the civilian Assembly were invariably rejected with contempt by this novel House of Lords, which, in its turn, originated nothing. That legislation was thus rendered impossible would have mattered little, where a strong administration was so much more needed, if a strong administration could have been formed. But it was just here that the battle of the factions raged most violently, and with the most fatal effect.

The government was to consist, as before, of two councils or committees, one legislative, to represent the Assembly when not in session, the other executive. It became the object of the civilian party to exclude the military element from these committees; and this, as far as their influence in the Assembly was concerned, they were strong enough to effect. The executive council, as constituted by the Assembly, consisted of Petrobey as president, and three continental *primates*: Zaimis, Karalampos, and Metaxas. A fifth place was not filled up, and was reserved for a representative of the islands.

Kolokotrones, however, with threats of violence, obtained the vacant place for himself. He attempted also to secure the election of his creature, Deliyanni, to the presidency of the legislative committee; and when this was filled by the choice of Mavrocordatos, he broke out in uncontrollable fury. The Phanariot, with his spectacles, his swallowtail coat, his European airs, and his talk of constitutional government, was an object of loathing to the savage old *klepht*. 'I won't allow you to be president!' he cried. 'If you accept, I will follow you step by step, and throw dirt at that fine European get-up of yours!' (Mendelssohn, i.).

Kolokotrones now saw that, unless he appealed to arms, his influence in the government would be lost. For a time, indeed, he and the other military chiefs submitted, grumbling; but on the 10th of April, a fresh aggression on the part of the civilians precipitated the crisis. It was now decided by the Assembly to deprive Kolokotrones of the supreme military command, and to vest this in a committee of three. This was but one more example of the unwisdom of making offensive proposals which there is no possibility of carrying through. Kolokotrones, in the face of this direct attempt to deprive him of his power, threw off the mask, and openly defied the National Assembly. Supported by his bands of *klephts* and *armatoli*, on whom he could always rely, he now forced the executive council to accompany him to Nauplia, where it was completely at his mercy; while the legislative committee wandered helplessly from place to place, in constant terror from the fierce followers of Kolokotrones, and stripped of all power. (Prokesch, i.)

At this period nothing but the unreadiness of the Ottomans to take advantage of the situation in Greece could have saved the Hellenes from destruction. A stroke of fortune had indeed once more helped their cause; for, early in 1823, the Ottoman magazine of Tophana had been destroyed by fire; and in this immense conflagration, the greatest that even Constantinople had ever witnessed, vast stores of war material had perished, besides some six thousand houses, and fifty mosques.

In spite of the huge loss and inconvenience caused by this accident, Mahmoud yet hoped to prosecute the war with vigour; and once more a double invasion of the Morea was projected. Mustai Pasha was to invade West Hellas, and advance upon Missolonghi; while, to prepare and cover this movement, Yussuf Pasha marched by way of Boeotia and Attica upon Salona and Lepanto, with a view to crossing thence to Patras. The moment was very favourable, both by sea and land. In the Morea the strife of parties was raging with full violence; and, at sea, the islanders were likewise turning their arms against each other. Hydriots and Spezziots were at daggers drawn; and Samos, under Lycourgos—of sinister memory in connection with Chios—was defending itself, by force ol arms, against the unjust aggressions of the Psariots. The Greek fleet had become a mere flotilla of pirate hulls, without organisation or discipline, and as ready to prey upon friend as foe; and not even Miaoulis could reduce it to order.

Khosrew Pasha, however, who commanded the Ottoman fleet which, at the end of May, sailed out of the Dardanelles, was not the man to take full advantage of the situation. He was in any case more suited to the council chamber than the quarter-deck, and, timid by nature, the fate of his predecessor, Kara Ali, had filled him with a perfect horror of the Greek fireships. (Finlay, ii.) His present cruise was not marked by any considerable results. He touched at Mitylene and Chios, embarked some troops at Tchesmé, and sailed for Euboea, where he arrived in time to relieve Karystos, then being besieged by Grisiotis. Thence he sailed past Hydra, threw supplies into Coron and Modon, and, on the 20th, landed some troops and a large sum of money at Patras. Instead, however, of remaining on the west coast of Greece to support the operations of Mustai, he hastened back to the Dardanelles.

Yussuf Pasha had meanwhile opened the campaign in East Hellas. Advancing from Thessaly with six thousand men, he marched into Phokis, occupied Salona, and, driving the Greeks out of the passes of Helikon and Parnassus, descended upon Levadia. The Pasha of Euboea, at the same time, with eight hundred horsemen, raided in the direction of Thebes, and swept off the harvest. Odysseus now entrusted the defence of the Acropolis to his lieutenant Gouras, who had lately married a beautiful girl of Lidoriki, (see chapter 12), and marched to occupy the defiles of Helikon, while the Athenians took refuge in the island of Salamis. The news of the Ottoman invasion had, moreover, put an end for the time to the feuds in the Morea; and Kolokotrones and Niketas now advanced to Megara with a force of Moreots. Other bands also speedily collected, and succeeded by a bold guerilla war in driving the Turks back into the plain of the Kephisisos. The *seraskier* himself crossed over into Euboea; and, as Odysseus took no measures to prevent it, he was able to drive the Greeks out of the northern half of the island. The Ottoman plan of campaign in East Hellas was, however, shattered.

For the invasion of West Hellas, meanwhile, Mustai Pasha had assembled at Ochrida an army consisting entirely of Albanian tribesmen. Of these five thousand were Mussulman Ghegs, and three thousand Roman Catholic Miridits, whose hatred of the Orthodox Greeks had made them the close allies of the Mohammedans. As usual, the Greeks, occupied with their own quarrels, had neglected to guard the passes; and the army of Mustai advanced as far as Karpenisi without encountering any serious opposition. Here, however, it met with a disaster which constituted for the Greeks one of the most brilliant exploits of the war.

On the night of the 21st of August, Marko Botzares, the Suliot hero, with three hundred and fifty of his clansmen, surprised the camp of Djelaleddin Bey, who commanded the Ottoman vanguard. Four thousand Mussulman Ghegs and Catholic Miridits were in the camp; but so complete was the surprise that little opposition was offered when, slaying and plundering, the Suliots rushed among their panic-stricken enemies. Botzares himself made straight for the tent of the Bey, which had been pitched within a small enclosure surrounded by a wall. Raising his head above the wall to see how an entrance could be effected, the Suliot's head became visible against the sky, and he received a bullet through the brain.

The death of their beloved leader was a terrible blow to the Suliots, and put a stop to their proceedings, but not before they had slain some two thousand of the enemy. Taking up the body of Botzares, and laden with an immense booty, they retired without molestation. Had the Ætolian *Armatoli* taken part in the attack, as had been arranged, the force of Djelaleddin must have been annihilated; but their jealousy of Botzares and his Albanians had kept them idle spectators; and, as it was, the Ottoman commander kept command of the ground, and Mustai's march was hardly delayed.

At the end of September, the Ottoman commander-in-chief formed, at Vrachori, a junction with Omer Vrioni, who commanded an army of some four thousand Mussulman Tosks, an Albanian tribe speaking a dialect distinct from that of the Ghegs, with whom it was by no means on friendly terms. With this heterogeneous force Mustai, in October, proceeded to lay siege to Anatoliko, a small town in the

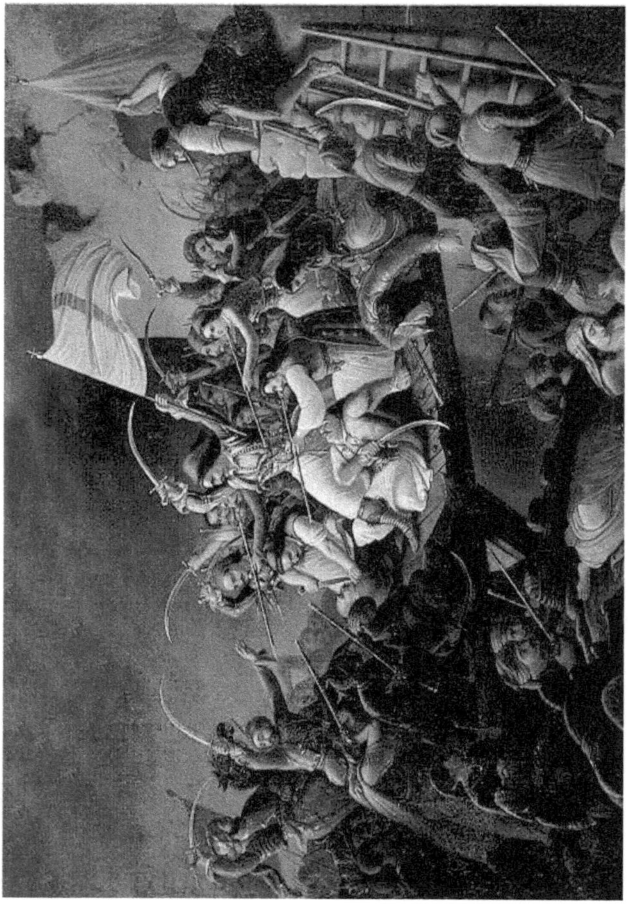

Ætolian lagoons, about five miles west of Missolonghi. The place was garrisoned by some six hundred men, and entirely unfortified. It had, however, a small battery of six old-fashioned cannon, commanded by William Martin, an English seaman, who had deserted from some ship of war, and who succeeded with these in dismounting the only Turkish gun. The *pashas* now could do nothing but bombard the place with a couple of mortars, which did but little damage, the garrison, in fact, suffering much more from thirst than from the Ottoman shells.

In this strait, the angel Michael came to their assistance. A bomb from the Turkish mortars fell into the church of the archangel, shattering the pavement; and lo! from the hole thus made there bubbled up a plentiful spring of pure water. (Gordon, ii). Encouraged by this miracle, the Greeks made so stout a resistance, that on the 11th of December Mustai raised the siege. The second half of the Ottoman plan of campaign had thus also broken down; and the year closed in triumph for the Greeks.

No sooner was the danger from the Turks at an end than the Greeks resumed the internecine struggle which the common peril had interrupted. Mavrocordatos, supported by the party of the primates, and by the islands, determined to make another effort to break the power of Kolokotrones. The executive committee was now entirely in the hands of the military party. Zaimis, indeed, had left it and thrown in his lot with the other primates; but Petrobey, after wavering awhile, had definitely declared for Kolokotrones, whose authority was now supreme. The legislative committee, stripped of all power, had broken up; and the remnant of it, which had established itself in Argos, now opened the struggle by sending to the executive to demand a statement of accounts.

For only reply, Petrobey sent a band of his Mainotes, who dealt with the Hump of the legislative committee as Cromwell had dealt with that of the Long Parliament. The members thereupon fled to Kranidi, opposite the island of Hydra, and put themselves under the protection of the Hydriots. Greece was thus, at the end of 1823, divided into three sections. In East Hellas, Odysseus reigned supreme; West Hellas was held by Mavrocordatos for the government at Kranidi; while Kolokotrones, established in Nauplia, and in the Acrocorinthos, which had surrendered on the 7th of November, aimed at subjecting the Morea to military rule.

★★★★★★

It is pleasant to record that on this occasion the firmness of Niketas prevented the capitulation being violated. The Moslems were embarked on an Austrian ship, and allowed to carry away their arms and a small sum of money. See Gordon, ii.

✶✶✶✶✶✶

Thus far the violence of Kolokotrones seemed to have triumphed; but the government at Kranidi possessed many elements of strength which, now that it was removed from the immediate danger of intimidation at the hands of the military chiefs, began to assert themselves. It had the prestige of legitimacy; it possessed in Mavrocordatos a man who was regarded by the opinion of Europe as the constitutional leader of Greece, and in Kolettes the only one of the Greek chiefs who could combine the spirit of the old barbarism with that of the new culture; (Prokesch, i.), and, above all, it alone would dispose of the loans which were at this time being raised in Europe, of which the arrival was already rumoured abroad. This last indeed, was the factor that ultimately determined the victory of the government; for, in Greece, even more than elsewhere, he who held the purse-strings held the reins of power.

The government now determined to make a vigorous effort to reassert its authority. It had already opened the struggle by demanding the surrender of Nauplia, and openly accusing Kolokotrones of peculation. It now put Petrobey and Karalampos on their trial, deposed Metaxas, and deprived Kolokotrones of the supreme command of the forces; while a new executive council was created, with Konduriottes, a wealthy Hydriot ship-owner, as President, but Kolettes, the astute Epirote, as its moving spirit.

To this action of the government Kolokotrones replied by collecting some thirty-five members of the Assembly at Tripolitza, and there setting up an opposition government. At the same time, he began to collect his bands in Elis and Arcadia, strengthened the defences of the Acrocorinthos, and handed over the command of Nauplia to his son Panos; while the influence of Petrobey assured him the support of the Mainotes in Messenia. The government, on the other hand, could reckon, in the Morea, only on the support of Corinth, which was held by Notaras, and of Achaia and a part of Arcadia, where the influence of the primates Londos and Zaimis was supreme. East Hellas was still held by Odysseus, who played of course entirely for his own hand, and could be relied upon by neither party. West Hellas, on the other hand, remained, under Mavrocordatos, true to the government.

Konduriottes, the new President, owed his elevation solely to his great wealth, which gave him an influence quite out of proportion to his capacity. In private life he was jovial and good-tempered, and, as a statesman, his riches placed him above the suspicion of corruption; but he was dull, obstinate, and ignorant, and, above all, full of Hydriot prejudices, which he was at no pains to disguise. (Gordon, ii.). Kolettes, who had been physician to Ali Pasha, and combined a certain amount of European culture with a thorough knowledge of the best way to deal with barbarous or half-civilised people, was the only man of any capacity in the new administration; and it was under his influence that, to counteract the military preponderance of Kolokotrones in the Morea, the government now introduced bands of Rumeliot and Bulgarian mercenaries, who invaded the Peloponnese by way of the Isthmus, and treated it as an enemy's country.

By March 1824 the government had everywhere the upper hand, and Kolokotrones began to feel himself hard pressed. Nauplia was closely invested; and a Hydriot force, under Miaoulis, marched into Argolis, seized the mills of Lerna, and captured Argos. Kolokotrones himself was shortly afterwards defeated before Tripolitza by the united forces of the Bulgarian Hadji Christos and the Moreots; and, after one or two more fights of less importance, was compelled to open negotiations with the primates Zaimis and Londos. Through their mediation, an arrangement was ultimately come to by which Kolokotrones submitted to the government, and surrendered Nauplia in return for an equivalent in money.

The government was now everywhere triumphant; but in its very victory were contained the seeds of future troubles. Zaimis and Londos were accused of making too favourable terms with Kolokotrones; (Gordon, ii.), and the first symptoms of a rupture between the islanders and the Moreot primates became apparent. To the disgust of the Peloponnesians, the Suliot Photomaras was made governor of Nauplia; and this first instance of the undue favour, which the administration of Konduriottes was about to show to the continental Greeks and the islanders, so offended Londos and Zaimis, that they withdrew from Nauplia in dudgeon.

CHAPTER 8

The Second Civil War

In the autumn of 1823, when the civil dissensions were at their height, Lord Byron arrived in Greece. Even before he publicly announced his intention of joining the Greek cause, he had exercised an immense influence in arousing the Philhellenic enthusiasm of Europe; and now that the genius whose fame extended throughout the length and breadth of Christendom, proclaimed that he was prepared to devote health and fortune, and, if need be, life itself, to his ideal of a free Hellas, the eyes of the civilised world were directed with a new interest on the affairs of Greece.

It was largely owing to the influence of Byron that the two first Greek loans had recently been floated in London. It is the surest proof of the genuineness of the Philhellenic sentiment in England at that time, that two loans, one of 800,000*l.* and the other of 2,000,000*l.*, should have been floated without difficulty, within a few days of each other, only on such very unsatisfactory security as could be offered by an insurgent government constantly at feud within itself. Byron himself brought out with him the first instalment of 40,000*l.*; and, when he realised the actual condition of Greece, he felt serious qualms at having helped to induce people to invest in so doubtful a speculation.

For the time being, indeed, the money was not handed over to the Greek Government, but banked at Zante, where, after Byron's death, it was detained for a still further period by order of the authorities of the Ionian Islands. The question of what became of it when it was ultimately handed over to the Greek Government, or what was the destination of the subsequent instalments, has some light thrown upon it by the statement of the Philhellene General Gordon, who says, 'With perhaps the exception of Zaimis, the members of the Executive were no better than public robbers.' (Gordon, ii.). A considerable sum was,

LORD BYRON IN ALBANIAN DRESS

indeed, saved from the greed of the Greeks by being expended, more or less wisely, in the national interest before it reached their hands. (But according to Mendelssohn as much as 1,000,000*l*. was absorbed by *jobbery* in London and New York. See also Finlay, ii.).

The services of Lord Cochrane, the celebrated sailor, who had made a great name for himself in the naval wars of South America, were engaged by a retaining fee of 37,000*l*.; though it was not till 1827 that he made his appearance in Greece. Four steamers were also ordered, at a cost of 150,000l.; but of these only the *Karteria* arrived in time to be of any service; while, of the two frigates which Captain Lallemande, a French cavalry officer, had been sent to America to buy for the Greek navy, only one, the *Hellas*, ever arrived in Greek waters, and cost 160,000*l*.

By far the greater part of the loans was, however, scrambled for by the factions in Greece itself; and, as one main result of the generosity of Europe, the partisans of the victorious party swaggered about the streets of Nauplia, their clothes glittering with gold embroidery, and their belts lined with English sovereigns. (Finlay, ii.). It is certain that, whatever else may have happened, the unfortunate creditors never received one penny either of the principal or of the interest that had been 'secured' to them.

Byron himself was, from the moment of his landing, under no illusion as to the character of the people he had come to serve. During the autumn of 1823, he had remained in Cephalonia, one of the Ionian islands then under the British flag, to gather information with a view to seeing where his help could best be given. To the Greeks, meanwhile, the wealthy English '*milordos*' was interesting mainly as a gold mine, to be worked for their own personal advantage; and, during his residence in the island, nearly every statesman or general of any pretensions wrote to him to solicit his favour, his influence, or his money. Kolokotrones in Salamis, Mavrocordatos in Hydra, and Metaxas in Missolonghi competed for his presence; for only where each of them chanced to be could Greece be served. Petrobey, more naively honest, said, straight out, that the best way to save Hellas was to give him, the Bey of the Maina, a thousand pounds. Byron wrote:

> Of the Greeks, I can't say much good hitherto, and I do not like to speak ill of them, though they do of each other.—Moore's *Life of Byron*.

In the face of so much disillusion and discouragement, the attitude of Byron is full of a singular and pathetic interest. Under circumstances which would have crushed the enthusiasm of a man of less sympathetic imagination, he displayed a wide-minded generosity, a steadfastness of purpose, and withal a shrewd common-sense, which could scarcely have been expected of his wayward genius. The glorious Hellas of his dreams had faded, for the time, in the hard, grey light of a day of sordid realities. Yet here, beneath his eyes, was a Hellas, human, pitiful, bleeding from many wounds; it was not for him to gather his poet's robe about him, and pass by on the other side. Many had come out to fight for the cause of Greece thinking to find a country peopled with the heroic types of old, had found instead a race of brigands, and departed in disgust.

Many more had remained, their eyes so blinded by Philhellenic prejudice that they were content to gloss over the worst crimes of the Greeks with classical allusions. Byron belonged to neither of these classes. He knew that half-barbarous peoples are full of vices, and that emancipated slaves are not of the stuff that makes heroes. He saw in a very clear light the dishonesty, the meanness, the selfishness of the Greeks; and yet he did not despair of Greece. He wrote, on the 7th of October, from Cephalonia:

> I was a fool to come here, but, having come here, I must see what can be done.—Moore's *Life*.

Once out of the realm of dreams, and brought face to face with facts, the activity of Byron on behalf of Greece was characterised by good sense as well as generosity. Nothing is now heard or seen of the three beautiful classical helmets which he had caused to be made for him before he came out to Greece; but with practical advice and wisely bestowed material help he is ever ready. He refused, indeed, to squander his money on unworthy objects, or to become, as so many of the Philhellenes had done, the dupe and instrument of a selfish faction. He writes:

> I offered to advance 1,000 dollars a month for the succour of Missolonghi and the Suliots under Botzari (since killed); but the government have answered me that they wish to confer with me previously, which is in fact saying that they wish me to expend my money in some other direction. I will take care that it is for the public cause, otherwise I will not advance a para. The Opposition say they want to cajole me, and the party in power say the others wish to seduce me, so between the two I have a

difficult part to play; however, I will have nothing to do with the factions unless to reconcile them if possible.—Moore's *Life*.

His efforts to bring about a cessation of the ruinous civil strife were as unceasing as they were ineffective he said:

> The Greeks have no enemies in heaven or earth to be dreaded but their own discords.—*Ibid*.

He besought the government to bring about a reconciliation between the parties, and threatened that, if union could not be restored, the payment of the loan would be indefinitely postponed. To Mavrocordatos he wrote:

> Greece is placed between three measures; either to reconquer her liberty, to become a dependence of the sovereigns of Europe, or to return to a Turkish province. Civil war is but a road which leads to the two latter. If she is desirous of the fate of Wallachia and the Crimea, she may obtain it tomorrow; if of that of Italy, the day after; but if she wishes to become truly Greece, free and independent, she must resolve today, or she will never again have the opportunity. (Dated December 2, 1822, from Cephalonia. Moore).

All his prayers and admonitions, however, fell on deaf ears. The Greek factions wanted his money, not his advice; and, failing the appearance of the former, they rejected the latter with scorn.

At last, in January 1824, Byron decided to take a more active part in the war, and sailed for Missolonghi. With characteristic perversity, he had chosen, for the scene of his activity, in spite of the entreaties and warnings of his friends, one of the most unhealthy spots in Greece. For one whose health was already undermined to settle amid the fever-breeding marshes of the Acarnanian coast was, indeed, to court death; and Byron went to meet his fate with a certain deliberation. He had openly expressed his willingness to surrender his life for the cause of Greece, and, perhaps, he felt that this could be better served by his death than by his life. He regarded himself, to use his own simile, as but one of the many waves that must break and die upon the shore, before the tide they help to advance can reach its full mark.

The voyage to Missolonghi was not without its adventures, and twice the military career of the erratic genius was nearly cut short. Once, during a sea fog, the Greek brig which carried him nearly collided with a Turkish frigate; and, but for the fact that the latter took it for a fire-ship, and sheered off in alarm, he must have been captured. A day or two later he was all but wrecked on the coast of Acarnania, the vessel having twice actually run upon the rocks. However, in due course he arrived safely at Missolonghi; though the vessel containing his money and stores was captured by the Turks, and towed into Patras. Here it was detained for a few days, but ultimately very generously restored by Yussuf Pasha to its owner.

★★★★★★

Byron himself affected that the Turks had done no more than they were compelled to do in restoring his ship, which was sailing under the English flag. But it was notoriously laden with stores and money to be used against the Turks; and these at any rate they would have been justified in retaining. It is certain that, under similar circumstances, the Greeks would have done so. As it was, the Ottoman authorities restored the whole of their capture, greatly to the astonishment of the British ambassador at Constantinople, Lord Strangford, who even thought it necessary to protest to the Porte against this action, as forming a bad precedent.

There is no doubt that the protection of the British flag was grossly abused during the war by the English Philhellenes. Lord Cochrane, after he became High Admiral of Greece, though he himself sailed under the Hellenic ensign, was constantly accompanied by his private yacht, flying the English colours, on which, for safety's sake, he kept all his money and valuables! In the present instance, the Reis-Effendi, replying to Lord Strangford's remonstrances, said: 'Yussuf Pasha has understood the views of the *Sultan*; it is better to suffer than to open the door to injustice, which would happen if *pashas* were allowed to search European ships.' See Prokesch, i.

★★★★★★

Byron's activity at Missolonghi was not sufficiently prolonged to be of any great importance in affecting the fortunes of the war. He took the Suliots, who had been left leaderless by the death of Marko Botzares, into his pay. Fifty of these he formed into a bodyguard to protect his own person; while some five hundred were enrolled as a regiment of which he took the command. Their lawlessness, greed, and insolence, however, soon compelled him to disband the latter, though he retained his select guard to the last. For the most part, he devoted his money and energy to strengthening the fortifications of the town, being aided in this work by the engineer Parry. He also planned an attack on Lepanto; but its execution was prevented by the insubordination of the Suliots; and his remaining weeks of life were embittered by the feuds and broils of which he was compelled to be the helpless witness.

A regular war broke out between Anatoliko and Missolonghi. Karaiskakis marched, with three hundred men, from the former place, and in revenge for some injury received, carried off two primates from Missolonghi; while the dismissed Suliots returned and seized the fort of Vasiladi, which commanded the town from the lagoon.

Prostrated by sickness and racked with pain, Byron preserved among all these troubles, which he was powerless to prevent, the same unshaken fortitude and unbroken spirit. Even on his death-bed, his cool courage and indomitable will cowed into silence the fierce Suliot warriors, who had burst, with brandished knives and wild threats, into his room. It may perhaps be doubted whether he would, had he lived, have proved a really effective general, or have been able to reunite the shattered fragments of Greece, before they were once more welded together by the blows of a common misfortune. It is certain that his death was the best service that he could have rendered to the cause he had at heart; for all Europe felt that he had died an exalted martyr to his faith in the future of Hellas; and no martyr, however humble, ever yet died quite in vain.

By the Greeks the news of the death of Byron, which took place on the 19th of April, was received with a becoming regret, which was, however, speedily swallowed up by anxiety as to the fate of the loan of which he had been the trustee. It was, in fact, the prospect of the arrival of this loan which had done more than anything else to secure the victory of the government in the first civil war; for the contending factions had hastened to make peace, so as not to be absent from the expected division of the spoil. Only Odysseus, planning deep schemes of his own, had held aloof. The presence of Byron at Missolonghi had inspired the wily *Klepht* with the idea of getting the English poet into his hands, and securing, by an astute diplomacy, the lion's share of the loan for himself. He was enthusiastically seconded by Colonel Stanhope (Earl of Harrington), whose fanatical Philhellenism made him the blind instrument of the Greek hero's unscrupulous intrigues.

★★★★★★

For Colonel Stanhope's benefit Odysseus affected to be an ardent partisan of liberty. 'His conversation was of newspapers and schools, the rights of the people, and a museum of antiquities.' One morning, while the colonel and Odysseus were sitting together in the latter's quarters, Dr. Sophienopoulo entered, handed the general a report on the state of the hospital, and answered various queries about it. No hospital existed!—Gordon, i.

******

A meeting had actually been arranged between Byron and Odysseus at Salona, when the poet's death put a stop to the plot. Odysseus now, fearing lest he should lose all share in the loan, gave up suddenly all his schemes of independent action, and hurried to Nauplia to pay court to the government.

After the death of Byron, the first instalment of the loan, amounting to 40,000*l.*, which had been banked by him at Zante, had been, to the dismay and disgust of the Greeks, detained by the English administration of the Ionian Islands. After the destruction of Psara by the Turks, (see the next chapter), on the 2nd of July, however, the money had been handed over to the Greek Government; and, at the news, not only Odysseus, but Kolokotrones, Niketas, and every other chieftain, great or small, who could formulate the shadow of a claim, hastened to Nauplia to share in the spoil. For the government, however, duty and interest for once coincided; and they determined to fit out a squadron to avenge the disaster of Psara; a decision which it was all the easier for them to make, as it would benefit their main supporters, the Hydriot ship-owners. Any funds that might be left over, they determined to hold in reserve.

For the disappointed chieftains and primates, this put the coping-stone on the edifice of the misdeeds of the government. (Prokesch, i.). Konduriottes had used his powers as President throughout to favour the islanders at the expense of the other Hellenes; he had thrust his friends, the Hydriot sea captains, into all the most important military and civil commands; and now the pure stream of British gold was to flow into the same dirty channel! This was more than the disinterested patriotism of the Moreot primates and the *Klephts* of the mainland could stand. Furious with jealous rage and disappointed greed, they retired, with their bands of armed followers, from Nauplia.

Odysseus was the first to leave. Kolokotrones followed, and with him went the Moreot primates, who, in the last civil war, had been his main opponents: Sissinis of Gastuni, the great landowner of Elis, who lived upon his estates with more than feudal splendour: (Finlay, ii. The peasants had to fall on their knees whenever they addressed him, even in reply to a simple question) Londos, the friend of Byron, whose influence was paramount in Achaia: and Zaimis, who could always reckon on the support of a large part of Arcadia. Again Greece was about to be plunged into civil war: a war, this time, of the Moreots against the islanders.

By the autumn, the whole of the Morea was in flames; but the conflagration, this time, did not last long. Kolettes, the only member of the government who possessed either firmness or ability, had hitherto let the folly and incompetence of Konduriottes have full play, because he desired to undermine his authority; but, now that serious danger threatened, he took the reins of government into his own hands. The possession of the English gold, and, still more, the prospect of the speedy arrival of a second and larger instalment of the loan, was a tower of strength to the Administration.

Kolettes, with promises of plentiful reward, induced the Rumeliots to come to the aid of the government; and 3,000 men, under Gouras and Karaiskakis, crossed the Isthmus into the Morea. Against this host the scattered forces of the Moreots could do nothing; and in less than fourteen days the rebellion was at an end. The Rumeliot bands harried and wasted the country as though they were fighting the Turk and not their own countrymen. The country houses of Londos and the other primates were burnt, and they themselves forced to fly. (Prokesch, i).

The death of his son Panos, in a skirmish before Tripolitza, broke the spirit of Kolokotrones; he surrendered to the government, and was imprisoned in a monastery in Hydra. Here, for the time, he languished in a studied neglect, unwashed and unshorn, and prophesying moodily to sympathetic visitors that the time was not far distant when his ungrateful country would supplicate, on bended knees, for his assistance.

Odysseus, meanwhile, had recrossed the Isthmus, and had taken advantage of the absence of his lieutenant Gouras and of Karaiskakis to make peace with the Turks. In December 1824, he made an arrangement by which, as the price of his treason, he was to be guaranteed the captaincy of East Hellas by the Ottoman Government. As an open traitor, however, his career was not of long duration. In April 1825, Gouras returned to East Hellas, and attacked his former chief and a body of Turks under Abbas Pasha, at Daulis. Odysseus and his allies were defeated, and driven to Cheroneia. Deserted by his followers, and distrusted by the Turks, the power of Odysseus was now completely broken; and, on the 25th of April, he was compelled to surrender at discretion to his former lieutenant. (Mendelssohn, i.). He had declared himself the enemy not only of the government, but of Greece, and he could have little hope of mercy. A convicted traitor, stained with innumerable crimes, his death by process of law might have been regarded as an act of stern justice. As it was, he was imprisoned in the Acropolis for several months, and finally, on the 16th of July, murdered there by Gouras, who had succeeded to the place forfeited by his treason.

★★★★★★

Finlay, ii. In view of the growing unpopularity of the Government of Konduriottes, Gouras was afraid lest Odysseus should escape and regain his power. This, and not the satisfaction of justice, was the motive of the murder.

★★★★★★

At the beginning of the year 1825, then, the Government of Konduriottes and Kolettes was everywhere victorious. Supported by the islands, by European opinion, and by the Phanariot Greeks, it was now at the height of its power; all resistance to its authority was broken; and it seemed as though Greece were at last to be united under a powerful administration. But, meanwhile, a storm had been gathering over Hellas from without, which, when it burst, would have shattered to its foundations a far more substantial edifice of power than this government of selfish factions.

CHAPTER 9

Insurrection in Crete

While the Greeks were finding an ally in the Philhellenic sentiment of Europe, Sultan Mahmoud sought aid in another direction. With the keenness of view that characterised him, he had studied the causes of the failure of the Ottoman arms, and determined on a new plan of action. To master the insurrection, he realised the absolute necessity for obtaining the command of the sea, and of opposing the untrained valour of the Greeks with the discipline of drilled troops; but all attempts to reform the Ottoman Army had hitherto failed, owing to the fierce opposition of the *janissaries* to any interference with their privileges and immunities; and the Turkish Navy, owing to the causes mentioned elsewhere, had not proved itself efficient in war, though it was now in a far better condition than at the outbreak of the revolt, and doubtless in time the vastly greater resources of the Ottoman Empire might have worn out the naval power of Greece.

Under these circumstances, the *Sultan's* thoughts turned to his vassal Mehemet Ali, Pasha of Egypt; and to him he determined to apply for aid. This remarkable man, who had raised himself from the lowest ranks of the people to sovereign power, was already plotting those vast schemes of ambition which subsequently brought him into collision with the Ottoman Empire; and, in preparation for these, he had organised an army on the European model, and a magnificently appointed fleet.

The *Sultan*, fully awake to the importance of modern methods in warfare, had viewed these preparations of his powerful vassal with considerable misgiving; and, in proposing to him to help in the suppression of the Greek revolt, he doubtless hoped to serve a twofold object, in using the instrument which seemed the most effective for his immediate purpose, and at the same time, perhaps, blunting a weapon which he suspected would, sooner or later, be directed against himself.

He, therefore, now proposed to Mehemet Ali to use these newly disciplined forces for the suppression of the Greek rebellion, and promised, in return, to hand over to him the Island of Crete, and to invest his son Ibrahim with the Pashalik of the Morea. Mehemet, whose plans of wider ambition were not yet ripe, and who still maintained towards his *suzerain* the attitude of a loyal and dutiful subject, was nothing loth to respond to an appeal which was so flattering to his pride, and so pregnant with future possibilities; and the bargain was soon concluded.

Crete, the price of his interference, was the first to feel the weight of Mehemet Ali's power. The insurrection in the island had, so far, been singularly successful. At Therison, at Crepa, and at Haliarkae the insurgents had been victorious; the Mussulmans had been swept from the hills and the open country, and confined to the three coast towns. But success had been followed by the customary quarrels between the victors. The hillsmen fought with the lowlanders; and both combined to resist the authority of the Russian Afentulis, who had been sent as his representative by Demetrius Hypsilanti. In November 1822, the Hydriot Tombazes arrived, and replaced Afentulis; but the quarrels continued, and the short intervals of peace were spent in empty discussions on abstract questions of constitutional government.

While the Cretans were wasting their time in quarrelling and oratory, Mehemet Ali was making vigorous preparations for taking possession of his new province. In June 1823, his son-in-law, Hussein Bey Djeritli, landed at Suda; and forthwith the 'pacification' of the island began. Against the disciplined Egyptian troops, the guerilla warriors of Crete were powerless. Step by step, the island was reduced, with admirable method, and barbarous cruelty; and the Cretans, defeated in the open and driven from their villages, sought refuge in their mountain caves. But even here they were not safe. In the cave of Melato 2,000 souls had sought refuge; and of these thirty men capable of bearing arms and all the old women were slain; the rest were sold into slavery. Still more ghastly was the tragedy of the Grotto of Melidoni, whither some 370 souls had fled for safety. The narrow entrance of the cave was held by armed men, and all the efforts of the Arabs to storm it failed.

At last the discovery of a hole in the roof of the grotto inspired the latter with a brilliant idea for reducing the garrison. They now proceeded to block up the entrance to the cave, and, when this was accomplished, thrust masses of burning material through the hole in the roof. The wretched defenders fled from point to point of their place of refuge, now become a dreadful death trap, to escape from the advancing horror of suffocating smoke; but every outlet had been carefully closed, and when, after a certain time, the Arabs entered the cave, not a soul of all the defenders was left alive.

★★★★★★

The Cretan 'Christians' appear to have used this incident as a precedent during the recent massacres at Sitia, when many Moslems, who had taken refuge in a cave, were killed just in the same way. See 'Side Lights on the Cretan Insurrection', by Mr. Ernest Bennett, *Nineteenth Century* for May 1897.

★★★★★★

By April 1824, the severe measures of Hussein had succeeded in reducing the island to submission; and only in some of the remoter mountain fastnesses, which had, like the Maina, ever defied the Ottoman power, did a few bands of the Cretans still assert their independence. Tombazes, with a crowd of refugees, was taken off by a squadron of Hydriot ships. Hussein, the object of his cruelty being accomplished, exchanged it for a politic clemency, and, while disarming the people, issued a general pardon, and attempted to reconcile the Cretans to the Egyptian rule by a considerable remission of taxation.

Crete being thus in the hands of the Egyptians, Mehemet Ali determined to make it the base of the expedition which, under his son Ibrahim Pasha, he was now preparing against the Morea. For months past the dockyards and arsenal of Alexandria had been the scene of extraordinary activity; and, by the beginning of June, one of the most magnificent fleets that had ever been seen in the Mediterranean was assembled in the port; while, outside the town, an army of 15,000 disciplined troops was encamped, in readiness to sail for the suppression of the infidel revolt.

Before the transports were ready to embark the troops, the impatience of Mehemet caused him to fit out a squadron for the purpose of striking a blow at the Greek islanders. Three frigates and ten corvettes, commanded by Ismail Djebel Akhdar, and carrying 3,000 Albanian troops under Hussein Bey, were ordered to sail against the island of Kasos, a nest of pirates, which had earned a peculiarly evil reputation in the Archipelago. The ruthless cruelty of the Kasiots was remarkable even among the barbarous corsairs of the Ægean, and to their sinister activity was ascribed the disappearance of numberless merchantmen on the high seas. (Jurien de la Gravière, *Station du Levant*, i).

Believing themselves safe from all attack on their seagirt fortress—a barren rock some three leagues in length, and surrounded on all sides by inaccessible cliffs—the Kasiots had made no adequate preparations for defence; and had even carried their negligence so far as not to take the slightest precaution against being surprised. During the night of the 19th of June, therefore, Hussein had no difficulty in landing a strong body of his Albanians on the west coast of the island; and the hardy mountaineers scrambled with ease up the precipitous crags, and occupied the heights of the island.

The Kasiots, completely taken by surprise, and scattered in four villages, could make no effective resistance. The slaughter began at midnight, and lasted till dawn. Every man capable of bearing arms was mercilessly cut down; the young women and children were embarked the same morning for Egypt; and the slave markets of Alexandria were glutted with human wares whose plastic beauty, moulded by the sun and the pure air of the southern seas, gave them a high value as commodities. Besides thousands of slaves, the Arabs captured large quantities of stores, the accumulated proceeds of piracy, and fifteen armed and forty unarmed vessels. The neighbouring islands also, terrified by to signal an example, now sent in their submission.

Meanwhile the preparations of Mehemet Ali had been completed, and on the same day, the 19th of June, that Hussein landed in Kasos, the fleet of Ibrahim sailed from Alexandria. Seldom had a more imposing armada been borne upon the waters of the Mediterranean. Two hundred ships of war and transports, carrying 18,000 men, followed the flagship of Ibrahim to sea. The whole sea between Alexandria and Rhodes was now covered with scattered ships; for the prevailing north winds compelled the Egyptians to beat up the coast in detached squadrons; and had the Greeks been animated with the spirit of our own Drakes and Frobishers, their light sailing cruisers might have done, under these conditions, endless havoc among the hostile fleet. As long, however, as the danger was not actually at their doors, they were too busy with their own quarrels to pay much attention to the proceedings of the enemy; and Ibrahim had no difficulty in uniting his scattered fleet at Rhodes.

The Egyptian commander-in-chief cast anchor in the Bay of Makry, where he proceeded to celebrate the great Mohammedan festival of *Bairam* with exceptional solemnity, so as to impress upon the soldiers the religious character of the enterprise on which they were about to embark. The whole army was drawn up along the shore of the bay; and, as the red rim of the sun disappeared beneath the horizon, coloured lanterns were hoisted at every masthead, and the guns of the fleet thundered out a salute, while volley after volley of musketry re-echoed from the hills. Then there fell a sudden silence, and, as the smoke clouds cleared away, the warriors of Islam saw the crescent moon floating, surrounded by glittering stars, in the darkening vault of the sky. From twenty thousand throats a mighty shout went up; and to the simple faith of the Arab soldiers it seemed as though *Allah* himself had set his seal upon their enterprise.

While Ibrahim was confirming the courage and enthusiasm of his troops by this effective *coup de théatre*, the Ottoman fleet, under Khosrew Pasha, had been unusually active, and on the 2nd of July struck a blow which at last awakened the Greeks to some sense of their danger. Of all the Ægean islands, none had been more energetic and active in carrying on the war than the little rock of Psara. The courage and, it may be added, the cruelty of the Psariot seamen had rendered them peculiarly obnoxious to the Turks; the Mussulmans of the Asiatic seaboard especially, whose fields they had harried, and whose towns they had burned for years past, hating them with a perfect hate. (Gordon, ii.). Their Greek neighbours also had suffered not a little from their meddlesome pride and overbearing conduct; yet, on the whole, no Hellenic community had deserved better of its country, or taken a bolder part in its liberation, than Psara; and its destruction was felt to be a national disaster of the first order.

The continued successes of their vessels at sea had filled the Psariots with an overweening belief in their own prowess, and a corresponding contempt for the Turks, which was to cost them dear. It never entered their heads to take any effective measures for guarding their island against the attacks of so despicable a foe; and they boasted that, if the whole power of the *Capitan Pasha* were to land upon the island, they could easily sweep it into the sea. Their boast was soon to be put to the proof.

On the 2nd of July, Khosrew Pasha, favoured by a sudden change of wind, which disguised his movements from the enemy, succeeded in landing a strong force on the northern side of the island, where the coast was apparently so inaccessible that it had been thought unnecessary to protect it by more than a weak battery. Completely surprised, this was carried at the first rush; and the Albanians proceeded to climb the precipitous sides of the mountains, and in due course reached the heights looking down on the town of Psara, and commanding the rear of the Psariot batteries. On the opposite side of the island, meanwhile, Khosrew with the Ottoman fleet had attacked the town and the ships in the harbour.

Surprised and outflanked, the Psariots made a desperate resistance; but their batteries were ill placed, they themselves little accustomed to fighting on land, and quite incapable of effective combination. Only a few succeeded in reaching the vessels in the harbour, and making their escape; the majority were put to the sword. A small band, under Dimitri Prazano, retreated to the fort of Palaeocastro, and defended it till further resistance was hopeless; they then received the communion, and as the Turks swarmed over the defences, the Greek leader fired his pistol into the powder magazine, and buried the defenders and some 2,000 of the enemy under the ruins of the fort. (Prokesch, i.).

The news of the destruction of Psara spread dismay among the Greeks, and, for the time, inspired the selfish government at Nauplia with some energy against the common enemy. It was now that the Lord Commissioner of the Ionian Islands allowed the first instalment of the loan to be handed over to the Greek Government; and this, as has already been mentioned, was used in fitting out a squadron of ships in the harbours of Hydra and Spezzia. With these Miaoulis now sailed to Psara, and destroyed the vessels which Khosrew had left to hold the place. The return of the Ottoman fleet, however, compelled him to retire; and the island remained, for the time, in the hands of the Turks. It never again recovered its former prosperity; and the activity of the surviving Psariots was more than ever directed to piracy pure and simple.

Encouraged by his success against Psara, Khosrew next decided to attempt the reduction of the important island of Samos, which had long acted as a breakwater against the tide of Ottoman conquest. But the Greeks, warned by the catastrophe of Psara, were now thoroughly on the alert; and a strong squadron, under Miaoulis and Sachtouris, cruised night and day round the island. On the 14th of August, Miaoulis had gone on a hasty cruise to watch the Egyptian fleet at Rhodes, and, in his absence, Khosrew appeared off the southern point of Samos; at the same time, a fleet of forty transports, carrying 4,000 men, started from the mainland to try and effect a landing on the island. They were, however, attached by the Greek squadron under Sachtouris, who, having the advantage of the weather-gage, succeeded in sinking two of the transports, capturing two, and compelling the rest to retire.

A second attempt of the Turks to cross the strait also failed; and on the 16th and 17th of August, the arrival of one Psariot and nine Spezziot ships enabled the Greek admiral to attack the Ottoman fleet with success. As usual, the Greeks relied mainly on their fire-ships; and Kanaris succeeded in burning a Turkish frigate of fifty-four guns. Two others were likewise destroyed in the same way; and 2,000 of the enemy perished. Discouraged by these losses, Khosrew gave up the idea of reducing Samos, and sailed away to effect a junction with Ibrahim, which he effected, on the 1st of September, off Budrun. (Prokesch, i.).

The united Turkish and Egyptian fleets should now have been able with ease to sweep the Greeks from the open sea. Besides the battleship of seventy-four guns, bearing the flag of Khosrew, there were twenty frigates, twenty-five *corvettes*, and forty brigs and schooners, with nearly 300 transports of all sizes and shapes. The Ottoman fleet, moreover, though still far from being in good order, had very greatly improved since the beginning of the war. But the relations between Ibrahim and the *Capitan Pasha* were by no means cordial; the Egyptian prince resented the authoritative attitude which Khosrew's technical superiority of rank entitled him to assume; and he noticed with suspicion and contempt that, when it came to action, the Egyptians were allowed to bear the brunt of the fighting, while the Ottoman admiral always discovered some pretext for remaining at a discreet distance from the danger. Even when the Turks did go into action, the practice of their gunners was so bad that the Greeks received very little damage. (Finlay, ii. Lord Byron said, 'These Turks, with so many guns, would be dangerous enemies, if they should happen to fire without taking aim.')

The Egyptian and Turkish fleets being now united, the object of the allies was to convoy their great fleet of transports safely to Crete; and no effort of courage or patience on the part of the Greeks should have been spared to prevent the success of this enterprise. On the 5th of September, a Greek fleet of between seventy and eighty sail, under Miaoulis, appeared in the channel between Kos and the island of Kappari; and the Ottoman fleet stood out to engage it. All day the battle raged, with great violence, but very little result. In the end, such advantage as there was lay with the Ottomans, though, beyond the loss of a couple of fireships by the Greeks, neither side had suffered appreciably during the whole day's cannonade.

★★★★★★

The Turks seem to have suffered more from their own bad

seamanship than from the Greeks. 'Their principal care was to avoid running foul of each other, which, nevertheless, they continually did.' 'They had few killed or wounded, but many of their ships were disabled by mutual collision.' Gordon, ii. The English blue-jackets used to say that the Ottoman fleet was 'adrift in the Archipelago.'

★★★★★★

The Greeks, however, noticed with dismay that their fireships had fewer terrors for the well-trained Egyptian seamen than for the ill-disciplined Turks. Where the latter had fallen into panic and confusion at the approach of the dreaded engines of destruction, the Egyptians simply manoeuvred out of their way, and allowed them to drift harmlessly to leeward; or, if by chance they succeeded in attaching themselves, cut them adrift before they could do any damage. From this time forward, the superiority at sea which the Greeks had owed to their skill in this particular form of warfare began to decline; and such successes as they gained later in the war were due more often to their possession of the steamer *Karteria*, purchased on the advice of the Philhellene Captain Hastings, and to their use of heavy ordnance and charges of red-hot shot.

On the 10th of September, the Ottoman fleet again stood out from Budrun, and a battle followed in which the Greeks obtained slightly the advantage. A Turkish frigate and a corvette were destroyed by fireships; and these losses so terrified the Turks, that they hauled off, and both fleets returned to their former anchorages. The Greeks, however, though they had inflicted considerable loss upon the enemy, had only done so at great cost to themselves; for some of their own vessels had been destroyed, and many fire-ships had been sacrificed in vain. Their success, therefore, was scarce marked enough to dissipate the sense of discouragement which had seized them after the battle of the 5th.

A renewed effort of Khosrew to reach Samos met with but very ineffective resistance on their part; and its success was only prevented by a storm which dispersed the Turkish fleet. The *Capitan Pasha* thereupon retired once more into the Dardanelles; and only a few Turkish vessels remained with the fleet of Ibrahim.

Early in November, Ibrahim again made an attempt to reach Suda, where a considerable force, transported direct from Alexandria, had already collected. On the 13th, however, as his fleet, convoying the transports, was approaching Crete, Miaoulis with a Greek squadron bore down upon them. The Egyptian captains had neglected to keep, in accordance with their orders, to windward of the transports, which were sailing far in advance of the ships of war. Miaoulis was therefore able to attack them before the warships could come to the rescue. Several were destroyed, several captured, and the rest so completely dispersed that some of them even returned to Alexandria.

A Turkish frigate also nearly fell into the hands of the Greeks; and, surrounded by five or six Hydriot brigs, it only escaped owing to the invincible objection of the Greeks to coming to close quarters with the enemy. The next day at dawn, Ibrahim, seeing the necessity for once more postponing his enterprise, collected the remnants of his convoy under the shelter of Scarpanto, and two days later cast anchor in the deep Bay of Marmorice, on the west coast of Rhodes.

The Greeks now thought that, the season being far advanced, Ibrahim would give up, for the present, all idea of reaching Crete. The pay of the Hydriot seamen was a month or two in arrear, and they were eager to return home and enjoy some of the fruits of their victory. Miaoulis, inspired by a clearer perception of the threatened danger to Hellas, and by a purer patriotism, was anxious not to lose sight of the Egyptian fleet even now; and he besought his mutinous seamen, by their love of country, by their faith, by the shades of their ancestors, and by their good name among posterity, not to abandon their task. His prayers and entreaties fell on deaf ears.

The Hydriot seamen wanted neither glory nor the blessings of posterity, but their arrears of pay; they were not slaves or Turks to work for nothing. The Egyptians had been swept from the sea; let them now have their money, or they would return to their islands, orders or no orders. Miaoulis was obliged to yield; and the Greek fleet sailed for Nauplia, leaving the sea unguarded. (Cf. Lemaître).

The Greeks had not yet realised the character of the enemy they had now to deal with, nor had experience of Ibrahim's dogged tenacity of purpose; or they would never have dreamed themselves safe as long as the Egyptian fleet was not utterly destroyed. As it was, on the 5th of December, Ibrahim again set sail, and this time reached Suda without falling in with a single Greek ship.

A couple of months were now spent by the Egyptian commander in making elaborate preparations for the invasion of the Morea; and to the European officers of the staff he remarked that, having out-manoeuvred the Greeks at sea, he should meet with little difficulty in crushing them on land. (Finlay, ii.). When he had embarked at Alexandria, he had sworn never to set foot on dry land before reaching the

Morea; and now European travellers saw him seated upon his quarterdeck, cooling his rage and impatience on his unhappy subordinates with kicks, blows, and bullets. (Mendelssohn, i.).

At last all was prepared; and on February 24, 1825, he landed at Modon, at the extreme southern point of the Peloponnese, with an army of 4,000 regular infantry, and 500 cavalry. The transports were sent back to Crete; and soon afterwards, without meeting with any opposition from the Greeks, they brought over a second force of 6,000 infantry and 500 cavalry, besides artillery. The tide of war had turned against the Greeks.

Chapter 10

Siege of Navarino

The Greeks were far from realising the full import of Ibrahim's invasion. Their success against the Turks had given them an overweening confidence in their own prowess; while the misfortunes of such trained battalions as they had possessed had filled them with contempt for regular troops. After the disastrous Battle of Peta every semblance of military discipline had vanished from their forces in the field; and now they boasted loudly that the Arabs would run away at the mere sight of the bold *armatoli*, who had always been victorious over the *Sultan's* armies. Of effective military preparation, even on their own irregular lines, there was none.

The English loans, or such part of them as had not been spent in buying rotten hulks from the Hydriot shipowners for the use of the navy, or embezzled by the members of the government, had been squandered in maintaining a host of greedy adventurers, whose only title to be considered soldiers lay in the fact that they swaggered about in the streets of Nauplia, resplendent in gold-embroidered Albanian costumes and silver-mounted arms. Even so, of the 30,000 soldiers whom the government had in its pay, only some 8,000 could be mustered when at last the President, Konduriottes, determined to march against the invader.

The brief career of Konduriottes as a general is strongly reminiscent of comic opera.

> As he passed under the lofty arched gateway of Nauplia on the 28th of March, the cannon from the ramparts and from the fortress above pealed out their loud salutations, and were answered by the batteries on the shore and the shipping in the harbour.—*Historical Sketch of the Greek Revolution*, by Dr. S. G.

Home, who was present at this scene.

He was habited with barbaric magnificence, and followed by a long train of secretaries, guards, grooms, and pipe-bearers; but the dignity of his appearance was somewhat compromised by the fact that, as an islander, he was unaccustomed to riding, and had therefore to be held on his mettled charger by a groom on either side. The campaign thus magnificently begun was not fruitful of great results. The enemy being in the south, Konduriottes proceeded to march northward, until, at last, hearing that Ibrahim was besieging Navarino, he turned, and, by a circuitous route, led his army back to—Nauplia! Having thus earned sufficient military glory, he resigned his command, and appointed a Hydriot sea-captain named Skourti commander of the land forces.

Meanwhile Ibrahim had been proving himself a leader of a different stamp. No sooner were the troops landed than, without a moment's unnecessary delay, he advanced on Navarino, and on the 21st of March opened the siege of this important fortress, as well as of the old castle of Pylos, which commanded the narrow channel to the north of Sphakteria.

A Greek Army under Skourti now advanced to attempt the relief of these two places. It was composed of 7,000 men, the flower of the Hellenic forces, consisting of a band of Suliots under Djavellas and Constantine Botzares, of Rumeliot Armatoli under Karaiskakis, and a force of Albanians from the plain of Argolis under the immediate command of Skourti. There was, besides, a body of Bulgarian and Wallach irregular horse under Hadji Christos. This force was attacked on the 19th of April by Ibrahim with a detachment of 3,000 regular infantry, 400 cavalry, and four guns.

The affair of Krommydi was the first serious encounter between the Greeks and regular troops, and it resulted in an easy victory for the latter. The Greeks had established themselves, in a position selected by themselves, as usual, behind their shallow entrenchments; and these Ibrahim, after a brief reconnaissance, ordered his Arab infantry to storm at the point of the bayonet. The regulars, for the most part mere raw recruits, advanced up the slope towards the Greek entrenchments without wavering, though many fell. When they approached the enemy, their officers ordered them to advance at the double, and led them cheering to the attack. The veteran warriors of Greece, skilled in all the arts of irregular warfare, were unable to stand against the onset of disciplined battalions. With scarce a moment's resistance they fled, leaving 600 dead upon the field.

Ibrahim was now free to push the siege of Navarino and Pylos, without fear of further interruption from the Greeks on land. Shortly after the Battle of Krommydi, Hussein Bey, the conqueror of Crete, arrived in the Egyptian camp; and his keen judgment at once noticed the defects in Ibrahim's dispositions. Without having read Thucydides, or knowing anything of the immortal struggle between the Spartans and Athenians for the possession of the island, he realised that Sphakteria was the key of Navarino, and that the possession of this would involve in the end that of the fortress; and on his pointing this out to Ibrahim, the Egyptian commander ordered him to take possession of the island.

The Greeks, too, had realised, though late, the extreme importance of this position, had hastily occupied it with a few hundred troops, and erected a couple of weak batteries. They had, however, forgotten, what the Spartans had learned to their cost two thousand years before, that Sphakteria could only be held by the power commanding the sea. The Greek fleet had, as usual, been delayed by the selfishness and insubordination of the Hydriot seamen, and in the harbour were only five brigs; and when, therefore, on the 8th of May, the Egyptian fleet of ninety sail entered the bay, all hope was lost of holding Sphakteria or saving Navarino.

Under cover of a heavy cannonade from the Egyptian ships, Hussein landed, with a regiment of Arab regulars and Moreot Mussulmans, on the southern point of the island, and at once advanced to the assault of the Greek entrenchments. Again the Greeks fled, almost without striking a blow, before the Arab bayonets; and only the brave Hydriot captain Tsammados, with two or three others, among whom was the gallant Piedmontese exile Santa Rosa, died at their posts. Of the others, Mavrocordatos and Sachtouris, the governor of Navarino, succeeded in escaping on board a Greek vessel. Some 200 Greeks were taken prisoners, and about 350 slain, amongst the latter being the *klepht* Anagnostaras.

Scarcely three days after the occupation of Sphakteria by the Egyptians, Pylos capitulated; and the 800 men of the garrison were allowed to depart, after laying down their arms. Ibrahim now also offered honourable terms to the garrison of Navarino, and in spite of the strenuous opposition of George Mavromichales, afterwards the assassin of Capodistrias, the unexpected clemency of the Egyptian commander to the garrison of Pylos had its due effect, and the Rumeliot Armatoli

BATTLE OF NAVARINO

insisted on the surrender of the place. In view of the hideous scenes which had been enacted at Navarino a few years before, the Greeks may well have had some doubt as to whether the capitulation would, in their case, be strictly observed.

Among the crowd, through which they would have to pass on their way to the ships on which they were to be embarked, were the fathers, husbands, and brothers of the unfortunate Mussulmans who had been massacred and outraged by them, or their co-religionists, four years before; and their own evil conscience inspired them with terrors which proved to be groundless. The presence of Ibrahim's regular troops insured the terms of the capitulation being observed; the soldiers of the garrison were marched down to the quay, surrounded by a strong escort of cavalry, and thence transferred to Kalamata in neutral ships, escorted by a French and an Austrian man-of-war.

When all was over, a Greek squadron under Miaoulis at last appeared upon the scene; and, seeing that he was too late to save Navarino, the Hydriot admiral proceeded to Modon, where he succeeded in destroying with fire-ships several of the Egyptian vessels in the harbour, including the fine frigate *Asia*, and also in burning a considerable quantity of stores; but this success of the Greeks had no effect in delaying Ibrahim's movements.

Hitherto the vanity and overweening self-confidence of the Greeks at the centre of government had been fed by false reports of victories, and bombastic promises of the speedy expulsion of the Egyptians from the Morea. The fall of so important a fortress as Navarino, however, was a misfortune which not even the most plausible Levantine could interpret as a success; and the arrival of the news at Nauplia was followed by a wild outburst of rage and alarm. The incapacity of Konduriottes was violently denounced; and the primates and chiefs clamoured for the recall of Kolokotrones, as the only leader capable of organising an effective resistance to the invader.

Konduriottes was compelled to yield; for the Rumeliot *armatoli*, upon whose support his power had mainly rested, had now been drawn from the Morea by the report of Reshid Pasha's advance into West Hellas. The Archimandrite Dikaios (Pappa Phlesas) also, who was now Minister of the Interior, joined in the popular outcry, and in the meantime asked that he himself should be allowed to march against the enemy, the recall of Kolokotrones to be the reward of victory. The harassed government was not unwilling to let the turbulent ecclesiastic go; in the same spirit as that in which the Athenians had once allowed Cleon to have a command, in the hope that they would thus rid themselves either of the enemy or of their general.

With a body of 3,000 troops, Dikaios marched southward, and at Maniaki, on a spur of Mount Malia, took up a position commanding a view of the plain towards Navarino, and there awaited the arrival of the Egyptians. Presently the plain below them seemed to be covered with marching battalions; and, when the Greeks saw an apparently innumerable host advancing upon them with a steadiness and fateful deliberation as disconcerting as it was strange to their experience, many of them lost courage and fled. About a thousand, however, held their ground; and Dikaios stimulated their courage with the eloquence which had made him so great a power in the revolt. Victory was always possible, he cried, but if they fell, many Turks would also bite the dust, and this battle would be as famous among posterity as the immortal stand of Leonidas and his three hundred Spartans.

For once, courageous words were followed by courageous deeds. The Arabs advanced to the attack; but the Greeks held their ill-constructed entrenchments with obstinate valour. At last, however, the discipline and numbers of the enemy prevailed; but not before 800 of the Greeks and 400 Mussulmans had fallen. Dikaios himself fought like a lion; and the headless trunk of the burly priest was discovered surrounded by piles of slain Arabs. Ibrahim caused the head to be sought; and, when it was found, had it set upon the trunk, and the figure of the dead leader placed upright against a post. For a while he stood silently regarding it; then at last he said, 'That was a brave and honourable man! Better have spent twice as many lives to have saved his; he would have served us well!' Such was the heroic end of one who had hitherto been mainly known as a dissolute priest and a dishonest politician. (Mendelssohn, i.).

This exploit of Dikaios revived the drooping courage of the Greeks; and when Kolokotrones, raised from his prison to the supreme command, took the field, he made his dispositions with a certain confidence. But in generalship he was no match for Ibrahim. The rapid movements of the Egyptians bewildered those who had been accustomed to the dilatory methods of Turkish warfare.

Kolokotrones had occupied the pass of Makryplagi, to bar the road to Tripolitza; but Ibrahim outflanked him, advanced on the town, and took it, without meeting with any serious opposition. He hoped from this base, by a rapid movement, to secure Nauplia, before it could be put into a state of defence; but at the mills of Lerna, which were

Battle of Navarino

occupied by some 250 Greeks, under Makriyanni, Constantine Mavromichales, and Hypsilanti, he met with so stout a resistance, that he realised the impossibility of seizing Nauplia without a regular siege; and, as at the present moment he was not prepared to undertake this, he returned to Tripolitza.

Kolokotrones now hoped to repeat in the case of Ibrahim the strategy which he had once employed so successfully against Dramali, and, by occupying the mountain passes, to blockade the Egyptians in Tripolitza, and starve them into surrender. But Ibrahim was awake to this danger; and, on the 6th of July, he anticipated the designs of Kolokotrones by making a simultaneous attack on all his positions, and forcing him to retire. The mills of Daria, Zerekovia, and Piana, which the Greeks had neglected to fortify, fell into his hands; and the Egyptian army was secured plentiful supplies.

The war, from this point, ceased to have the character of a contest between equal forces. Ibrahim, using Tripolitza as his base, crossed and recrossed the country, harrying and devastating; and it seemed as though his deliberate policy were to destroy by famine and disease the remnant of the population which the sword had spared, in order that the Morea, cleared of its inhabitants, might be repeopled by Mohammedan negroes and *fellaheen*. The Greeks, utterly discouraged, no longer ventured to meet the enemy in the open, but carried on a guerilla warfare, cutting off his supplies, and harassing his march. For effective aid Hellas could look no longer to her own children, but turned despairing eyes abroad. Such was the desperate state of the fortunes of Greece, when Mehemet Ali sent orders to Ibrahim, who on September 30, 1825, had gone into winter quarters at Modon, to advance to the assistance of Reshid Pasha, who for eight months had been in vain besieging Missolonghi.

Chapter 11

The Siege of Missolonghi

The defence of Missolonghi must always rank as one of the most heroic and soul-stirring episodes, not only in the war of Greek independence, but in all history. It seemed as though Greek patriotism, flying from the selfishness, the intrigues, and civil broils which elsewhere disgraced the cause of freedom, had concentrated itself in this little city of the lagoons, where a garrison of peasants, burghers, and simple fishermen defied for months the whole power of the Ottoman Empire.

Sultan Mahmoud remembered with bitterness the failure of his troops before Missolonghi three years before. He determined now to make another attempt to reduce the stubborn rebels; and to make sure that this time there should be no failure, he entrusted the task to Reshid 'Kiutayeh,' Pasha of Janina, who had commanded the Ottoman Army at the Battle of Peta, and who was at once an able general and a man of singular determination of character. At the same time, he thought it expedient to warn him that either Missolonghi or his head must fall.

Reshid set about the task with great thoroughness. The wild Albanian tribes were won over by the usual presents; and on the 6th of April he led an army of twenty thousand men through the pass of Makrynoros, the Thermopylae of Western Hellas, which the Greeks had, as usual, left undefended. On the 27th of April he reached Missolonghi, and on the 7th of May formally commenced the siege by opening the first parallel.

The town was now in a far better state of defence than during the former investment. The earth wall had, mainly owing to the exertions of Lord Byron, been strengthened by a couple of bastions and other defensive works. A covered gallery had been constructed outside the ditch, and, flanking the wall, in the lagoon the island of Marmora had been fortified. At the outset, moreover, the besieged were much better provided with artillery than the besiegers. Reshid, indeed, in this respect was so badly off that he had at first to trust mainly to the spade, and gradually advance his parallels nearer the walls.

The garrison of the town consisted of four thousand men, under some of the best captains in Greece; but there were in addition to these some twelve thousand non-combatants, who formed a serious drain on the resources of the besieged. The veteran Notaris Botzares commanded the forces of the defence; the heroic Papadiamantopulos, a Moreot primate, presided over the civil government of the town.

In June Reshid received some reinforcements of artillery, but was prevented from pressing the siege with proportionate vigour owing to lack of ammunition. The supply of bombs having run out, the mortars were reduced to hurling rocks; and the practice of the gunners was, moreover, so bad that very little damage was done. An attack on the island of Marmora was repulsed. On the 10th of June, a squadron of seven Hydriot ships sailed into the harbour, bringing plentiful supplies, some reinforcements from the Morea, and promising the speedy arrival of further succour.

A month later the Greek watchman reported a fleet in the offing, and the hard-pressed Missolonghiots thought that the promised relief had arrived. Their joy was, however, premature; for the fleet turned out to be that of Khosrew Pasha, who brought Reshid much-needed supplies, and, above all, large stores of ammunition. At the same time, Yussuf Pasha had sent from Patras a flotilla of flat-bottomed gun-boats for use in the shallow waters of the lagoons, and these Reshid now used to seize the islets off the shore, and to invest the town by sea as well as by land.

Every fresh advance of the besiegers, however, only seemed to raise to a higher pitch the courage and determination of the defence. The town was now exposed to a hail of shot and shell, which speedily reduced it to a mass of ruins. On the 23rd of July a bombardment more violent than usual seemed to herald a general attack. On the 28th a mine exploded under the bastion Botzares, and the Turks advanced into the breach. Twice they planted the banner of the Crescent on the summit of the ruins, and twice they were hurled back into the ditch. For that day they gave up the attempt.

On the 1st of August, and again on the following day, they renewed their efforts to storm the town, but with no better success. Five hundred of their number had fallen, and still Missolonghi seemed as far as ever from being taken. Reshid vented his wrath on some unhappy prisoners, whom he caused to be taken before the walls and beheaded.

In spite of their triumphant resistance, however, the position of the Missolonghiots seemed now to be desperate. The garrison was weakened by hunger, and, worse still, the supply of ammunition was all but exhausted. There were only two small kegs of powder left in the town, and, should Reshid return at once to the attack, the result could not be doubtful.

At this critical moment the arrival of the Greek fleet, so long expected, was at last signalled. It appeared that the Hydriot seamen had refused to sail without double pay in advance; and the timely arrival of a loan from England had alone revived their venal patriotism, and saved the Missolonghiots.

On the 3rd of August the Greek fleet attacked that of Khosrew. For two hours the hostile squadrons manoeuvred to win the weathergage. At last the Greeks got to windward, and sent down their fireships on the vessel of the *Capitan Pasha*. But Khosrew had a peculiar dislike to this form of warfare, which might prepare for him the fate that had befallen his predecessor, Kara Ali, at the hands of Kanaris. No sooner did he see the hated craft bearing down upon him than, with his whole fleet, he stood out to sea, and, on pretence of forming a junction with the Egyptian fleet, never slackened sail until he reached Alexandria. Nevertheless, with true Oriental complacency, he claimed the victory, on the plea that his ships had received no damage!

Reshid Pasha had, however, been abandoned to his fate; and, before Missolonghi, the tables were now completely turned. Admiral Miaoulis destroyed Yussuf's flotilla of gunboats, and threw a plentiful supply of ammunition and provisions into the town; while a sortie of the garrison, under Karaiskakis, succeeded in regaining the islets in the lagoons and destroying the Turkish works. The blockade was now completely raised; and the Greek fleet, leaving seven vessels to keep the command of the sea, sailed away in pursuit of Khosrew.

Kiutayeh, without ammunition, without money, and with but little food, was now in an evil plight; yet his courage and determination never faltered. Failing other means, he took again to the spade, and rolled an immense mound of earth against one of the bastions. The Greeks had hailed this primitive siege operation with shouts of derision; but it was so far successful that the bastion was taken, only, however, to be immediately recaptured, and the labour of three weeks destroyed. On the 21st of September and the 13th of October two vigorous sorties were made by the garrison. The troops were followed by crowds of the inhabitants with spades and pickaxes, who proceeded, while the soldiers drove back the Turks, to demolish the Ottoman earthworks.

What the Greeks left unfinished the autumn rains completed, and Reshid saw the whole labour of the year destroyed. Under present conditions any further effort against the town was out of the question. By death and desertion his army was now reduced to some three thousand men; and it was necessary to wait for help. He determined, therefore, to withdraw from the immediate neighbourhood of the town, which the malarial swamps rendered extremely unhealthy, and, entrenching himself at the foot of Mount Zygos, to act strictly on the defensive.

The position of the Ottomans was now extremely critical, and nothing but the fatuousness of the Greeks saved them from utter ruin. In their rear the mountain passes were held by strong bands of Greek Armatoli; in front was Missolonghi. Had the garrison of the latter combined with the mountaineers in a simultaneous attack on the Turkish camp, the Ottoman Army would have been annihilated. But the chiefs of *Armatoli* were too much occupied with their own quarrels; and the Missolonghiots were so well content with the success they had hitherto achieved that, so far from dreaming of any offensive action, they neglected even to reprovision the city, or make any arrangements for the future. Probably, too, they thought that the Turks, in accordance with their usual custom, would retire homeward before the winter.

In this, however, they were greatly mistaken; for Reshid knew well that he must either conquer Missolonghi or perish before the walls. On the 18th of November the fleet of the *Capitan Pasha* returned, just in time to save the Turks from starvation; and the small Greek squadron being unable to hold its own against the Ottomans, they once more regained the command of the sea.

At this juncture Ibrahim received orders to join Reshid before Missolonghi. With his accustomed promptness he advanced from Navarino by forced marches, crossed the important pass of Kleidi without encountering any opposition, and at Pyrgos and Gastuni seized the stores of corn which had been intended for Missolonghi. On the 27th of November he held a council of war with Reshid and Yussuf Pasha. Between Ibrahim and Kiutayeh there was no love lost. The mere presence of the Egyptian was a wound to Reshid's pride, and Ibrahim rubbed salt into the sore.

'What!' he cried, when he saw Missolonghi, 'were you kept out eight months by this fence? Why, I took Navarino in eight *days!*' (Mendelssohn, i.).

He boasted that, within a fortnight, he would reduce the town, without Reshid's assistance. Kiutayeh accepted the offer, and vented his ill-humour on some wretched Greek women and boys, whom he impaled, as spies, before the walls.

The appearance of Ibrahim before Missolonghi threw the Greek Government into the greatest state of alarm. With the fate of the gallant Missolonghiots that of Greece seemed now to be inextricably involved, and it became urgently necessary to take measures to relieve the town; but the treasury was empty, and all attempts to float a new loan failed. It was proposed to sell the public lands, already pledged as security for the national debt; but the suggestion merely destroyed the last vestiges of the government credit. Personal patriotism now came to the rescue, and by private subscription a sufficient sum was raised to enable Miaoulis to fit out a fleet for the relief of Missolonghi.

On the 21st of January he arrived off the beleaguered town, and succeeded in lauding some stores on the island of Vasiladi. Here, however, he was attacked by the combined Turkish and Egyptian fleets, and compelled to draw off. On the night of the 27th the Greeks succeeded in destroying with a fireship an Ottoman *corvette*. On the 28th a battle with the Turkish and Egyptian fleets resulted in a victory for the Greeks. Miaoulis was enabled to throw two months' provisions into the town, before, at the beginning of February, he was compelled by the insubordination of the Hydriot seamen to sail home.

Ibrahim, whose proceedings during the winter had been stopped by floods and rains, which made the marshes about the town impassable, now commenced operations in earnest. He determined first to attempt to take the place by assault, trusting that his drilled regiments might succeed where Reshid's undisciplined horde had failed. On the 25th of February a heavy cannonade began; and, for three days, a hail of iron descended on the devoted town. On the 28th the Egyptians advanced to the attack of the bastion Botzares. Three times the Arab guard gained a footing on the walls; three times they recoiled before the furious onslaught of the Greeks; and at midday the attempt was relinquished. Ibrahim was beside himself with rage. Reshid, not altogether displeased, asked him what he now thought of the 'fence'!

It was now determined to invest the place once more by sea, as well as by land. The selfishness of the Hydriot sailors, who had refused to remain without pay in advance, had forced Miaoulis to leave the Turks in command of the sea. They now again prepared a flotilla of flat-bottomed boats, and proceeded to make a systematic attack on the islands of the lagoons. On the 9th of March, Fort Vasiladi fell. On the 21st, after a seven hours' fight, the Egyptians captured the sand-bank of Dolma; and thereupon the town of Anatoliko, which had so far shared the fortunes of Missolonghi, capitulated. Its three thousand inhabitants were transported to Arta, in accordance with the terms of the capitulation.

To Greek and Turk alike this seemed the beginning of the end; and Ibrahim seized the opportunity to offer the Missolonghiots honourable terms. The garrison was to be allowed to withdraw, the inhabitants either to follow, or to remain undisturbed under the protection of the *Sultan*. But the undaunted defenders were determined to hold out. What the future had in store for them or their foes, they answered, God only knew; but of terms they would have none, and were determined to live, or die, free.

★★★★★★

Cf. Lemaître. He ascribes this attitude solely to the Missolonghiots' distrust of Ibrahim's promises, which they regarded as a trap. He is right when he says that their fear of being massacred was idle. I find only one instance during the war of the Turks having violated a capitulation—that of the surrender of the monastery of Seko by Pharmakidi (see chap. 3.), when the promise given by the Ottoman officers was held to be overruled by the special orders of the *Sultan*, which arrived subsequently. The Greeks, of course, did so frequently; and, possibly, they judged others by themselves. I prefer, however, to believe that in this case their motive was a higher one.

★★★★★★

A last gleam of brilliant success illuminated the darkening fortunes of the Greeks. In all the lagoons, only the little island of Klissova, garrisoned by about two hundred men, under the brave Djavellas, remained now in their hands. On the 6th of April this was attacked by some two thousand of Kiutayeh's Albanians. Even the flat-bottomed boats of the enemy were, however, unable to come close in land; and the soldiers were compelled to leap into the water and wade ashore through the mud, while, from behind their low entrenchments, the

Greeks met them with a deadly fire. The water was soon cumbered with the bodies of those who fell. The rest scrambled back into the boats, and made off.

Ibrahim now thought he would like to prove the superiority of his disciplined troops, and, in his turn, made an attack on the island. But the Arabs met with no better success than the Albanians. Three times they advanced to the assault, and three times the volleys of the Greeks threw them into confusion and drove them back. Hussein, the conqueror of Kasos, of Crete, and of Sphakteria, fell mortally wounded while directing the third assault. The Greeks, with the loss of thirty-five men, remained masters of the island. Of the Turks, a thousand had fallen in vain.

Had the Missolonghiots taken advantage of the discouragement of the besiegers, caused by this reverse, to throw themselves *en masse* upon the enemy, and cut their way through, the attempt would probably have succeeded. But, though reduced now to the greatest straits, they still looked forward confidently to the arrival of the fleet with relief. On the 31st of March, Admiral Miaoulis actually did appear; but his fleet was small, poorly armed, and undermanned. The combined navy of the Turks and Egyptians lay, in overwhelming strength, across his course; and, in the absence of flat-bottomed boats, he could make no attempt to throw provisions into the town by way of the lagoons. Reluctantly he was compelled to relinquish his enterprise, and leave Missolonghi to its fate.

This could now be no longer delayed. The town was reduced to the most miserable plight. The starved inhabitants wandered amid the ruins of their homes, looking more like ghosts than living men. For days they had been reduced to subsisting upon the most loathsome food; and now even rats and mice were luxuries no longer obtainable. The sick and wounded, for whose care it was impossible to make provision, lay in neglect and filth, rotting in a living death. The brave defenders of the shattered walls, weakened by hunger, could scarcely any longer bear the weight of their arms. And now, even of the most miserable food, rations remained for only two more days. Yet no voice was raised in favour of surrender. The men of Missolonghi were determined, come what might, to be true to their vow to live or die as free men.

There remained but one chance: to cut their way to life and freedom through the lines of the enemy; and a sortie of the garrison and all the inhabitants of the town was accordingly arranged for the night of the 22nd of April. It was hoped that in the surprise and confusion of the attack a large portion, at any rate, of the besieged might fight their way to liberty. Those who fell would at least die gloriously as free men.

Botzares' plan was well conceived, and by no means hopeless of success. Communication was opened with Karaiskakis, and that chief was asked to send a strong body of Armatoli to the slopes of Mount Zygos, to feign an attack on the rear of the Turkish camp, and draw off the attention of the besiegers. The sound of the firing was to be the signal for the sortie to begin. The Missolonghiots were to be divided into two bands: one was to attack the camp of Reshid; the other, with the women and children, to attempt to cut its way through the Egyptians. Once beyond the Mussulman lines, they could join hands with the Armatoli on Mount Zygos, and seek safety in the mountains.

The plan, however, was betrayed to Ibrahim by a Bulgarian deserter. Karaiskakis, too, was unable to carry out his share of the programme. The messenger of Botzares found him lying ill in his tent, and the other chiefs of Armatoli too much occupied with their own selfish quarrels to care much about the fate of the heroic Missolonghiots. Only about two hundred men, under Noti Botzares, proceeded on the afternoon of the 22nd to Mount Zygos, only, however, to fall into an ambush of some two thousand Albanians, whom Ibrahim had posted there for the purpose of cutting them off. The sound of the firing was taken by the Missolonghiots to mean that the *Armatoli* had reached the place arranged.

Unfortunately, it also warned Ibrahim that the sortie might be expected that night, a belief which was confirmed by the unwonted stir and clamour in the town. He made his dispositions accordingly. The troops lay under arms in the trenches; and, in case the Greeks should succeed in breaking through, strong bodies of cavalry were held in reserve to fall upon them in the open ground beyond the camp.

At nightfall the preparations of Botzares began. The soldiers were ordered to lie in the shallow moat in front of the wall until the signal should be given. Across this moat were thrown three bridges, and behind these were massed all those of the inhabitants who could walk—the men on the outside, the women and children in the midst. All were armed. The women were dressed as men; the very children carried pistols. As yet there was no sign of wavering, and all alike seemed inspired by the same heroic resolution, the same steadfast patience. But hour after hour passed, and still the expected signal from Mount Zygos was not given. At last, about midnight, the moon rose. The excited warriors, their nerves strung to the utmost tension, seemed to take this as a signal to begin. With a wild shout they sprang out of the ditch, and rushed upon the hostile lines. At the same time the masses of men, women, and children began to crowd across the bridges.

The Greek charge was met with a murderous fusillade from the Turkish trenches, and at the same time the Ottoman guns opened fire on the packed masses of humanity on the bridges. For a while these continued to advance without confusion; but presently, as the hail of shot fell thick about them, those in the rear began to press forward, and in the crush that ensued some were in danger of being pushed off the edge into the ditch. One or more of these cried out 'Back! Back!' in a frightened voice. (Finlay, ii. This seems the most reasonable explanation of the panic. By some the cry of 'Back!' has been ascribed to treason). The word was passed from mouth to mouth with increasing terror. A panic seized the majority of those who had not yet crossed, and, believing that all was lost, or acting only on a blind impulse of fear, they turned and rushed wildly back into the town. The Mussulmans, with loud cries of '*Allah! Allah!*' leaped from their trenches, and entered the town together with the wretched fugitives.

★★★★★★

Lemaître says the Arabs waited till dawn before entering the town, which they did only that they might exchange their cold tents for warm houses! They were fired upon from the windows, and, not till several had been killed, did the massacre begin. But M. Lemaître can only sometimes be taken seriously.

★★★★★★

Then began a slaughter grim and great. From a cloudless sky the moon gazed calmly down on the awful scene of carnage. It seemed as though hell had been suddenly let loose on earth. The still air of the spring night was filled with the sound of yells and shrieks, the crackling of flames, and the crash of falling timbers. Yet this night of lurid horror was not without its brighter episodes, its stirring examples of cool courage and steadfast heroism. In the bastion Botzares a lame man sat, linstock in hand, and waited the coming of the Turks. As the enemy swarmed over the battlements he set the light to the powder-magazine, and blew himself and them into eternity. The Primate Kapsalis took up his post in the cartridge factory.

A large body of Turks in search of plunder swarmed into the building; the heroic Greek set fire to the powder, and perished with them in the explosion. Papadiamantopulos, more noble than most of his class, had deliberately returned to Missolonghi, when the fate of the town could not be doubted, in order to set an example of fortitude to the people whose government he had conducted. He perished in the sack. Truly, had Byron lived to see this night, he would have admitted, in spite of all his former disillusion and disappointment, that at last '*Grecian mothers had given birth to men.*'

To return to those bands of the Greeks who had not been carried by the panic back into the town. Their first furious onset carried all before it. Led by the veteran Botzares, by Makris, and Djavellas, the hero of Klissova, they leaped into the Turkish trenches, and cutting and slashing with their *yataghans*, succeeded with comparatively little loss in hewing their way through the Ottoman lines. The confusion and the dim light helped them; and doubtless also the liberty to sack and murder in the doomed town had more attraction for the brutal soldiery than a struggle with desperate men.

Once beyond the Turkish lines the Greeks imagined themselves safe. They were, however, woefully mistaken. No sooner did they appear in the open than the cavalry, which Ibrahim had held in reserve for the purpose, fell upon them and scattered their already broken ranks. They met this new and unexpected danger, indeed, with dauntless courage; but what could a confused crowd of foot soldiers do against cavalry?

Individual acts of heroism are recorded. A girl, who was carrying her wounded brother, was attacked by a Turkish horseman. Putting down her burden, she took his gun, aimed with great coolness, and brought the Ottoman from his saddle. Then lifting her brother, she resumed her flight. (Gordon, ii.) But escape was all but impossible where the, treacherous moonlight betrayed every movement of the fugitives; and only a broken remnant of the Greeks reached the rugged slopes of Mount Zygos, where the nature of the ground rendered the pursuit of cavalry impossible.

Here at last they hoped to be safe; for here, according to the plan, Karaiskakis and his Armatoli were to have awaited them. No Greeks, however, appeared; and their signals were unanswered. At last, wearied out with the fight and their former privations, they halted in the deep shadows of the forest to rest, and to collect their scattered forces. Suddenly on all sides of them the thick undergrowth was ablaze with the flashes of muskets, and a deadly hail of lead fell once more among their broken ranks. Instead of falling among the friendly *armatoli*, they had stumbled into an ambuscade of Kiutayeh's Albanians. There was no attempt at resistance. Many fell at the first volley. The rest, favoured by the darkness, continued their weary flight up the mountain.

Of all the defenders of Missolonghi only some thirteen hundred souls, including about seven women and a few children, ultimately reached a place of safety. Many who had escaped the sword of the Turks perished of hunger and exposure in the mountains. Plain and forest were strewn with the bodies of the dead, and in Missolonghi itself Ibrahim erected a ghastly trophy of three thousand heads. But, living or dead, the Missolonghiots had kept their word, and were free.

The fall of Missolonghi marks an epoch in the story of the Hellenic revolt. Even after the lapse of seventy years, (as at 1897), it is impossible to read the account of the heroic defence of the town, and of its terrible fate, without emotion. At the time the effect of the news was profound. All Europe had been watching with breathless interest every phase of the titanic struggle. Missolonghi, the scene of Byron's romantic activity, the site of his grave, appealed in itself to the imagination of a world which had not yet shaken off the spell of the poet's genius; and, even without this, the heroism of its inhabitants would have sufficed to win for it the enthusiastic sympathies of Christendom. The defence and fall of Missolonghi then gave an immense impetus to the wave of Philhellenic feeling which was already sweeping all before it throughout Europe.

The crimes, the follies, the selfishness of the Greeks were forgotten. The public opinion of Europe, itself growing restless under the yoke of Metternich's reactionary policy, saw only the spectacle of a gallant people struggling 'against fearful odds' for the liberty which is the birthright of all men; and, not in England only, but throughout Europe, an active propaganda was carried on in favour of the cause of Hellas. On the continent, where the Greeks were not recognised as belligerents, subscriptions were collected, ostensibly to provide funds for the ransom of Greek slaves, really for the purposes of the war. Throughout France, Germany, nay in Austria itself, societies were formed for this purpose. The smaller German princes, 'sentimental' professors, poets, and tradesmen alike, joined in a work which Metternich rightly felt was a practical revolt against his own policy of reaction.

In spite of his protests, however, and of his police, he was unable to curb a movement for which even the Crown Prince of Prussia and Ludwig of Bavaria openly expressed their sympathy. The empty coffers of the Greek Government continued to be replenished with

European gold, and the Greek armies reinforced by European volunteers, till Reshid Pasha could exclaim, with bitterness and with truth, 'We are no longer fighting the Greeks, but all Europe!'

CHAPTER 12

Defeat of the Greeks Before Athens

The fall of Missolonglii removed the barrier which had kept the Ottoman forces pent up in the western corner of Greece, and the flood of war now rolled eastwards. Ibrahim, indeed, not altogether to Reshid's sorrow, refused to join in the invasion of Eastern Hellas. Mehemet Ali had already spent vast sums on the war, and felt no inclination to incur further expenditure with no immediate benefit to himself. Ibrahim then returned to his own *pashalik* of the Morea, where, inadequately supplied with funds and reinforcements, he spent the rest of the summer in comparative inactivity.

Kiutayeh, on the other hand, freed from the presence of his hated rival, pushed the war with his accustomed vigour. Western Hellas was soon pacified. Many renowned chiefs of *armatoli*, among them Varnakiotes, who had taken part in the shameful massacre of Vrachori early in the war, gave in their submission; and in July the Turkish commander was free to push forward into Eastern Hellas. He occupied the passes over the mountains without meeting with serious resistance, strengthened the garrison of Thebes, and formed a junction with the forces of Omer Vrioni in Euboea. The united army of the Ottomans, 8,000 strong, with plentiful cavalry and guns, then marched into Attica, before the ingathering of the harvest.

Odysseus, the hero of so many exploits, who had been supreme in this part of Greece during the earlier phases of the struggle, was now no more; and, in the Acropolis, his former lieutenant, Gouras, commanded in his place.

The rule of Gouras, who now governed Eastern Hellas in the name of the Greek State, was that of a brigand chief rather than of a civilised administrator. His tyranny and exactions were worse than the worst experiences of Ottoman misrule, and when the Turks at last appeared, they were welcomed by the miserable peasantry of Attica as deliverers. Kiutayeh sought to strengthen this impression. He made grants of public lands to the peasants, and even enrolled them in an organised police force to resist the incursions of the Greeks. (Cf. Gordon, ii.).

Having by this wise and politic generosity won the sympathies of the inhabitants of the open country, the Ottoman commander advanced, without delay, on Athens, and laid siege to the town. On the approach of the Turks, Gouras with his immediate followers deserted the city, and threw himself into the Acropolis. The townspeople, who sought to follow him, he repulsed with brutal callousness. Thus left to their fate, they made no long resistance, and on the 25th of August the Turks carried the town by storm. A stream of fugitives fled to the Acropolis, and this time Gouras could not refuse to admit them.

All eyes were now centred on the Acropolis, as they had once been on Missolonghi. The historic rock, crowned with immortal memories, and still bearing on its summit the glorious monuments of the great days of Greece, seemed the only remaining bulwark of Hellenic freedom. If it fell, nothing would be left to prevent the Turk from sweeping across the Isthmus into the Morea, where there was now no force capable of resisting his attack. But as long as the Acropolis held out, the Peloponnese was safe; for Reshid could not advance, leaving an unreduced fortress in his rear.

At last the fatuous Government of Greece awoke to the imminence of the danger. The Greeks had cursed the selfishness and supineness of their rulers to which Missolonghi had been sacrificed. If the Acropolis fell, there would be no rulers left to curse. For a moment, in the presence of a common peril, the warring factions laid aside their quarrels.

One man was now pointed out by a consensus of public opinion as alone capable, if he wished, of saving Greece. If he wished—for the previous career of Karaiskakis had not been altogether such as to inspire unlimited confidence. In the character of this extraordinary man were present in full measure all those strange and vivid contrasts of light and shade, of baseness and nobility, which give to the actors in the story of the Greek revolt such remarkable dramatic interest. Bred among the wild brigand tribes of Epirus, he had, from his youth up, been distinguished by his dauntless courage and his ready wit.

These would seem to have earned him the special regard of old Ali Pasha, who, though not given to the exercise of clemency, twice commuted a sentence of death which had been passed on the young brigand, and even enrolled him in his body-guard. Trained thus in the school of the Pasha of Janina, a character naturally fierce and subtle had received, as yet, little impress of higher and nobler influences. After the fall of Ali, Karaiskakis took once more to the mountains, and, as a chief of *klephts*, ultimately threw in his lot with the cause of the Greeks. His patriotism had, however, not been above suspicion. More than once he had entered into relations with the Turks, and was suspected, not without justice, of playing the same selfish game as Odysseus. But of his courage, his skill as a leader, and his immense influence over the wild hillsmen, there could be no doubt.

Among the *arniatoli* his name had passed into a proverb. 'Why are you running, fool,' they would cry out when anyone fled, 'as though Karaiskakis were after you?'

'Karaiskakis,' said the Albanians of Kiutayeh's army, 'is the only Romaic captain whom we fear.'

To this man the Hellenic government decided, not without misgiving, to entrust the command of the Greek forces in Attica. Zaïmis, the President, Karaiskakis's personal enemy, agreed to forget old grudges in the face of the common danger, embraced him in public, and formally handed over to him the leadership of the troops. Karaiskakis knew that he was distrusted, and with reason, he said:

> Hitherto, I know I have been devil and angel by turns. Henceforward I am determined to be all angel.—Mendelssohn, i.

He kept his word. It seemed as though the new sense of a great responsibility, the consciousness that on his efforts rested the main hopes of the cause of his people, wrought in his character, as in that of many others in the course of the national uprising, a complete revolution. From a selfish partisan chief, he became a great national leader, and from this time, until he sealed his devotion with his death, gave himself up heart and soul to the service of his country.

The immediate object of Karaiskakis was now to advance upon Athens, and raise the siege of the Acropolis. At Eleusis he gathered a band of some two thousand irregular warriors. Besides these, the French Colonel Fabvier was also present at the head of a thousand drilled troops; and together they advanced as far as Chaidari in the direction of Athens. Here, however, they were attacked by the Ottoman forces. Karaiskakis's hillsmen, entrenched behind their shallow *tamburias*, repulsed the onslaught of the enemy; but the regulars, either from pride or laziness, had neglected to entrench themselves, and were thrown into confusion by the Turkish horse. Their defeat involved also

Camp of Georgios Karaiskakis

that of the irregulars, who were outflanked and compelled to retreat. The advance upon Athens had, for the present, to be abandoned.

Meanwhile the defence of the Acropolis, on which so much depended, was in danger of collapsing. The brigands and mercenaries, who formed the greater part of the garrison, were no Missolonghiots, to dare all for the sake of their country. As the siege was pressed, and the conditions of life within the narrow citadel grew more and more intolerable, desertions became increasingly frequent, and more than once the troops broke out into open mutiny. Gouras was compelled to harass the enemy night and day with an unceasing fusillade, to keep them on the alert, and so prevent his own men slipping through their lines under cover of the darkness. At last, on the 13th of October, Gouras himself was killed.

At first it seemed as though this misfortune would involve the fall of the fortress. But the heroic wife of the dead chieftain harangued the soldiers, upbraiding them for their cowardice, and, aided by her husband's lieutenant, Makriyanni, succeeded in persuading them to continue the defence. On the 23rd they were encouraged by the arrival of Kriezotes, who with 300 men had cut his way through the investing force. Two months later, Colonel Fabvier, with six hundred men, also succeeded in entering the fortress, bringing with him a supply of powder, but no provisions. As, however, he was unable, in spite of all his attempts, to cut his way out again, so large an additional force proved a severe strain on the already somewhat straitened resources of the garrison.

Meanwhile Karaiskakis was endeavouring to repeat, against Kiutayeh in Attica, the plan which Kolokotrones had used, in Argolis, so successfully against Dramali. His design was to seize all the passes between Eleusis and Marathon, in this way to cut off the Ottomans from their base of supplies, and so starve them out of Attica. But Reshid was a better general than Dramali; he saw the supreme importance of keeping his communications open, and sent out in good time a sufficient force to secure them. Karaiskakis was beaten, and had for the present to give up his plan. But though out-generalled by the Turkish commander-in-chief, he gained over one of his lieutenants a signal success, which did much to retrieve his defeat, and revive the courage of the Greeks.

On the 5th of December he succeeded in cutting off, in a mountain pass near Arachova, a detachment of some 2,000 Turkish troops under Mustapha Bey. Surrounded by hordes of savage hillsmen, the

Ottomans defended themselves for some time with their accustomed valour. At last a violent snowstorm seemed to give them an opportunity for abandoning an untenable position. Getting into such formation as was possible under the circumstances, they prepared to make their way out of the trap into which they had been led. The main road, however, being now held by the enemy in force, they were compelled to take to the steep mountain-tracks which, even in fine weather, gave but a very insecure foothold. Struggling through the blinding snow, up these dizzy paths, they were attacked by the Greek mountaineers, who were in hot pursuit.

The matchlocks of the Greeks had been rendered useless by the storm, and the soldiers used only their *yataghans*. Amid the swirling snow the work of butchery proceeded in ghastly silence. When, their labour accomplished, the pursuers returned to Arachova, the inhabitants, who had heard no sound of firing, asked what had become of the Turks. For only answer the Greeks held up their bloody knives. Of the Ottoman force scarce three hundred succeeded in making their escape.

In February 1827 Karaiskakis added to his prestige by another victory, repulsing Omer Vrioni from Distomo, with the loss of all his baggage and artillery. These and other lesser successes made him appear invincible to the wild tribesmen. The chiefs of *Armatoli*, who had but lately submitted to Kiutayeh, once more changed their fickle allegiance, and joined the Greek leader with all their forces. Beyond the immediate reach of Reshid's army, and excepting Missolonghi, Anatoliko, Lepanto, and Vonitza, all continental Greece was now again restored to the Hellenic cause. Karaiskakis had more than justified the confidence reposed in him.

Meanwhile, however, new actors had appeared upon the scene. The Hellenic Government was now almost wholly dependent on the sympathy of the Philhellenes of Europe for the means of carrying on the war; and in the first outburst of despair that followed the fall of Missolonghi, it had even been proposed in the National Assembly to place Greece formally under the protection of England. The timely arrival of General Gordon with a sum of 14,000*l*. alone saved the country from ruin. With the help of this sum a fleet of sixty vessels of war and twenty-one fire-ships had been fitted out, the regular troops reorganised under Colonel Fabvier, and some nine thousand Armatoli taken into the pay of the government.

Early in 1827 Lord Cochrane and Sir Richard Church arrived in the Morea, and were appointed high admiral of the fleet and generalissimo of the land forces respectively. The veteran Miaoulis, in spite of his well-earned fame, consented, with a rare disinterestedness, to accept a subordinate post under the English admiral; and when, in April, Lord Cochrane and Sir Richard Church arrived at Phalerum, Karaiskakis added to his laurels by agreeing without demur to serve under the orders of the new general.

Already, on February 5, 1827, General Gordon had landed and entrenched himself on the hill of Munychia, near the ancient harbour of Athens. His plan was to fortify this as a base for an advance on the Ottoman camp, while the attention of the Turks was diverted by a demonstration from Eleusis in the direction of Menidi. This latter ended in disaster. An advanced guard of 800 *armatoli*, under the brave and enthusiastic Colonel Brake, was fallen upon by a superior Turkish force, and cut up. Five hundred of the Greeks, with their heroic leader, fell in this engagement; while the rear guard of 2,000 men, under Notaras and Vassos, fled without coming in sight of the enemy.

After this success Reshid, on the 11th of February, advanced on Munychia to attempt to dislodge General Gordon. The onset of the Turks was, however, repulsed, partly by the vigorous resistance of the Greeks, but still more owing to a hail of shot and shell poured upon them by the steamer *Karteria* which, under the command of the brave Philhellene Captain Hastings, had entered the bay.

On the arrival of Cochrane and Church at Phalerum, a council of war was at once held to settle on the plan of campaign. Karaiskakis proposed to have recourse to the plan which he had already unsuccessfully attempted; to occupy the mountain passes leading into the plain of Attica, and starve the Turks out. With the increased forces now at the command of the Greeks, the country at their backs no longer hostile, and the command of the sea, this plan, had it been accepted, would not improbably have been crowned with success. But Cochrane's whole temperament disinclined him to cautious measures, and Church, as his subsequent proceedings proved, was incapable of grasping the true conditions of the war he had undertaken to conduct. Karaiskakis was overruled, and it was determined to make a direct attack on the Ottoman position at Athens.

On the 20th of April a body of troops under Major Urquhart landed at Munychia; and on the 25th a chance skirmish brought on a general engagement with the Ottoman troops stationed near the monastery of Saint Spiridion. Cochrane, seeing his opportunity, put himself at the head of the Greeks, and, armed only with a telescope, led them in person against the Turkish entrenchments. The impetuous onrush of the Greeks carried all before it; and, before the victorious soldiery stopped, seven of the smaller Turkish redoubts had been captured, communication established between the Greek camps at Phalerum and Munychia, and Kiutayeh's vanguard isolated in the promontory of the Piraeus.

In the monastery of Saint Spiridion, however, a band of 300 Albanians still held out, and these it now became necessary to reduce. For two days the brave defenders repulsed every effort to storm their position; but on the third day want of water compelled them to capitulate; and General Church granted them honourable terms. Unfortunately, he had taken very inadequate measures to insure the terms being observed. They were to march out with the honours of war, Karaiskakis and one or two other leaders as hostages in their midst. When the Albanians emerged from the gate of the monastery they were at once surrounded by an angry and excited mob of Greek soldiery.

Some chance altercation led to a shot being fired; and immediately there began a hideous slaughter. In vain Karaiskakis sought to stop the bloodshed. The Albanians broke and fled, pursued by the furious Greeks. Karaiskakis cried out to them, in his horror and disgust, to kill him, as was their right. The panic-stricken wretches, however, were thinking only of their own safety. A few succeeded in escaping to the Turkish lines, but the greater number were slain.

This ghastly breach of faith on the part of the Greeks was an ill-omened beginning of their campaign. Cochrane was furious; Church apologetic. A certain measure of responsibility undoubtedly rests upon the head of the English general; for, knowing the fierce and unreliable character of the Greeks, he should have taken measures to prevent his soldiers coming anywhere near the Albanians during their outmarch; and, above all, he should himself have been present to see that the terms of the capitulation were honourably observed.

The 5th of May was fixed for the general attack on the Turkish camp; but an untoward event led to its being postponed till the 6th. Strict orders had been issued that there was to be no outpost skirmishing on the day before the battle. To hold fire within sight of their enemy was, however, more than the hot-blooded *armatoli* could achieve; and Karaiskakis, lying ill and feverish in his tent, was suddenly aroused by the sound of firing. Rushing out to discover the cause, he found a Greek outpost engaged in a sharp encounter with a small party of the

GREEK TROOPS

enemy. He at once joined in the fray, to try and drive back the enemy and stop the fight. In the eagerness of pursuit, however, he advanced too far, and was isolated from his men. Surrounded by foes, before his soldiers could come to his rescue, he received a bullet in the body, and was carried mortally wounded from the field.

When the news of this misfortune spread abroad the effect was profound. The Greeks, who till now had been eager for the battle, and, if anything, overconfident as to its result, were overcome with grief, and filled with despair and the gloomiest foreboding. In the Ottoman camp the exultation was correspondingly great; and the Albanian outposts shouted over in derision to the Greeks: 'You must put on mourning; Karaiskakis is dead!' All night the wounded hero lay dying. While breath remained in his body his soldiers swore they would not leave his side; but, even if they could have been induced to move, it would have been impossible to undertake a serious military enterprise with troops in such a temper; and it was accordingly decided to postpone the attack for another day, and give the soldiery time to recover their spirits.

Between Munychia and Athens the ground was covered with olive yards and gardens, which would have afforded excellent cover for the advance of irregular troops. But for some unexplained, and perhaps inexplicable, reason, Church had transferred his base from the Piraeus to the eastern end of the Bay of Phalerum, and here on the morning of the 6th of May the main body of the attacking force was landed. Between it and the enemy lay a stretch of open downs, affording no cover for infantry, but excellent manoeuvring ground for the Ottoman cavalry. Church was still on his yacht, where 'in most unmilitary' fashion, (Finlay ii.), he had made his headquarters. The Greeks, sullen and depressed, advanced across the open in a straggling line, without order and with no eagerness. Suddenly, from a ravine where they had been concealed by the Ottoman commander, a large body of Turkish cavalry burst upon them; and the Greeks, with hardly a pretence of resistance, broke and fled.

Cochrane and Church had just landed from their yachts when the crowd of fugitives, close pressed by the Ottomans, rushed helter-skelter to the shore.

The English officers had barely time to wade into the sea, and scramble into their boats, before the panic-stricken mob reached them. For the rest, all that could be done was to turn the guns of the ships upon the victorious Turks, and hold them at bay till the fugitives could be taken off by the boats. As it was, 1,500 Greeks perished in this disgraceful rout.

The effects of the defeat were out of all proportion to the importance of the battle. The English officers, whose arrival had been hailed with such unbounded hope and enthusiasm, fell into discredit; for it was felt, with some justice, that the reverse was in great part due to their defective judgment and their lack of a true grasp of the situation. The army of irregular warriors, which had only been held together by the commanding personality of Karaiskakis, now melted away like snow; and all hope of driving Kiutayeh from Attica, or of raising the siege of the Acropolis, had to be abandoned.

Of all the positions which had been won in the recent fights, Munychia alone remained in the hands of the Greeks. Here Church held out for three weeks longer, more for honour's sake than for any end it could serve. On the 27th of May, he abandoned this post also, and, before leaving, he sent orders to the garrison of the Acropolis to surrender the fortress. They refused with scorn. 'We are Greeks,' they answered, 'and determined to live or die free. If Reshid wants our arms, let him come and fetch them!'

In spite of these heroics, however, they thought better of it. Negotiations were opened with the Turkish commander-in-chief through the intervention of the French Admiral de Rigny, who chanced to be in the harbour; and a rumour that Ibrahim was approaching from the Morea made Reshid more amenable to terms; for the proud Ottoman did not feel inclined to yield the laurels of victory a second time to the hated Egyptian. On the 5th of June the garrison of the Acropolis marched out with the honours of war, Reshid himself, at the head of a strong body of cavalry, keeping the line of march, and seeing that the terms of the capitulation were observed.

******

Mendelssohn, i. Jurien de la Gravière, *Station du Levant, ii*. The conduct of Reshid throughout the negotiations for the surrender of the Acropolis was marked by a moderation and straightforwardness which did him great credit. See Finlay, ii.

******

The Turks were now once more masters of the whole of continental Greece, and had Kiutayeh advanced at once across the Isthmus, the insurrection must have been finally crushed. Happily, for Greece, his jealousy of Ibrahim prevented him from doing anything to aid him in reducing his *pashalik* to order; and instead of advancing into the

Morea, he returned to Janina, where he employed himself in consolidating the provinces he had reconquered. Once more the Greeks had been saved in spite of themselves.

CHAPTER 13

Successes of the Greeks

After the fall of Missolonghi, the interest of the war during the year 1826 had been centred in Attica. In July, indeed, Miaoulis had sailed, with the fleet fitted out with the money brought by General Gordon, to the relief of Samos. On the 11th and 12th of September he had engaged the Turks in a running fight, the Greek sailors once more displaying their superior seamanship, and had forced them to take refuge under the guns of the Dardanelles. On land, however, no decisive action was fought. Ibrahim for the time was powerless; Mehemet Ali had sent him no reinforcements; his troops were worn out and demoralised; and in November he retired into winter quarters at Modon, where he remained until April 1827. The Greeks, relieved from the most pressing dangers, were free to waste their energies in talk, and their strength in suicidal strife.

The fall of Missolonghi had brought to a head the furious discontent of the people with the selfish and incompetent government of Konduriottes, who was compelled to bow to the storm, and resign the Presidency. Zaimis was elected in his place, and a governing committee of eight members formed, from which both Konduriottes and Kolokotrones were excluded. This was the signal for the beginning of a still more furious war of parties; and even the Philhellenic sympathies of Europe were torn to shreds to form the ensigns of hostile factions, which dubbed themselves English, French, or Russian, according to the nation whose interference they most favoured.

It was characteristic also that the party divisions, even under these alien designations, followed local divisions. Miaoulis, Mavrocordatos, and the islanders generally were 'English.' The Moreots declared for Russia, following the lead of Kolokotrones, who hated both Mavrocordatos and the Hydriots, who had held him prisoner. The Rumeliots, or continental Greeks, were 'French.'

In November the National Assembly, which was powerless amid the strife of armed factions at Piada, was transferred by Zaimis to the island of Ægina. Konduriottes and Kolokotrones, patching up a temporary truce in their common hatred of Zaimis, now summoned a second Assembly at Kastri, and, in February 1827, elected Sissinis President. Once more Hellas, already bleeding from so many wounds, seemed in danger of being torn asunder by civil war. At this crisis, however, Lord Cochrane and Sir Richard Church appeared upon the scene, and their earnest remonstrances succeeded in once more uniting the rival parties.

Both Assemblies were dissolved, and, in March 1827, a new one called together at Damala, near the ancient Troezene. Zaimis and Sissinis also now both resigned, and the Assembly proceeded to the election of a new President. The choice fell upon Count Capodistrias, the ex-minister of Russia, for whose election Kolokotrones and the 'Russian' party had long been intriguing. (Mendelssohn, i.). The appointment was to be for seven years, and until the arrival of the new President, the government was placed in the hands of a committee of three. George Mavromichales, Miliaitis, and Nakos were the commissioners chosen.

In May 1827 was published the Constitution of Troezene, the charter of the liberties of Greece. This was in many ways a document of singular interest. As an instrument of effective government, indeed, it was stillborn, but as a manifesto embodying the ideal of the Hellenic race it was full of significance; for it proclaimed in the face of Europe that, whatever fate the diplomacy of the Cabinets might have in store for Greece, she herself would never rest content until the whole of those members of the Hellenic race who had risen in arms against the Turk had obtained their liberty.

The limits of the new Greek State were to include Albania, Thessaly, Samos, and Crete! Apart from this pronounced Panhellenism, the constitution was remarkable for an enunciation of democratic ideas far in advance of those of any State of Europe, including as it did the principle of government by the people, the equality of all before the law, freedom of opinion and of the press, and provisions against arbitrary taxation and imprisonment without trial. (Mendelssohn, i.).

The actual condition of Greece was indeed a curious commentary on these ambitious and high-soaring sentiments. When, on the 17th of May, the Assembly dissolved, its work dissolved with it. In the actual state of the country force was the only principle of government that found recognition; and every adventurer who could command a dozen cut-throats thought himself entitled to a share in the spoils of office. The provisional government, which had been appointed till the arrival of Capodistrias, was as corrupt as it was incompetent; and it was indeed characteristic of the state of Greek politics that this had been entrusted to two rogues and a fool. George Mavromichales and Miliaitis, intent only on making their fortunes while they might, found the readiest way to this end in selling their countenance to the pirates who had now begun to swarm in the Ægean, a scandal which Nakos was too imbecile to prevent. (George Mavromichales, who afterwards murdered Capodistrias, had the virtues and the vices of a brig-and chief, as a Mainote he could have no objection to piracy).

The Senate which, under the terms of the constitution, had been elected for three years, was a mere debating club, and hardly even that. Kolokotrones, in derision, had insisted in forcing its presidency on Dr. Reniaris, a deaf old Cretan, who at the time of his election had in vain sought to escape from the dangerous honour by hiding behind an almond tree! (Mendelssohn, i.).

Even had the government been honest and competent, the task that lay before it might well have proved too much for its strength. The country was utterly exhausted; no taxes could be collected; no customs levied; and, save for the contributions of the Philhellenes, the coffers of the State were empty. Everywhere, too, the wildest anarchy reigned supreme. The islanders, weary of an unprofitable war, had taken to piracy, and turned their arms against the commerce of all nations. Spezziots and Hydriots did what seemed good in their own eyes.

The Psariots made Ægina itself the centre of their depredations; and the fugitive Cretans in the Cyclades had established pirate strongholds, from which they issued to scour the narrow seas. On the mainland, too, the fortresses in the possession of the Greeks had been converted into robbers' nests. J. Mavromichales in Monemvasia, Djavellas in Acrocorinthos, levied blackmail on the wretched peasants of the surrounding country.

In Nauplia the castles of Itsch-kalé and Palamidi were held by rival bands of Suliots and Rumeliots, under their chiefs Photomaras and Grivas, who, when not engaged in bombarding each other, agreed in wringing contributions from the miserable inhabitants of the town by torture and imprisonment. In the open country wandering bands of

Armatoli passed hither and thither, plundering what the devastating columns of Ibrahim had spared; and the wretched peasants fled to the mountains, or here and there turned desperately on their tormentors. At Argos the townsmen threw barricades across the roads, and fired on every soldier who appeared in sight. (Mendelssohn, i.).

In June civil war seemed once more on the point of breaking out. To plundering in the abstract the Moreot *Klephts* had, of course, no objection. But they could not endure that a Peloponnesian town should be laid under contribution by Rumeliots. The position of Photomaras and Grivas in Nauplia was gall and wormwood to them; and they determined to make an effort to expel them. To this end they devised a plot which, in men themselves so treacherous and shifty, displayed a touching simplicity and trust. An officer of Grivas was bribed, with the gift of a pair of gold-mounted pistols, to admit the younger Kolokotrones and a party into the fort of Palamidi. The officer agreed, kept the pistols, and betrayed the plot to his chief.

The night of the 9th of June was chosen for the enterprise. A postern in the wall of the lower town had purposely been left open by Photomaras. Through this Kolokotrones, with a body of 250 men, penetrated into the town; while Tsokris, with another band, climbed the steep ascent to Palamidi. Arrived at the castle, the latter found the door unlocked as agreed, and passed through it with his men. But he was scarcely inside before a murderous volley was opened upon him at close quarters. Completely taken by surprise, and wounded at the first discharge, he turned and fled out of the mouth of the trap, pursued down the hill by the laughter and the bullets of the Rumeliots. Meanwhile Kolokotrones had fared no better. Surrounded, in a house which he had seized, by the superior forces of Photomaras, he had to ransom himself and his men by signing a bond for 60,000 *piastres*.

Scarcely had the Rumeliot chiefs got rid of this danger, however, when they began once more to quarrel with each other. Accusations brought against Kolettes, who was accused of receiving Ottoman bribes, had raised party spirit to white heat, and Photomaras and Grivas plunged into the fray, on opposite sides. The guns of the forts of Nauplia were now turned against each other, and for days a vigorous bombardment was kept up. On the 13th of July alone, more than two hundred bombs and shot were discharged. The wretched townsmen, already stripped by the rival gangs of ruffians of nearly all they possessed, now saw their homes reduced to ruin solely to prove which robber should have the right to deprive them of the rest. The town caught fire in several places, and a hundred souls perished in the flames. The inhabitants tried to escape into the open country; but the gates were occupied by soldiery, who drove them back, or only sold the right to leave the town at a high tariff.

To this hotbed of anarchy, the government had been transferred a month before. The provisional committee now fled, and was followed speedily by the Senate, which on the 14th of July had lost three of its members by the bursting of a bomb in its midst.

Once more the situation was saved by foreign intervention. During the height of the bombardment Admiral Codrington had arrived off Nauplia, and now interfered on behalf of the townspeople, whom he persuaded the chiefs to allow to depart. The city was soon deserted by all its inhabitants; and, of all the Greek leaders, only Demetrius Hypsilanti remained, obedient to what he considered his duty, in his bullet-riddled house.

On the 19th of July a conference was arranged between the rival chieftains on board Captain Hamilton's ship. It was represented to them strongly by the British officer how fatal the continuance of their course of action would be to the Greek cause, since, however willing the powers might be to interfere on behalf of Greece, it was impossible for them to negotiate with a government terrorised by armed factions. Sir Richard Church, who had meanwhile also arrived, added his representations to those of the admiral.

Photomaras, who had had rather the worst of the bombardment, made a virtue of necessity, and yielded his stronghold to the government. Grivas, however, still held out, and refused to evacuate Palamidi, except for payment of a million *piastres*; and, since no one had the power to force him, he remained for the time master of the situation.

Meanwhile, after five months of inactivity Ibrahim had, on the 18th of April, once more taken the field, and marched northwards into Elis. For three weeks he was detained before the castle of Klemutsi, into which Sissinis had hastily thrown himself on the news of the Egyptian advance; but, at the end of the third week, want of water compelled the garrison to capitulate, and the Egyptians continued their march to Rhium. Ibrahim, who had hitherto raged like a lion, now changed his policy, and began to play the fox. Everywhere he treated the peasantry with the greatest forbearance, leaving them their seed corn, and paying them for all his provender. This new and unlookedfor generosity bore fruit; and whole districts, weary of the homeless struggle, sent in their submission, and returned to the Ottoman allegiance. Nenekos of

Zabati, who had first set the example of defection, even raised a corps of irregulars to act as auxiliaries to the Egyptians.

The news of this treason and of the defection of so many whole eparchies from the Greek cause roused the old lion Kolokotrones from his lair. Casting aside at the call of patriotism the miserable intrigues and quarrels in which he had been immersed, he threw himself, with his accustomed fierce energy, into the task of resisting the victorious advance of the Egyptians. He issued a proclamation calling on all men capable of bearing arms, between the ages of sixteen and sixty, to rise for the defence of their country. A corps was despatched against the traitor Nenekos. Another, under Niketas, marched southward into Messenia, to attack Ibrahim's base. Two more, under Gennaios, (*i.e.* the 'brave,' a nickname given him by the *armatoli* for his courage), Kolokotrones and Paploutas, were deputed to hold the mountain passes in the centre of the Morea. Kolokotrones himself marched to Corinth and the lake of Phonia, to join Notaras and his Corinthians in watching Ibrahim's further movements.

In the irregular warfare that followed the advantage remained on the side of the Greeks. An attempt of Ibrahim to seize the monastery of Megaspilaion was frustrated by the valour of the militant monks. He then tried to penetrate into Karytaena; but the forces of Gennaios and Paploutas held the passes, and he was compelled to turn back. He retired baffled into Messenia; and the Greeks were correspondingly elated.

Further triumphs awaited them in the north. On the 15th, and again on the 29th, of July Kolokotrones defeated the combined forces of Nenekos and Achmet Bey at St. Vlasi and the Cloister of Saint John. He lacked the means, however, to take full advantage of his victory and attack Patras. In vain he urged the Hellenic Government to send him supplies of food and ammunition, he wrote indignantly:

> I cannot feed my soldiers with air, turn earth into powder, or rocks into bread!

The government paid no attention to his urgent messages, either because they had no supplies to send, or because they were too much occupied with their own selfish ends to care about the conduct of the war. The Greeks as well as the Turks were, therefore, compelled to live upon the unhappy peasants, who thus found themselves ground between the upper and the nether millstone.

Ibrahim, hearing that Kolokotrones was about to make an effort to reconquer the districts which had submitted to the Ottoman rule, now sent reinforcements by sea to Patras. Achmet Bey also once more led an expedition out of Patras, and, guided by Nenekos, marched along the coast of Achaia, with a view to securing the current harvest. But Kolokotrones was prepared. At Vostitza his lieutenant Paploutas defeated the Turkish force, and hurled it back on Patras; and shortly afterwards another body of Ottomans was defeated by Gennaios amid the vineyards of Divri, and driven back on Pyrgos. On the news of these victories, the districts which had fallen away from the national cause once more threw in their lot with the Greeks.

A new danger now loomed in the South-West, where Ibrahim was threatening the reduction of Arcadia and the Maina; and Kolokotrones hastened southward to the aid of Niketas. But the wild Mainotes, invincible in their own mountain fastnesses, held the passes successfully against all the Egyptians' efforts to force them; and Ibrahim, furious at these continuous checks, now let loose his hordes of savages once more over the open country. Not only life itself, but everything that could support life was to be destroyed. His devastating columns crossed and recrossed the country in every direction, the line of their march being marked by clouds of smoke and flame. In this ruthless campaign of destruction more than sixty thousand fig and olive trees, the staple support of the country people, were destroyed.

It was, however, too late for any barbarous cruelty to succeed in crushing the liberties of Greece. The enthusiasm of the peoples of Europe had at last borne fruit, and stronger hands were about to take up the sword which Hellas had all but let slip from her weakening grasp. Soon the thunder of the guns in the bay of Navarino would proclaim to all the world that Europe had at last recognised the right of a heroic people to freedom.

CHAPTER 14

Treaty of London

For years the attempts of the powers to arrive at some mutual understanding, with a view to the settlement of the Greek question, had dragged on without leading to any generally acceptable proposals. At first the policy of the Holy Alliance, the Concert of Europe for the suppression of 'revolution' and 'impiety,' had been supreme; and, under the influence of Metternich, the revolt of the Greeks had been put under the ban of the European Cabinets. The open sympathy of Canning for the Greeks had been the first sign of a coming change, and led the Russian Government to believe that England might herself soon take up the championship of the Hellenic cause, which Russia, under the influence of Metternich and Canning's predecessor, Castlereagh, had hitherto declined.

But if the Greeks were to find a friend, it was intolerable that that friend should be England, and the *Czar's* government determined to anticipate her possible action. In January 1824, accordingly, a proposal, which has already been mentioned, was laid before the various courts by the Russian representatives. (Prokesch-Osten, i.). This plan, however, which proposed to erect the three provinces of the Morea, and East and West Hellas, into tributary principalities on the model of Moldavia and Wallachia, found favour with no one. The Greeks themselves rejected it with scorn and indignation; and Canning refused to consider any scheme that did not recognise the right of the Greeks to mould their own destinies. (*Ibid*).

Conferences were indeed opened at St. Petersburg to attempt to reach an agreement; but Canning ordered the British representative to withdraw, (*ibid*), and, though the other plenipotentiaries remained, the diplomatic debate dragged on without arriving at any result. The motive underlying the Russian proposals was indeed too clear to deceive anyone, much less the astute diplomacy of Metternich, who, while, in the interests of the Holy Alliance, he desired to humour the Czar, had no desire to see Russia playing in the Levant the role of patron which she had assumed in the Danubian Principalities. After sitting for some time without effecting anything, the Conference was adjourned for several months. In February 1825 it met again, and Metternich now declared through the Austrian plenipotentiary that the court of Vienna could recognise only one of two alternatives, either the complete subjection or the complete independence of Greece. (Prokesch-Osten, i.; Mendelssohn, i.)

With the idea of a group of vassal States, which Russia desired to force upon the Porte, he flatly refused to have anything to do. France had been won over to his views during a visit he had paid to Charles X. in Paris, in the spring of 1825. (Mendelssohn, i.) Under these circumstances Russia had no choice but to yield; and the sole result of the St. Petersburg Conferences was that, on the 13th of March, it was resolved to present a joint note to the Porte inviting it to accept the mediation of the Powers in the settlement of the Greek question. (Prokesch, i.). Needless to say, in the absence of any threat of compulsion, this proposal was indignantly refused by the Ottoman Government.

On the relations of the powers themselves, however, the effect of the conferences was more important. The spell which the genius and personal charm of Metternich seemed to have thrown over the mind of the Emperor Alexander was broken, and the relations between the courts of St. Petersburg and Vienna were strained almost to snapping. As France and Prussia both inclined to favour the Austrian policy, Russia now found herself compelled to court the sympathies of England. For the present, indeed, the sharp divergence of the ultimate aims of the two powers forbade any actual alliance.

A certain distance, however, either might proceed without clashing with the views of the other; and Canning was not ill-content when, in a note dated August 18, 1825, Alexander announced to the great Powers his intention of taking matters into his own hands. (Mendelssohn, i.). A journey which, at this time, the *Czar* made to the south of Russia was generally looked upon as connected with warlike preparations directed against Turkey.

The unexpected death of Alexander, however, which occurred at Taganrog on the 1st of December, threw everything again into uncertainty. The new *Czar* might reverse the policy of his predecessor; and it was not even known who the new *Czar* was to be. Constantine, the eldest son of the late emperor, and rightful heir to the throne, was a mere unlettered savage. In 1820, moreover, he had divorced his wife, and contracted a morganatic union with a certain Countess Grudzinska. This circumstance, and perhaps some consciousness of his own utter unfitness to rule, had induced him, in 1823, to sign a resignation of his claim to the crown in favour of his second brother, the Grand Duke Nicholas, who was married to the Prussian Princess Charlotte.

The Czar Alexander had agreed to this arrangement, and the formal documents had been duly executed, and deposited in the archives at Moscow and St. Petersburg, but with such secrecy that the transaction had not become generally known, and Nicholas himself had received no official intimation of it.

When, therefore, the news of Alexander's death reached St. Petersburg, Nicholas himself took the oath of allegiance to Constantine, and administered it also to the imperial guard. Not till this was done were the documents unsealed which appointed Nicholas heir to the Empire. Even now he refused to mount the throne, unless he received from Constantine a renewal of his abdication. The result of this delay and uncertainty was an inevitable confusion, of which the forces of discontent were quick to avail themselves.

For some years before the death of Alexander the army had been honeycombed with secret societies having for their object the overthrow of the autocratic power of the *Czars*. Outside military circles these plots had met with little support; but amongst the officers, and especially those who had been exposed to the influences of Western Liberalism during the three years passed by the Russian Army in France, revolutionary ideas had obtained a strong foothold. The objects aimed at by the conspirators were by no means uniform.

Some, like Nicholas Turgeniew, desired only by the gradual spread of education and enlightenment to pave the way for constitutional government. Others dreamed of a Russian republic, and, like Colonel Pestel, wished to have recourse to a military rising. Various plans for an outbreak had been projected even during Alexander's lifetime, but unforeseen circumstances had always arisen to prevent their coming to a head. The confusion and uncertainty which now followed the death of the *Czar*, however, seemed an opportunity not to be neglected, and led the conspirators to precipitate their action.

For the mass of the common soldiers, of course, the word 'Constitution' had no meaning whatever. An instrument for working upon them, however, was discovered in the double oath which, in the course of a few days, they were required to take. It was pointed out to them that to swear allegiance to Nicholas was a breach of the oath which they had already taken to Constantine. The 26th of December was the day fixed for the administration of the new oath to the army. Several regiments, however, refused to take it, and with flying colours and rolling drums, marched into the square opposite the Senate house, shouting for Constantine and Constitution, which latter they had been told was the name of Constantine's wife! (Mendelssohn, i.).

The revolt threatened to spread among the rest of the troops, and ominous signs were not wanting of unrest even among the civil population. But the firmness of Nicholas prevented the most serious consequences. The mutineers were surrounded by a strong force of reliable troops, and summoned to lay down their arms. At first they refused, and shot down General Miloradovitch, who was endeavouring to bring them to reason. The *Czar* then ordered the artillery to be turned against them; and three rounds of grape sufficed to quell the mutiny.

Five of the ringleaders, including Colonel Pestel, were arrested and executed. Many of the subordinate agents were transported to Siberia; and the whole conspiracy was completely broken up. The revelation of this widespread disaffection in the army was, however, a disagreeable discovery, and inclined the *Czar* more and more to the idea of a Turkish war, as a means of restoring the morale of his troops.

The course of events at St. Petersburg had been a severe blow to Metternich. When Alexander died, he knew nothing of the alteration made in the succession, and had written to congratulate Constantine with unconcealed joy. He knew that from Constantine the cause of the Greeks would have little to expect; that he hated England, despised France, loathed Prussia as a hotbed of revolutionary intrigue, and was wholly devoted to Austria. (Metternich to Baron Ottenfels, December 18, 1825. Prokesch, Appendix, vi.). He wrote exultingly:

> The Russian romance is at an end, now begins Russian history.—*Ibid*, '*L'histoire de la Russie va commencer là ou vient de finir le roman.*'

And now Constantine had given place to Nicholas, who, in every important respect, was the exact reverse of his brother. Nicholas, indeed, who in character seemed half Puritan, half drill-sergeant, had little enough sympathy for the Greeks. 'Don't speak to me of Greeks!'

he is said to have exclaimed, 'I call them rebels!'

Nevertheless, the course to which personal inclination would never have led him was being gradually forced on him by the logic of political necessity; for, apart from the military reasons already mentioned, and which would have made the need for the active intervention of Russia in the affairs of the East not unwelcome to the *Czar*, the growing influence of England in the Levant was beginning to fill him with anxiety. Russia could not afford to see her own prestige completely overshadowed by that of a power which was already recognised as her great rival in the East.

During the moment of supreme peril, when Ibrahim stood on the heights above Nauplia, in July 1825, the Greek National Assembly had offered to place Hellas formally under British protection. Canning had refused; but at the same time his policy had now become so markedly favourable to the Greeks, that Lord Strangford, the Turcophile ambassador at Constantinople, resigned. (Prokesch, i.) He was replaced by Stratford Canning (Lord Stratford de Redcliffe), to whom instructions were given to enter into relations with the Hellenic Government. In January 1826 a conference took place between the British ambassador and representatives of Greece at Perivolakia, opposite the island of Hydra.

The Greeks, discouraged by the unfavourable turn the war had taken, were at this time prepared to consider the Russian proposal of vassal States. Canning now determined once more to open direct negotiations with the *Czar*, of whose favourable disposition he had been previously assured in some private conversations with Baron Lieven, the Russian ambassador in London. In March 1826, accordingly, the Duke of Wellington was sent to St. Petersburg to congratulate the *Czar* on his accession, and at the same time to invite him to take part in some joint demonstration on behalf of Greece.

The English proposal placed the *Czar* in a somewhat awkward position. Only a few days before, on the 17th of March, he had sent an ultimatum to the Porte demanding, with the threat of war in case of refusal, the immediate despatch of plenipotentiaries to Russia to discuss certain grievances of which the *Czar's* government had to complain. It was possible, of course, that the *Sultan* might reject the ultimatum. If, however, he were to accept it, it would be difficult for the *Czar* immediately to advance a new and entirely different series of claims.

In spite of this objection, however, Nicholas, on the 4th of April, and before the answer of the Porte accepting the ultimatum arrived, signed the so-called Protocol of St. Petersburg, according to which England was empowered to offer to the Ottoman Government a settlement of the Hellenic question based on the terms agreed to by the Greek representatives at Perivolakia, Russia in any case promising her support. (Holland).

The publication of this protocol produced a perfect storm of indignation. The *Sultan*, having accepted the Russian ultimatum, naturally resented the sudden intrusion of an entirely fresh demand; and Metternich, who stigmatised the protocol as a compound of feebleness and folly, (*'Une oeuvre pleine de faiblesse et de ridicule.'*—Metternich to Baron Ottenfels. Prokesch), encouraged the Porte to resist. Sultan Mahmoud's stubborn temper, indeed, showed no signs of yielding; and at Constantinople the preparations for the long-projected reforms in the organisation of the army were pushed forward with new vigour. The measures taken to achieve this recoiled on the Ottoman Government itself. On the 15th of June, the *janissaries*, whose old-established privileges were most affected by the reforms, rose in open insurrection. Their opposition had, however, been foreseen.

They were overwhelmed by masses of Anatolian troops, whom the *Sultan* had collected in the capital for the purpose, driven back into their barracks, and there cut down to a man. Sultan Mahmoud was thus rid at a stroke of those proud and turbulent warriors who for centuries had played in Constantinople the part of the *Praetorian* guards at Rome. But, though he was now free to pursue his schemes of military reform, the destruction of the *janissaries* had seriously weakened his available forces; and he found himself compelled, in spite of the new demands of the *Czar*, to send his representatives, in accordance with the Russian ultimatum, to meet those of Russia at Akkerman. Here, on the 26th of October, an arrangement was come to by which Turkey granted all the demands of Russia with regard to certain outstanding questions in Servia and Roumania, the navigation of the Dardanelles and Bosphorus, and the handing over of some Circassian fortresses.

During all this time the British ambassador to the Porte had refrained from presenting the Protocol of St. Petersburg, though as early as May the *Sultan* had received private intimation of its contents. Meanwhile there had been an active interchange of views between the European Cabinets, and the situation had been to a considerable extent modified. Metternich still took up an irreconcilable attitude;

Prussia only agreed to co-operate in case of a complete unanimity of the Powers; but France, where the Catholic zeal of Charles X. inclined him to emulate St. Louis in forwarding a crusade against the *infidel*, had agreed to support the protocol. (Baron de Damns to Lord Granville. Prokesch, Appendix, vii.).

In the spring of 1827 further conferences took place in London, in which Austria consented to take part. But when Metternich found that he could not influence the decision of the other powers, he withdrew his representative in wrath. On April 4, 1827, the British and Russian ambassadors handed to the *grand vizier* the joint protocol of the powers.

The *vizier*, in the name of the *Sultan*, angrily refused to admit the right of foreign governments to interfere between the and his subjects, and, in view of the Treaty of Akkerman, complained bitterly of this new move on the part of Russia. The protocol having been thus refused, it became necessary to proceed a step further; and, on the initiative of France, the Protocol of St. Petersburg was, on the 6th of July, converted into the Treaty of London, by which the contracting parties bound themselves to secure the autonomy of Greece, under the suzerainty of the *Sultan*, but without breaking off friendly relations with the Porte. (For the text, cf. Holland).

For this purpose, the fleets of the three allied powers were, under Admirals Codrington, de Rigny, and von Heyden, to establish a blockade of the Morea against all Turkish and Egyptian ships, and thus to compel Ibrahim to return to Egypt. The intention of using force was disclaimed, but, as without this the attainment of the object of the blockade seemed doubtful, a wide discretion was left to the admirals.

The ambassadors of the three powers were still in Constantinople, and on the 16th of August they presented to the Porte a final note, calling on the Ottoman Government to arrange an armistice with the Greeks, and threatening, in case of refusal, to take any measures necessary to enforce it. (Prokesch, Appendix, viii.). The Porte hesitated for a moment in face of the determined attitude of the powers, and Metternich used the moment's delay for a last desperate diplomatic move. The death of Canning, too, which took place on the 8th of August, promised to modify the policy of England, and gave him some hope of still being able to reconstruct the shattered edifice of his diplomacy. He proposed to the Porte that Turkey should solicit the good offices of Austria for a settlement of her differences with the other powers. (*Ibid*, viii.).

The Ottoman Government, glad of any chance of retiring with dignity from a dangerous attitude, or of any pretext for delay, hesitated for a while, and finally, on the 20th of October, accepted the Austrian proposal. But it was too late. At midday on this same 20th of October, Admiral Codrington had sailed his fleet into the bay of Navarino, and before nightfall the proud armada of the Mussulmans, which was to have crushed out the last spark of Hellenic liberty, was drifting a mere tangled mass of broken wreckage on the face of the waters.

Chapter 15

The Battle of Navarino

At sea the events of the year 1827 had hitherto been as indecisive as on land. Lord Cochrane had done nothing to retrieve the disastrous impression produced by the fiasco before Athens. He was unable to prevent a Turkish fleet of twenty-eight sail joining, on the 14th of May, the Egyptian fleet in the harbour of Navarino. A vigorous naval demonstration off Patras, in connection with the movements of Kolokotrones, would probably now have been his best policy. He preferred, however, to play a more venturesome game, and to sail on an enterprise which could only have been justified by brilliant success.

At the beginning of June, he put to sea with a squadron of twenty-two war vessels and six fire-ships, without letting it be known what was his destination. Not till he had passed the island of Crete did he inform his captains that it was his intention to sail for Alexandria and attempt to destroy the fleet which Mehemet Ali was now fitting out in order to enable Ibrahim to crush the last remnants of the Greek sea-power. On the 17th of June Cochrane appeared off Alexandria. The Egyptians were utterly taken by surprise, and the guard-ship at the mouth of the port was destroyed before it could make its escape. Had the Greeks at once sailed boldly into the harbour, it is possible that they might have succeeded in destroying the Egyptian fleet, which was but half equipped and quite unprepared for an engagement.

Failure, however, would have meant utter destruction; and Cochrane did not venture to risk his ships through the narrow entrance to the port. He contented himself with hovering about outside; while Mehemet in person, furious at the insult to his capital, pressed on the armament of his ships, and, as soon as they were ready, stood out to sea to punish the presumption of the Greeks. These, however, did not care to risk an engagement with Mehemet's superior force, and made all sail for Greece, pursued for some distance by the Egyptians. This second fiasco destroyed what survived of Cochrane's prestige. The Greeks, weary of their continued ill-success at sea, took once more, with increased zest, to piracy pure and simple. It was reckoned that, at this time, more than a quarter of the population were engaged, in one way or another, in this lucrative pursuit. The *Spectateur d'Orient* said:

> Piracy is the only complete and systematised organisation which the Revolution of '21 has as yet produced.

At last, however, on the 1st of August, Cochrane did succeed in winning a victory at sea. Off Cape Papas he fell in with an Egyptian corvette and schooner, which he captured after a sharp engagement, and towed in triumph into the harbour of Nauplia. The effect of this success, the last achieved by the Greeks before the intervention of the Powers in the war, was heightened by the news which immediately followed.

On the 11th of August the terms of the Treaty of London were communicated to the French and English admirals at Smyrna. Admirals Codrington and de Rigny were now empowered to interpose in the war, and part the combatants, 'if possible, with trumpets; if necessary, with cannon.' The island of Melos was fixed upon as the place of rendezvous for the allied fleets; and meanwhile Codrington sailed to Nauplia to inform the Greek Government of the decision of the Powers. The news was received by the Greeks with the wildest demonstrations of delight; and there was no need to use any threat of force to induce them to agree to the armistice. In the present crisis of its fortunes the Hellenic Government was only too glad to accept the intervention of the Powers, and, on the advice of the British admiral, once more transferred its seat to the island of Ægina, in order to escape from the terrorism of the factions, and to have a free hand in dealing with the foreign representatives.

Meanwhile the armistice, accepted by the Greeks, had been rejected by the Turks with scorn. The Porte, indeed, refused to believe that the powers were in earnest, or that, in the last resort, they would appeal to force. At Constantinople a solemn farce was enacted to proclaim to all the world at once the determination and the clemency of the *Sultan*. The Greek patriarch was compelled formally to implore the Imperial forgiveness for such of the revolted provinces as had already submitted, and the prayer was ostentatiously granted. At the same time, a powerful armament was fitted out to proceed to the reduction of the islands of Hydra and Spezzia. Mehemet Ali, too, had now completed his great armada of ninety-two ships, fifty-one of them vessels of war; and, on the 7th of September, this sailed into the harbour of Navarino, raising the number of the Turko-Egyptian fleet in the bay to a hundred and twenty-six sail.

Five days later Admiral Codrington, who had been unable to intercept the Egyptian fleet, arrived off Navarino. He at once informed the Turkish admiral of the terms of the Treaty of London, and told him that any attempt on the part of the Turko-Egyptian fleet to leave the bay would be undertaken at its peril. Ibrahim, informed by the Capitan Bey of Admiral Codrington's ultimatum, took time to think; and, pending the arrival of the French admiral, no further action was taken. On the 22nd of September, Admiral de Rigny arrived, and on the 25th a conference was arranged with the Egyptian commander-in-chief. The instructions of the admirals were precise; and Ibrahim, on his side, professed himself unable to decide anything until he had received instructions from Constantinople.

It was calculated that it would take twenty-five days for these to arrive, and during this period Ibrahim agreed to keep his fleet in the harbour of Navarino, and to undertake no operations against Hydra or Spezzia. Small squadrons were, however, to be allowed to leave the bay in order to communicate with Suda and Patras. The admirals now believed that Ibrahim would yield, and that a demonstration in force would be sufficient to induce the Egyptian fleet to withdraw to Alexandria, without the need of having recourse to more violent measures. A couple of guard-ships were left to watch the entrance to the bay, and the allied fleet withdrew, de Rigny sailing to Elaphonesos, and Codrington, after dispatching a few of his ships to Malta, going northward to watch the proceedings of Cochrane, who was now cruising off the coast of Epirus.

The situation was now in the highest degree peculiar and strained. The Greeks, having accepted the armistice which the Ottomans had refused, now had the allies on their side; and, while Ibrahim's fleet was detained in forced inactivity in the harbour of Navarino, they were straining every nerve to make the best of the favourable conditions which the *Sultan's* obstinacy had created for them. The Turks complained bitterly that, while the armistice was enforced upon them, the Greeks were allowed a perfectly free hand, and that the allies, while affecting impartiality, were, in fact, actively engaged on the side of Greece.

This, indeed, to all intents and purposes, was actually the case. Yet, Greece having willingly accepted the armistice, it would have been absurd to have insisted on her remaining passive, while the Ottomans continued the war. As long, therefore, as the Turks maintained their present attitude, the Greeks could reap, unhindered, the full benefit of the coercive measures of the Powers, which were necessarily directed against that side only which had proved refractory.

Under these circumstances the war was carried on by the Greeks with renewed activity. An expedition under Colonel Fabvier was sent to the longsuffering island of Chios. Kriezotis and Karatasos were commissioned to stir up a rebellion in Thessaly and Macedonia. Crete was blockaded; and 2,000 Greek troops were landed at Grabusa to attempt once more to fan into a flame the slumbering embers of revolt. In Western Hellas several chiefs of Armatoli were again in arms; and an expedition was sent, under Church and Cochrane, to make an effort to reduce Missolonghi, and obtain a foothold in Albania.

The enterprises of Kriezotis and of Fabvier ended in quarrels and failure, the renewed rising of the Cretans only in some months of useless bloodshed. The expedition of Church and Cochrane, on the other hand, was of more importance, not only in its direct achievements, but because it led immediately to the active intervention of the allied fleet

The plan was for Church to advance, with a small army of 1,400 men, from the Isthmus of Corinth along the coast of the Gulf. Cochrane, meanwhile, with a squadron of twenty-three ships, was to sail round the Peloponnese, and, forming a junction with Church, to carry him over to Western Hellas. On the 10th of September Cochrane anchored before Missolonghi. Codrington, however, who, as stated above, had sailed up from Navarino to watch his movements, forbade him to disembark in Albania; and the original plan of campaign had therefore to be abandoned. Cochrane had to content himself with bombarding the fort of Vasilidi, without, however, producing any impression. He then returned to Syra in the Cyclades, leaving Captain Hastings, with a small. squadron, to join Church in the Gulf of Corinth.

Besides his own vessel, the steamship *Karteria*, Hastings had under his command the *Soter*, commanded by Captain Thomas, a couple of schooners and two gunboats. On the 23rd of September the *Soter*, accompanied by the schooners and gunboats, ran the gauntlet of the forts of Rhium, through the 'little Dardanelles,' under a hot fire. Hastings followed soon after in the *Karteria*, without suffering any damage, and proceeded to reconnoitre the hostile fleet, which was lying at anchor under the guns of several shore batteries at Salona. He found it to consist of eleven ships, five of them large, and including a schooner of sixteen and a brig of fourteen guns.

On the 30th of September he sailed to attack the Turkish fleet with the *Karteria*, the *Soter*, and a couple of gunboats. The Ottomans made no effort to avoid the engagements; indeed, their main anxiety was lest the Greek squadron should discover the immense disparity of their forces in time to escape what they supposed would be their total destruction. Hastings anchored the *Karteria* about five hundred yards from the shore, under a furious fire from the Turkish ships and batteries; while the rest of his little flotilla remained about two hundred yards further out. He proceeded with the greatest coolness and deliberation. Some rounds of cold shot were first fired from the small cannon, in order to discover the exact range. This having been done, Hastings loaded the long guns and carronades with bombs and red-hot balls, and poured in a murderous fire on the Turks.

The effect was instantaneous. A shot entered the magazine of the Turkish commodore, and blew him into the air; a brig was sunk, one schooner burnt, and another driven ashore; and within half an hour the Ottoman fleet was completely destroyed. The gunboats now ran in shore and silenced the Turkish batteries; and an attempt was made to haul off the stranded schooner. This, however, had to be abandoned, as the woods near the shore were occupied by Albanian sharp-shooters, who prevented any one from approaching the vessel. It was thereupon bombarded from a distance; and the work of destruction was complete.

This victory gave the Greeks once more the command of the Gulf of Corinth, and opened up their communications between the Morea and the mainland. Its importance, however, lay not so much in its immediate military as in its ultimate political effects; for it was the news of the career of Captain Hastings in the Gulf of Corinth, and of the destruction of the Ottoman squadron at Salona, which brought to a head the quarrel between Ibrahim and the admirals, and so led directly to the catastrophe of Navarino.

In view of the destructive activity of the Greeks, Ibrahim held himself to be no longer bound by the verbal agreement entered into on the 25th of September; and he determined to send a strong squadron to the Gulf to avenge the defeat at Salona, and put a stop to the proceedings of Hastings. On the 1st of October the frigate *Dartmouth*, which had been left to watch the Turkish fleet in Navarino, signalled the departure of a Mussulman squadron; and from the heights of Zante thirty Turkish warships were presently seen sailing, with a fair wind, in a north-westerly direction. This was the first division of the Egyptian fleet, under Mustapha Bey, bound for Patras.

In spite of a high sea that was running, Codrington at once put out from Zante in pursuit, and on the following day placed himself between the Turks and the Gulf of Patras. He now sent word to the Ottoman Admiral that he would fire on the first vessel trying to pass, and forced him to turn back, the British fleet accompanying him as far as the southern point of the island of Zante. On the evening of the 3rd the second division of the Ottoman fleet, consisting of three frigates, four corvettes, and seven brigs, was signalled.

On board one of the frigates Ibrahim himself was present; the other two were commanded by Tahir Pasha and Mohurrem Bey. After exchanging signals with Mustapha, this division also prepared to return to Navarino. Meanwhile, however, a stiff south-westerly wind had arisen against which it was impossible to beat up; and on the morning of the 4th three frigates and a number of smaller ships were still off Cape Papas, and endeavouring to make for Patras. Codrington now once more, in the teeth of the gale, went in pursuit. On the evening of the same day he overhauled the Turks, and, accusing Ibrahim of a gross breach of his word, threatened force if they did not at once return. Tahir replied that the truce had applied only to Hydra, and not to Patras; and Codrington now proceeded to fire on the foremost Ottoman ships, which had not hoisted their colours, and drove them back. In the night the gale increased to a hurricane, and both fleets were scattered. Ibrahim, however, made no further attempt to reach Patras, and returned to Navarino.

On his arrival he found the expected instructions from the Porte awaiting him. These, so far from counselling him to yield to the demands of the admirals, ordered him to redouble his exertions for the reduction of the Morea, and promised him the speedy support of Kiutayeh. Nothing could have better pleased the Egyptian commander-in-chief in his present temper; and, without delaying a day, he proceeded to wreak the consuming wrath, which he was powerless to exercise on the hated admirals, on the already thrice devastated country. The British officers watched from their ships the columns of flame and smoke which were the signal to the Powers of the Ottoman defiance.

As such, indeed, it was understood by Admiral Codrington. On the 13th, the Russian admiral, Count Heyden, and the French admiral, de

Rigny, arrived off Navarino; and the allied fleet was now complete. The British squadron numbered eleven, including three line-of-battle ships and four frigates, the French seven, with three line-of-battle ships and two frigates, the Russian eight, of which four were line-of-battle ships, and two frigates. The total number of guns amounted to one thousand two hundred and seventy.

A council of war was at once held, and it was decided to send an ultimatum to the Egyptian commander-in-chief. To continue a pacific blockade of the coast seemed, under the circumstances, useless; and even this it would soon be impossible to maintain, with the approach of winter, on a coast exposed to the fury of every storm that blew. The admirals had been allowed a wide margin for the use of their own discretion, and luckily Codrington, the senior in command, was not one to shrink from responsibility.

The ultimatum now presented to Ibrahim demanded fresh securities, the return home of the Turkish and Egyptian fleets, the prompt cessation of hostilities in the interior, and the evacuation of the Morea. The only reply received by the admirals was through Ibrahim's *dragoman*, who said that his master was away in the interior, and that it was impossible to convey any message to him. This sounded unsatisfactory enough; and on the 18th another council of war was held, in order to arrive at a final decision.

It was now determined, as the blockade from without had failed, that the allied fleet should make a further demonstration by sailing into the harbour, and it was hoped that this, combined with renewed representations to the Ottoman commander, might persuade the Turks that it was to their own interest to yield. But in spite of the pacific tone of the decision, Codrington was under no delusion as to the result of this move. He had already, on the 17th, had the harbour reconnoitred; and he now made every disposition for the eventuality of a fight, assigning to each ship its place in the line of battle, and concluding his general orders with the famous words of Lord Nelson that '*no captain can do wrong who lays his ship alongside that of an enemy.*'

The harbour of Navarino is formed by a large bay, three miles in length by about two in breadth. It is protected to the west by the celebrated island of Sphakteria, and only open to the sea at its south-western end, where it is entered by a channel some three quarters of a mile in width. The northern end of Sphakteria is separated from the mainland only by a narrow and shallow channel.

The Turkish fleet was anchored in the line of the bay, facing the entrance, forming rather more than a half circle, and having its extremities protected by the fortress of Navarino on the one side and the batteries of Sphakteria on the other. The ships, eighty-two in number, were arranged in a triple line, in such a way that the gaps in the front row were filled by those in the rear; and, on each flank of the foremost line, which consisted of twenty-two of the largest vessels, were posted three fire-ships. Though greatly superior both in number of ships and guns to the allied squadrons, the Ottoman fleet was inferior in the size of its vessels, there being only three line-of-battle ships as compared with the ten of the allies.

At about half-past one o'clock on the afternoon of the 20th, Admiral Codrington's flag-ship sailed into the harbour, followed by the whole of the allied fleet. As the entrance was too narrow to allow of any other formation than line ahead in passing in, the batteries commanding the mouth of the bay might, at the outset, have done great execution on the allied ships as they sailed past. Not a gun was fired, however, and it almost seemed as though the affair might, after all, have a peaceful termination. Without a sign of resistance being offered, the French and British ships took up the positions assigned to them, dropping their anchors and turning their broadsides to the enemy; and even the Russian fleet, though delayed an hour by a sudden dropping of the breeze, had plenty of time to take its place in the line.

The *Dartmouth* was now ordered by the British admiral to request the removal of a fire-ship, which was stationed to windward of the English flag-ship; and on the Turks refusing to alter its position, a boat was sent to cut its cables, and tow it aside. The attempt to do this was resisted by the Ottomans with volleys of musketry, and a French and an English ship answered with their guns. Admiral Codrington now sent a boat to carry a remonstrance to the Turkish admiral; but the boat was fired on, and the bullet struck the flag-ship. The battle now became general.

From the point of view of naval science the fight at Navarino has little importance, for cooped up within the limits of a narrow bay, there was no room for the display of tactics or seamanship. It was a mere question of 'hard pounding;' and sound discipline and good practice at the guns were the factors which determined the victory. It was not long doubtful on which side this lay. For two hours the cannonade continued, while, from the amphitheatre of hills around, twenty thousand of Ibrahim's troops watched the struggle. At the end of this time the flag-ship of the Capitan Bey and that of Mohurrem, which had been engaged by the *Asia*, cut their cables and drifted to leeward. Others of the Turks now began to follow suit, or fired and abandoned their ships; and by the evening the Turkish fleet was completely destroyed. (*M. B.* i. Codrington's despatch is given in full in Prokesch, Appendix, viii.)

The allies remained in the bay all night, experiencing considerable difficulty in saving their own ships from the burning wrecks which were drifting amongst them in every direction. In the morning it was found that, of all the Ottoman fleet, only twenty-nine vessels were still afloat. The whole bay was littered with a blackened and blood-stained tangle of broken wreckage, and with the mutilated remains of the poor wretches who had perished in the explosions of the Turkish ships; while the sea for some distance round was red with human gore. The loss of the allies had been comparatively slight, not more than five hundred and forty being killed or wounded; but of the Mussulmans no less than six thousand had perished.

Chapter 16

Policy of Wellington

The Battle of Navarino was important rather for its diplomatic than for its immediate military effects. Ibrahim, who had arrived in time to witness the destruction of the last of his fleet, is reported merely to have laughed grimly at the sight; and he exhibited, after as before the catastrophe, the same unshaken resolution. The allied admirals, immediately after the fight, renewed their demand that the Egyptians should evacuate the Morea, and threatened serious consequences in case of refusal. In spite, however, of the object lesson of the smoking wreck of his fleet scattered in the bay beneath his eyes, Ibrahim replied by stating his intention of remaining, until such time as he should be ordered to leave by his master the Sultan. The admirals were in no condition to enforce their fresh ultimatum. The ships of the allied fleet had suffered much in the battle, and it was necessary for them to refit; and for this purpose the British and Russian squadrons now sailed to Malta, the French to Toulon.

For Ibrahim, indeed, the destruction of his fleet had for the moment brought a sensible relief. It is true that his elaborate plans for the reduction of the Greek islands had been shattered; but, on the other hand, he was now freed from the intolerable presence of the admirals; a great deal of diplomatic fog which had hitherto obscured his path had been cleared away; and he was able to do his duty to the Ottoman cause without being hampered by considerations of international policy. He accordingly set to work without delay to make arrangements for passing the winter in the Morea.

With care, he could hope to make his available stores hold out till the next harvest, even should it be impossible to receive supplies from abroad. Of the surviving Turkish ships he made use to embark the sick, the wounded, and useless mouths generally, for Alexandria, and at the same time to forward several thousands of Greek captives for the supply of the slave markets of Egypt. (The fact that the British admiral did nothing to prevent this was made, later on, the pretext for depriving him of his command).

While the Egyptian leader was thus preparing, under adverse circumstances, to maintain his position in the Peloponnese, the news of Navarino had produced the most opposite effects upon the Cabinets and peoples of Europe. Metternich, giving voice to the opinions of the court of Vienna, denounced the action of the allied admirals as an unparalleled outrage, the destruction of the Ottoman fleet as an act of piracy and murder. In England the account of Admiral Codrington's action was received with very mixed feelings. To the weak Cabinet of Lord Goderich, which in a half-hearted manner had continued the policy of Canning, it was wholly unwelcome. They had babbled of peace, of friendly intervention, and pacific demonstrations; and now the prophecies of Metternich had come true, and they found themselves plunged, by the 'indiscretion' of the British admiral, and contrary to their desires or convictions, into war and war, moreover, with the power which it had hitherto been the policy of England to support, as the great barrier against the aggressive and ambitious schemes of Russia.

By the Tories, and the Tory press, the action of the allied admirals was denounced in no measured terms. *The Times* and the *Morning Post,* (Prokesch, ii., gives several articles in full), referred to it as an outrage on a friendly power, as worse than a crime, as a blunder, which had made the English fleet the instrument for the aggrandisement of Russia. It was argued at large whether Codrington should be rewarded, or tried by court martial; and though he did ultimately receive his G.C.B., the arguments by which his claims were supported sounded rather like a defence than a panegyric.

Meanwhile the news had been received in France with open, and in Russia with ill-concealed, delight. In France, indeed, the government of Charles X. had stood greatly in need of a little military glory to furbish up its tarnished reputation. Where it had been thought necessary to teach in the schools that Napoleon Bonaparte was a royalist general, who had gained victories for the monarchy during the temporary absence of the king from France, a real military success, won under the auspices of the Bourbon dynasty, could not but be welcome; and while the vanity of the French was flattered by the revived dream of military glory, Russia found it hard to disguise her satisfaction at a 'regrettable event' which had destroyed at a blow the entire sea-power of a nation with which she was then preparing, on her own account, to go to war.

Russia, indeed, proposed to the Allied Powers that the work of Navarino should be completed by presenting to the Porte a joint ultimatum embodying the terms of the Treaty of London. (Despatch of Count Nesselrode. Prokesch, Appendix, ix.). The English Cabinet, however, seemed utterly incapable of taking any vigorous action. There can be no doubt that its true policy would have been to have accepted the victory of Navarino as a fait accompli, and pushed it to its logical conclusion. Had the combined fleets, after destroying the Ottoman navy, forced the Dardanelles, and dictated terms in common to the *Sultan* under the walls of Constantinople, not only would two years of bloodshed have been avoided, but England would have been spared the blow to her prestige in the East which was dealt by the separate action of Russia.

In spite of the bloody barrier of Navarino, however, the British Government still affected to believe in the possibility of maintaining amicable relations with the Porte. While France was willing enough to support Russia, Lord Dudley, on behalf of England, replied to the Russian note, that the Treaty of London was peaceful in its intentions, and that only peaceful means should be used to enforce it. (Note of Lord Dudley. Prokesch, Appendix, ix.). In the king's speech, in 1828, the action of the admirals was referred to as 'an untoward event,' which, however, it was hoped would not disturb the harmony of the relations between

His Majesty's Government and that of the *Sultan*; (Hansard, xviii.), and to the Porte itself representations were made justifying Admiral Codrington's action on the ground that the Turks had themselves been the aggressors. When the Ottoman Government very naturally inquired by what right the allied fleet had entered the harbour of Navarino, at all, the reply was 'by the right which every fleet has to enter a friendly port in time of peace!'

The British ministers were in fact bound hand and foot to a policy which they hated. Even while Goderich was still at the head of affairs, Lord Dudley had confessed to the Austrian minister that he considered the Treaty of London an iniquity, but an iniquity in which it was unfortunately, for the present, necessary to persevere; (Mendelssohn, i.) and when, in January 1828, the Duke of Wellington succeeded Goderich at the head of the government, the policy of Canning was committed to the hands of a statesman who had hated him as a revolutionist, and who was heart and soul devoted to the methods of Metternich.

Under these circumstances it is hardly surprising that the policy of the English Government, after Navarino, was to the last degree vacillating and weak. They had neither the courage to throw over the Treaty of London, nor the will to make it effective in the only way possible. In the words of Baron von Prokesch-Osten, they sought to undo the 'evil' to which they had been appointed the unwilling heirs, 'not by soaring above the treaty, but by lagging as far as possible behind it.' That Greece was not ruined by their timid and unsympathetic policy was due to the uncompromising attitude of the Porte, which gave Russia the pretext which she desired for interfering single-handed in the affairs of the East.

The news of the Battle of Navarino reached the ambassadors of the powers at Constantinople, through a private channel, before it was known to the Porte. They immediately went to the *grand vizier*, and put to him as an abstract question, what the attitude of the Ottoman Government would be in the event of the allied fleets using force against the navy of Ibrahim. The *vizier* replied, diplomatically, that it was impossible to name an unborn child of which the sex was unknown. When, however, the Porte received official news of the destruction of its fleet, he told them that he could only describe it as a revolting outrage, for which redress would be demanded. (Mendelssohn, i.).

The Ottoman Government thereupon lodged with the ambassadors a claim for compensation, and a demand for an apology. Both were refused, even by the British Government, on the ground that, however deplorable the affair may have been, the Turks had been the actual aggressors. Some further futile *pourparlers* followed; but, in the end, the breach with the Porte was complete; and the ambassadors of the allied Powers were withdrawn from Constantinople. (Prokesch, ii.). At the same time all British, French, and Russian subjects were ordered to leave the Ottoman dominions; and twelve thousand Catholic Armenians were banished to Angora.

The sole offence of these unfortunate people was that they owed obedience to the Pope, that 'swine' who pretended to be the vicegerent on earth of the prophet Jesus, and might, therefore, be reasonably suspected of being devoted to the interests of the 'Franks.' When the *vizier* was remonstrated with for tearing these unfortunates in midwinter from their homes and occupations, he merely replied, with a sardonic smile, 'After all, Angora is not Siberia!' (*Ibid*. ii.)

In the breast of Sultan Mahmoud himself the news of the destruction of his fleet had stirred up a devouring wrath, which was only with difficulty restrained during the first negotiations with the Powers. As soon as the ambassadors had retired, and the necessity for an affected moderation of tone was past, it burst forth with unrestrained violence. On the 20th of December a solemn *Haiti-sheriff* was issued, calling on the Moslemin to rise for the defence of Islam, which the Christian Powers had united to destroy.

The cruelty as well as the perfidy of the European Governments was enlarged upon, who, with hypocritical professions of friendship on their lips, had done to death, in time of peace, six thousand of the true believers. Russia especially was singled out for denunciation; and the Treaty of Akkermann, which had recently been concluded with her, was declared null and void. Finally, it was announced that, in the defence of the faith, the followers of the prophet reckoned nothing of the odds that might be arrayed against them, feeling secure in the righteousness of their cause and in the protection of the Almighty. (Prokesch, Appendix, viii.).

Nothing could have been more welcome to Russia than this outburst; for the formal abrogation of the Treaty of Akkermann by the Porte gave her the pretext which she desired for going to war with Turkey on her own account. The working out of the Treaty of London 'by peaceful means' she was quite willing to leave to the other members of the Triple Alliance. The ruin of the Ottoman sea-power at Navarino had given her the undisputed mastery of the Black Sea; the dying flame of the Greek revolt could be fed into new life by Russian subsidies, and form a diversion in the south; while Russia, unhampered by allies, established herself in the Balkan peninsula.

In the Mediterranean, where military operations would have been costly and difficult, Russia readily consented to be bound by the terms of the Treaty of London. In return, France willingly, and England not without considerable misgiving, were prepared to let her have a free hand elsewhere. The reply then of Russia to the *haiti-sheriff*, was the declaration of her intention to occupy the Danubian principalities. Metternich's nightmare had come true, and the end of all the sentimental interference in the affairs of Greece was to be the aggrandisement of Russia in the east of Europe.

The Austrian statesman, indeed, still made desperate efforts to avert the catastrophe. He enlarged to the Porte, through his representative at

Constantinople, on the suicidal folly of its attitude, and besought it to modify its tone. The *grand vizier* replied, moodily, that it seemed that Austria too would soon be numbered among the enemies of Islam; but the importunity of Metternich so far prevailed, that the Ottoman Government was induced to explain away the *haiti-sheriff*, and even to consent to open negotiations on the basis of the Treaty of London. But it was too late. Russia had no desire to come to terms; and on the 6th of May her army crossed the Pruth.

For Greece, then, the direct result of the Battle of Navarino was that, after years of waiting and struggle, the great Orthodox power, from which in the early days of the revolution so much had been expected, had at last come to her rescue, none the less effectually that her motives were entirely selfish. After years of heroic effort, the Hellenes had begun to despair of success. Everywhere, in the islands, on the continent, and in the Morea, the Turks had once more gained the upper hand; the means for further resistance were exhausted; the heroes of the first hopeful years were dead; the reckless enthusiasm of the people crushed out under the accumulated weight of their misfortunes.

Indeed, the very people whom it was desired to free seemed no longer to exist. Of the once thriving population nothing was visible to the passing traveller, but here and there, some hollow-eyed shadows, wandering miserably among the ruins of burnt villages or the blackened stumps of the devastated orchards. Now, however, a new ray of hope shone through the lowering clouds of the national misfortunes. With the Powers of Europe arrayed on her side against the Porte, with Russia actively fighting her battles, there seemed no cause for despair; and Greece could look forward once more with confidence into the future. And to whom was it due that she had been saved from the fate which seemed to her children more dreadful than death?

Lord Salisbury in a recent speech declared that the very existence of Greece as a nation was due to the Concert of the Powers. Yet nothing can be more certain than that, if the question had been left to the Cabinets of Europe alone, Greece would never have been freed. Metternich was the typical statesman of the period, the ideal of all the chanceries of Europe; and to Metternich the diplomatic proprieties were of infinitely more importance than any national aspirations whatever; and no claims of abstract justice could be allowed for a moment to interfere with the rules of *haute politique*. (Metternich's judgment as to the result of interfering on behalf of the Greeks proved true enough. His capital error, politically speaking, lay in his underrating sentiment and public opinion as factors to be considered).

It was, as a matter of fact, to the peoples of Europe, and not to their governments, that Greece owed her liberty. The Battle of Navarino was the master stroke that cut the Gordian knot of her troubles; yet not one of the allied monarchs, not even Nicholas, would have ventured to give his admiral the order to fight.

> It was the public opinion of Europe which forced the unwilling courts into a peaceful intervention, and then swept away the admirals into their deed of blood at Navarino. Philhellenism had shown that it was no mere dream of pious enthusiasts, but a power; and while, astonished and thunderstruck, the Cabinets kept silence, the peoples rejoiced, and a deep sigh of satisfaction rose from all Christendom.—Mendelssohn Bartholdy, i.

CHAPTER 17

Piracy in the Ægean

In the midst of the excitement and enthusiasm aroused by the news of the Battle of Navarino, Count John Capodistrias arrived in Greece. He had indeed been in no hurry to take up the thorny and thankless task which had been assigned to him when, on April 11, 1827, the Assembly of Troezene had elected him president of Hellas. As early as July the ex-minister of Russia, in an interview with the Czar Nicholas at Zarscoëselo, had asked and received permission from his master to undertake the trust which the Greeks had offered him.

The pension which the *Czar* proposed to bestow upon him he refused; but he listened with all the greater attention to the instructions which the Autocrat of the Russias gave him for the guidance of his future conduct. If he had the imperial blessing on his enterprise, it was that he was regarded by the *Czar*, with justice, as Russian in his sympathies, and, above all, as one whose character and training would be the best guarantee against 'revolutionary' tendencies.

The next few months he had spent partly in Switzerland, where for some time he had made his home, partly in visiting the various European courts with a view to interesting them in the affairs of Greece, and, if possible, persuading them to supply the necessary sinews of war. He had met with but little sympathy and less material support; and when the tidings of Navarino led him to expect important developments in the East, he determined at last to start for his new sphere of labour. The British Government placed the frigate *Warspite* at his disposal to convey him to Greece, and a French and a Russian frigate were added by way of honourable escort.

On the 19th of January, then, after being driven by stress of weather for two or three days into the harbour of Nauplia, he arrived at Ægina, where the Hellenic Government now had its seat. As he landed, the three frigates fired a salute, and hoisted the Greek ensign at their tops, this being the first recognition by any of the powers of the Greek flag.

The arrival of the President was welcomed with the wildest demonstrations of joy by the people. The great reputation of Capodistrias, and, above all, the fact that he represented not only the national will of the Greeks, but the guaranteed support of Europe, made him appear as the long-expected Messiah of the Hellenic people. The ill will which the long delay of his coming had bred was forgotten in the joy of his actual arrival; and to the Greeks it seemed as though a new era had dawned with the moment he set foot on shore.

His first impression of the country he had come to govern was not indeed such as to inspire him with any great measure of hope or confidence. The short detention in Nauplia had itself been a revelation of inconceivable chaos and misery. Ibrahim's cavalry still scoured the country up to the very gates; and inside the walls the wretched town was given up to plague, famine, and a ceaseless war of factions. The chiefs Grivas and Photomaras again held their strongholds of Palamidi and Itsch-kalé; and a fresh bombardment was imminent. The arrival of the new President indeed, backed as he was by the support of the great powers, served for the time to put an end to the civil strife; and, at his command, the rival chieftains willingly surrendered their fortresses, submitted to be reconciled, and placed their forces at his disposal. Arrived at Ægina, however, he received from the ministers a report of the condition of the government and of the country which might well have made him repent the task he had undertaken.

In the Morea and in continental Greece the misery of the population and the devastations of the soldiery had made all organised government impossible; and in the islands anarchy reigned supreme. While the government was compelled to wander from Poros to Nauplia, and from Nauplia to Ægina, to escape from the violence of the warring factions, every private individual who could gather round him a band of hired ruffians was at liberty to play the tyrant in his own district. There was neither cultivation, nor commerce, nor industry remaining. The peasants no longer sowed, for the harvest would be reaped by the lawless soldiery; merchants would not venture to sea, for robbery and death awaited them there; and workmen would no longer labour, because they could not count on being paid.

The government itself was a government in little more than name, and could scarce command obedience even in Ægina itself. The treasury was empty, and the Minister of Finance could show only a budget of debts. The sole sources of revenue remaining were the tithes of certain of the islands, the customs, and the prizes brought in by the more than doubtful activity of the Greek privateers. As for the military strength of the government, some 1,500 men under G. Diovuniotes, and 2,500 under General Church were all that could be reckoned on. The castles and strong places were still in the hands of robber chieftains. The fleet, consisting for the most part of private vessels, was being used by the islanders mainly for their own ends, principally in piracy; and the squadron under the command of Admiral Cochrane was alone at the disposal of the government. Finally, for the administration of justice there existed, in all Greece, only two courts—the prize court in Ægina, and the commercial court in Syra.

To deal with this lamentable state of affairs Capodistrias had only his great reputation, his experience, and about 300,000 *fr.* in money subscribed by European Philhellenes for the ransom of captives. He had, indeed, the prestige of legitimacy, and of the support of the Powers, which secured him at the outset universal recognition, and made even the most turbulent spirits bow to his authority. But for the creation of a really strong government the essential materials were lacking. In the attempt to evolve order out of the chaos, he had, as he bitterly complained in later days to Lord Palmerston, (cf. Prokesch-Osten, ii.), to use the very instruments which had produced the confusion. In the absence of any one whom he could trust, he was thrown back upon himself; and the outward circumstances of his position seemed to exaggerate and to justify the arbitrary policy to which, by nature and training, he was already inclined.

An enlightened dictatorship was probably what would have been, at this time, the best form of government for Greece; but to have exercised it successfully would have required a rare combination of broad-mindedness and strength; and Capodistrias, though on the whole a man of high principles, was narrow in his sympathies, and the strength of character which he undoubtedly possessed bordered upon obstinacy. His experience of affairs, although great, had been very one-sided; and he had no imaginative sympathy to enable him to see beyond his own somewhat narrow circle of ideas. He was in fact a typical bureaucrat, and one, moreover, who had been trained in the corrupt school of Russian statecraft.

By such a man, with such antecedents, the problem of restoring the chaos of Greek affairs to order would be approached only in one way. He found a government, in theory democratic, liberal, and 'revolutionary,' in practice, impotent to create or to maintain a semblance of order. Not unnaturally he came to the conclusion that the practice was the result of the theory, and that the first thing to be done was to supersede the system which had been productive of nothing but anarchy and distress by one which should prove more effective in restoring order and prosperity. He set to work then without delay to substitute for constitutional government a bureaucratic regime based on the Russian model, with himself as its sole central and motive power.

His method of effecting the revolution was marked by characteristic disingenuousness. By a threat of immediate retirement in case of refusal, he first of all forced the Senate to abrogate the Constitution of Troezene. In a proclamation which he issued on the 1st of February, he then pretended that this had been done because the constitution had not given him sufficient powers to guarantee the independence of Greece; and he promised to summon a new National Convention for April, undertaking, meanwhile, to base his government on the principles of the three constitutions of Astros, Epidaurus, and Troezene. This last, however, was a mere blind to cover his intention of concentrating the whole functions of government in his own hands.

In place of the Senate he created a council of twenty-seven members, called the Panhellenium, nominated by himself, ostensibly to advise him in his public policy, really only to register his decrees. Besides this he established a General Secretarial Bureau, a sort of Privy Council, still more dependent upon himself, and which gradually absorbed all the business of the Panhellenium.

The crisis of the national affairs, and the prestige of foreign support, enabled Capodistrias to carry through his *coup d'état* without meeting with any serious opposition. A few voices here and there were raised in protest, but they were not heard in the outburst of joy and enthusiasm which greeted the President from all sides; and the more important of the old leaders, who might at the outset have proved troublesome, he had included in the government. Konduriottes, Zaimis, and Petrobey Mavromichales were made presidents of the three committees of the Panhellenium. Mavrocordatos the President attached to himself as financial adviser, with no particular office; and the powerful influence of Kolokotrones was secured by appointing him commander of the forces in the Morea.

Under such auspices it is possible that a wise and far-sighted statesman might have succeeded in carrying through his schemes of reform, and in founding a strong personal government based on the good-will and the gratitude of the people. But Capodistrias was neither wise nor far-seeing. He was a man of a cut-and-dried system, which he was determined to impose, at all hazards, upon the country he governed; and so, as his difficulties increased, and as the opposition, which had at first not ventured to make itself heard, gathered in force and bitterness, his government, from being merely irritating and oppressive, gradually developed into a tyranny.

Before long, and step by step, the whole machinery of Russian autocracy had been established on the free soil of Greece: an absolutely centralised government based on an elaborate system of espionage and of secret police, and supported by arbitrary imprisonment, censorship of the press, intimidation of local authorities, and all the other weapons of irresponsible rule. Even the immemorial communal liberties, which the Ottomans had suffered to survive, were now destroyed by the jealous distrust of the ex-Minister of Russia; and, in all Hellas, there was soon no power left to oppose, by constitutional means, the arbitrary will of the President.

The difficulties that faced him at the outset of his career might indeed easily have made a statesman of a more democratic temper intolerant of an opposition which may have appeared merely selfish and factious. Apart from the task of restoring some semblance of prosperity to the country, devastated by the war, there were a hundred questions, financial, military, and diplomatic, awaiting settlement. The war, too, though slumbering from the sheer exhaustion of the combatants, was by no means at an end. Ibrahim was still firmly established in the south of the Morea, with an army of 20,000 infantry and 4,000 cavalry.

In February he proved that he still had power to strike, by marching northwards on one of his great harrying expeditions, in the course of which he fell upon Tripolitza with fire and sword, razed it to the ground, blowing up the more solid buildings with gunpowder, and sowed the ruins with salt, He was only prevented from treating Nauplia in the same way by symptoms of mutiny among his troops. In vain Capodistrias, by direct negotiation and through the intervention of the admirals, endeavoured to persuade him to evacuate the country, he said grimly:

> If I go, it will be by way of the Isthmus, and my course shall be like that of the *simoon*, which overthrows cities, buries the inhabitants in the ruins, and dries up the trees to the roots!

Had he carried out this threat, the armies of Greece would have been in no condition to resist. It became a matter of urgent necessity to restore them to some degree of military efficiency; and the time was not unpropitious for such an undertaking. The wild soldiery were tamed by hunger, and hastened to obey, when the President ordered them to assemble under the command of the newly-appointed commander-in-chief, Prince Demetrius Hypsilanti, at Damala. Controlling as he did the only available food supplies, it would not have been difficult for the President to have compelled the *armatoli* to submit to some sort of European discipline. He was, however, quite unversed in military science himself, and the only man who could have carried out the reform successfully, the French Colonel Fabvier, he had recently, in the true spirit of autocratic jealousy, forced out of the Greek service. He contented himself then with dividing the army into unwieldy bodies of a thousand men, called *chiliarchies*, each under a colonel. Drill and discipline were allowed to take care of themselves.

At sea the condition of the Hellenic forces cried even more loudly for reform than on land. Soon after the arrival of the President, Hydra had sent a deputation with offers of assistance, but coupled with a demand for redress of grievances, and compensation for losses sustained in the national cause. To their haughty advances Capodistrias replied by a snub. Out of an empty treasury no compensation could be paid, even if it were due; as for their condescending offers, he had no need of them; they must obey his orders, or he would take care that they were not included in the terms of the treaty establishing Greek independence. (Mendelssohn, ii.). This episode was the first of a series which threw the islands ultimately into armed opposition to the President.

For the present the great question at sea was that of the suppression of piracy. For some time, the powers had winked at its continuance, because it gave them from time to time a ready pretext for interfering in the affairs of the Archipelago. But now the evil exceeded all bounds. Not only did vessels, which were virtually pirates, sail under letters of marque from the Greek Government, but regular corsair strongholds had been established on many islands of the Ægean; and now on Grabusa, off the coast of Crete, a flourishing town had sprung up which was solely supported by this nefarious traffic. This exhausted the patience of the powers, and in November 1827 the admirals received orders to clear the seas.

In January 1828, accordingly, Commodore Sir Thomas Staines appeared off Grabusa with a combined Anglo-French squadron, captured a dozen pirate ships, and destroyed the town. The inhabitants fled to Crete, and joined the insurgents under the Philhellenes Hahn and Urquhart. At the same time, Capodistrias dispatched the Greek fleet on a similar errand elsewhere. Whatever the sins of the government vessels themselves might be, there could be no question of the duty of suppressing pirates who dared to operate without lawful authority; and at Skopelos Admiral Miaoulis destroyed forty-one, and at Skiathos thirty-eight, pirate ships. After completing this work, he was sent to help Sachtouris blockade Ibrahim in Navarino, and try to cut off the supplies which, from time to time, he had received from Crete and from the Ionian Islands.

At every turn the President was hampered in his operations by lack of funds. He attempted, with but poor success, to establish at Ægina a national bank, to which, as he let it be plainly known, he expected the wealthier of the Greek leaders to contribute. In spite, however, of all the pressure he brought to bear, and of considerable deposits made by those indefatigable Philhellenes, King Ludwig of Bavaria and the banker Eynardt of Geneva, the project languished, in the absence of either credit or adequate securities.

The old Turkish system of farming the taxes, so fruitful of misery and corruption, had not been abolished; and, as they now fetched an increased price, a certain sum was made by putting these up once more to auction. It was decreed, moreover, that the taxes, which had hitherto been collected in kind, were in future to be paid in money: a regulation which resulted in giving over the peasantry into the hands of the usurers. The President addressed pitiful appeals for advances to the Cabinets of Europe, but for the present with very moderate success; and not till after the outbreak of the Russo-Turkish war did he receive subsidies on a large enough scale to relieve his embarrassments.

In his dislike and distrust of the men with whom he had to work, Capodistrias allowed himself to be misled into what was possibly the most fatal of all his many blunders. He thrust his own brothers into offices of great importance, for which they were wholly unfit, and surrounded himself more and more with compatriots of his own, members of the same semi-Venetian Corfiot aristocracy to which he himself belonged, who had taken no share in the war of Liberation, and were out of sympathy with the democratic ideas of the Greek people. His brother Viaro, a lawyer by profession, who had no quality either of brain or heart to recommend him, he made administrator of the Sporades, where his arrogance, folly, and absolute contempt for law or justice, made the wretched islanders long for the Turkish cadis back again.

Yet this man, of whose tyrannous dealings with the islands Capodistrias had been well acquainted, was, when shortly after his arrival Lord Cochrane resigned his command, appointed High Admiral. In the same way, his younger brother Agostino, without possessing one single qualification for the office, except perhaps an imposing presence, was appointed over the heads of Hypsilanti and Sir Richard Church to the supreme command of the army.

Such flagrant instances of nepotism could hardly fail to offend and alienate a people as jealous and ambitious as the Greeks; and if, for the time being, the position of Capodistrias was unshaken, it was that his presence among them was regarded as a pledge of the goodwill of Russia and of the Triple Alliance, from which alone they could now hope to obtain that for which they had fought and suffered. Should anything at any time occur to shake their faith in the good intentions of the powers, their disappointment would assuredly vent itself against the man who had done so much to make his government odious and oppressive.

CHAPTER 18

Greek Naval Operations

Metternich said:

> The Triple Alliance consists of one power at war, which at the same time poses as mediator; of another power which operates in a spirit of friendly hostility; and, finally, of a power friendly to the Porte, which is at the same time the ally of its declared enemy and the accomplice of its friendly foe! Europe has never experienced such an *imbroglio!*—Mendelssohn, ii.

The Russian declaration of war had indeed produced a strange diplomatic tangle, which it seemed, at first sight, almost hopeless to attempt to unravel.

The Triple Alliance appeared to be once more on the point of breaking up. The British Cabinet saw with horror and alarm the threatened destruction of the Ottoman power in Europe, the maintenance of which was one of the main articles of its political creed; yet it was bound, by treaty obligations, by public opinion, and, above all, by the 'untoward' fact of Navarino, to aid and abet in the fatal work. Wellington indeed declared roundly that, come what might, he would suffer no Russian aggrandisement. For the present, however, all that could be done was to attempt to counterbalance the expected victories of the *Czar's* forces by judicious tactics within the field of operation of the Alliance.

For the present, indeed, the alarm of England at the action of Russia was without grounds. As has often since been the case, the 'Sick Man,' who, according to wise diplomatic doctors, was at the point of dissolution, showed at the approach of danger a most unexpectedly vigorous vitality. Instead of the easy and triumphant march to Constantinople, which the Russians had looked forward to when they crossed the Pruth, it cost them two hardly-contested campaigns before they could bring the Ottomans to terms.

This, however, was as yet 'on the knees, and between the hands of the gods,' and, for the present, the other two powers of the Alliance feared to be outshone by the prestige of Russia in the East. It was proposed in the conference, which was still sitting in London, to intervene actively to secure the evacuation of the Morea by the Egyptian forces. England, indeed, at first refused to do anything that might still further embarrass the Porte; but the Prince de Polignac pointed out, in a diplomatic aside, that the intervention was regarded at Paris 'as a means for getting a free hand as regards Russia.'

The Russian representative for his part had no objection to a course which would create a further diversion in Russia's favour; and so finally it was decided, on the 19th of July, that France should occupy the Morea, and compel the withdrawal of Ibrahim. (Protocol of July 19. Prokesch, Appendix, ix.). England, out of friendly consideration for her old ally the *Sultan*, refused to share in the enterprise, and stipulated that, as soon as her work was done, France should withdraw her troops. The government of Charles X. eagerly accepted the task, only too glad of an opportunity for covering the ever-widening cracks in its foundations with fresh wreaths of military glory.

Meanwhile, however, circumstances, and the irrepressible activity of Codrington, once more interfered with the designs of the 'Conference. Capodistrias was now doubly anxious to rid the Morea of the presence of Ibrahim. The Russian invasion had withdrawn the mass of the Turkish troops from continental Greece; and it would have been easy to reconquer all that had been won from the Greeks by Reshid; but as long as Ibrahim remained in the south it was impossible for the Hellenic forces to leave the Morea. Under these circumstances the President once more earnestly pressed the admirals to compel the withdrawal of the Egyptian Army; and in July a conference was held by them at Zante, at which it was decided to:

> Facilitate the sailing of a fleet of transports from Alexandria, to carry away Ibrahim's forces. If, however, the hopes of Egyptian transports should prove deceptive, everything possible would have been done.

Admiral Codrington, without authority from above, and without consulting any one, determined that the hopes should not prove deceptive. He sailed to Alexandria, and, on the 9th of August, arranged a treaty with Mehemet Ali, providing for an exchange of prisoners, and for the immediate evacuation of the Morea. The strong and frank personality of the British admiral is said to have exercised a great influence over the mind of the viceroy; but the determining factor in the negotiations was of course the impending French expedition, which both were aware of, but neither mentioned! (Mendelssohn, ii.). It was the last interference on behalf of Greece of the clear-sighted and courageous admiral; and it came none too soon; for, on his return to Navarino, he found Sir Pulteney Malcolm, who had been sent out to supersede him.

******

The conduct of Admiral Codrington during his command had been violently criticised, and his independence had more than once forced the hand of the government. In the present instance, however, Lord Aberdeen paid in the House of Lords a high tribute to the skill with which the negotiations at Alexandria had been conducted. Cf. Hansard, xxiv.

******

In their eagerness for glory, the French had pushed on their preparations with unexpected haste; and on the 30th of August, before the transports which were to convey Ibrahim to Alexandria had arrived, General Maison landed with 14,000 men at Petalidi in the Gulf of Coron. To their infinite disgust, however, they found that the object of their expedition had already been achieved. The Egyptian Army showed not the slightest disposition to dispute their landing. On the contrary, Ibrahim called upon the French commander, and inspected the troops, which, instead of the expected glory, had to be content with some neatly-turned compliments on their smartness and military appearance.

On the 16th of September the transports arrived, and the Egyptian Army began to embark. On the 3rd of October Ibrahim himself left with the last of his troops. It had been stipulated that no prisoners were to be removed against their will, and French soldiers were drawn up on the quay to see that this provision was observed. Of the six hundred captives, however, only eleven elected to remain in their devastated country. For the rest the flesh-pots of Egypt seemed to hold out greater attractions; and in the end the scandal of such a desertion was avoided by their all being compelled to remain.

The ill-will of the French at being deprived of their laurels found vent in a breach of the convention which Codrington had arranged with Mehemet Ali, and which the French affected not to recognise. By the terms of the treaty for the evacuation of the country, Ibrahim was to be allowed to leave garrisons in such fortresses as had been in the occupation of the *Sultan's* forces at the time of his landing; and, in accordance with this provision, garrisons had been left in the castles of Coron, Modon, and Navarino, and in the fort of Rhium. These the French summoned to surrender.

The Turks refused, but, in the case of the first-named fortresses, suffered the besiegers to plant their ladders against the walls, and storm the defences without opposition. Only the fort of Rhium resisted, but, after a short bombardment, this also capitulated at discretion; and this, for the present, completed the warlike operations of the French in Greece. During the remainder of the occupation the troops were employed in the arts of peace: in making roads, tilling the devastated fields, clearing out the accumulated filth in the towns, and generally setting a good example, which it would have been well for the Greeks to have followed.

The French occupation was unpopular in Greece, and Capodistrias himself had not desired it; but, now that it was a *fait accompli*, he thought it might be put to still further uses. The withdrawal of Ibrahim had left him free to put an end to the practical armistice which had now for months obtained in East and West Hellas; and he now suggested that General Maison should march across the Isthmus, and drive the Ottomans into Macedonia. However, much he may have desired to do so, the French general, in face of his instructions, dared not accept; though probably, had he done so, the government at Paris would have gladly justified his action.

Any hesitation he may have had was set aside by another protocol of the Conference of London, that of the 16th of November, which declared the Morea, with the neighbouring islands and the Cyclades, under the protection of Europe, thereby tacitly excluding continental Greece from all share in the benefits won by the war. (For text see Prokesch, Appendix, ix.). The French now withdrew from Greece, leaving only a couple of battalions in the fortresses of Coron and Navarino to act as a guarantee of order.

The publication of the protocol of the 16th of November roused a storm of indignation throughout Greece. Capodistrias himself shared the popular feeling. The inclusion of continental Greece in the new State was vital to its very existence as a free country; and the President determined to press the war, in spite of conference and protocols. He wrote to General Haydeck:

> I agree with you, that if we had some well-served field pieces and a few squadrons of cavalry we could win our frontier in spite of the London protocol.—Mendelssohn, ii.

In prosecuting the war with vigour Capodistrias had a double object to serve. He desired to secure for Greece her natural boundary, and he wished also to effect a diversion in favour of Russia, which was now being hard pressed in the Balkan campaign.

If the inclusion of Athens and Thebes in the Hellenic State was an article of faith, that of the island of Crete could hardly be regarded as more than a pious aspiration. Yet, in the interests of Russia rather than those of Greece, Capodistrias had not hesitated to fan once more into a flame the ever smouldering embers of Cretan rebellion. Soon after the Russian declaration of war, he had sent the Philhellene Baron Reineck to replace the Cretan leader, Hadji-Michali, who had been killed at Francocastelli, and had entrusted him with a message characteristically diplomatic. Greece dare not, he said, call on the men of Sphakia to rise; but, if they did so of their own accord, a Greek commissary would be there to counsel and lead them. Much less would have sufficed to rouse the inflammable islanders.

The insurrection, once begun, swept with irresistible force over the island. At Nerokuro the Ottomans were defeated; the district of Apocorona was in the hands of the rebels; and the Turks were driven back upon Suda. Massacres of Greeks in the power of the Ottomans followed every Greek victory, the work of mutual slaughter proceeding uninterrupted until, in October, Admiral Malcolm, Codrington's successor, appeared off the island, and proposed an armistice in the name of the powers. Mustapha, the Turkish commander, at first refused, but ultimately was persuaded to accept the armistice; but in spite of this the plundering and murder went on on one side and the other, for some time longer.

The naval operations of the Greeks during the year 1828 were also, in the pursuit of the same policy as that which had stirred up the useless rising in Crete, directed primarily in the interests of Russia, and only indirectly in those of Greece. Russia, in declaring war on Turkey, had, as has already been mentioned, sought to reassure her allies by guaranteeing the neutrality of the Mediterranean; but, as her difficulties in the Balkan peninsula increased, she sought by one means or another to modify this arrangement, as far as such modification suited her own interests. (Prokesch, Appendix, ix.).

Count Heyden received orders to blockade the Dardanelles; and he even went so far as to capture two or three Egyptian vessels, on the plea that they were conveying munitions of war to Bulgaria. (*Ibid* x.). Owing, however, to the strenuous objections of the allied powers, the blockade was subsequently modified, and the captured ships were released. Under these circumstances Capodistrias did what he could to come to the assistance of Russia. He ordered Admiral Sachtouris, who was blockading Volo, to raise the blockade and sail to the Hellespont, on the pretext that this measure was necessary to secure the arrival of the necessary food supplies. At the same time, he issued letters of marque to a number of privateers, who promptly revived that piratical activity which at the beginning of the year Capodistrias had himself aided in suppressing. Among others, eight Austrian vessels were brought in and condemned by the prize court at Ægina; but, on the vigorous intervention of the Austrian Captain Dandolo, the booty had to be disgorged.

On land meanwhile operations had, during the summer, been at a standstill. As long as Ibrahim remained in the Morea, any action beyond the Isthmus was impossible; and Hypsilanti had remained in camp at Megara. He was, however, only waiting till the withdrawal of the Egyptian troops became a certainty; and in October accordingly, when the news of Ibrahim's embarkation reached him, he broke up his camp and advanced into Attica. The country had been denuded of troops by the Russian war, and the advance of the Greeks was rapid and victorious. Attica was immediately overrun; and, after two successes gained at Stevenikos and Martini, Boeotia with its capital Levadia, and Salona fell into their hands. The possession of East Hellas seemed now assured to the Greeks, and the season being far advanced, Hypsilanti concentrated his forces round Thebes.

In Western Hellas also military operations had, for the greater part of the year, been practically at a standstill. Shortly after the Battle of Navarino, Captain Hastings had transported a small body of troops, under General Church, to Dragomesti on the coast of Acarnania; and subsequently another force crossed the Gulf of Corinth and occupied the site of a Greek fort on the mainland, opposite the island of Trisognia. But the troops were utterly demoralised; the peasants were in general hostile to them; and nothing was done. Captain Hastings had, on December 29, 1827, bombarded and captured the fort of Vasiladi; but, not long afterwards, he had retired in dudgeon from active operations, owing to the fact, which Church was powerless to prevent, that the Greek chiefs were carrying on a brisk trade with the Turks at Patras in the rations supplied to them by the Philhellenes! After the arrival of Capodistrias, he had indeed again allowed himself to be persuaded to resume operations; but an attack which, on the 25th of May, he made on Anatoliko was repulsed; and he himself, to the great sorrow of the Greeks, whom he had served with such unselfish courage and devotion, was mortally wounded.

A month later, on the 27th of June, Capodistrias himself arrived off the coast of Acarnania on board the *Warspite*, and proceeded to visit the camp of Sir Richard Church. He found the troops in an even worse condition than those he had reviewed not long before at Troezene, and he was not careful to disguise his opinion. When Church proposed to introduce the officers of his force, the President refused, he said:

> I know these gentlemen. You have fought the Turks for nine years, you say! You have stolen sheep and goats! That is all you have done!—Mendelssohn, ii.

Yet one at least of these officers, the Frenchman Manche, had taken part in the heroic defence of Missolonghi. Capodistrias was indeed distinguished for the possession of a biting tongue, which he kept but imperfectly under control; and it made him many enemies.

Church, however, was glad enough of the incentive given by the President's visit to exchange the wearisome inactivity of the last months for active operations. In September the Greeks advanced to the Gulf of Arta, and occupied Loutraki. An attempt of the Corsican adventurer Pasano, who had been appointed by Capodistrias to succeed Captain Hastings, to force an entrance to the Gulf of Arta failed; but the Greek officers, who believed this failure to have been due to the admiral's cowardice, subsequently made another attempt, without waiting for orders, and passed gallantly under the batteries of Prevesa. This secured to the Greeks the command of the Gulf of Arta. Pasano was now recalled, and the courageous and capable Hydriot admiral, Kriezes, appointed to succeed him. On the 29th of December the town of Vonitza fell into the hands of the Greeks; but the almost defenceless Venetian castle did not surrender till March 17, 1829.

Chapter 19

Indignation of the Greeks

While the conference of the powers was consulting in London, a commission, consisting of the three ambassadors who had retired from Constantinople, had been sitting at Poros for the purpose of collecting evidence and reporting. They had applied to Count Capodistrias for statistics of the condition of Greece, and he had furnished them, as far as the confused and disorganised state of the country would allow. At the same time, he had insisted on the Greek views with regard to the boundary question, and had suggested Prince Leopold of Coburg, afterwards first King of the Belgians, as a candidate for the sovereignty of Hellas.

In December 1828 the commissioners reported, and their memorandum, known as the Protocol of Poros, formed the basis of a protocol signed, on behalf of all the powers, at London on March 22, 1829, the provisions of which did not differ very greatly from the measures which were adopted when Greece was ultimately established as an independent kingdom.

> The frontier of the new Hellenic State was to be drawn from the Gulf of Volo to the Gulf of Arta, and among the islands it was to include Euboea and the Cyclades. An annual tribute of about 30,000 was to be paid to the Porte. The Turks who had owned land in Greece were to be allowed to sell their property, or to be otherwise compensated. The Hellenic State was to enjoy perfect autonomy under the *suzerainty* of the *Sultan*, and was to be governed by an hereditary prince selected by the Porte and the powers.—Prokesch, Appendix, x.

This plan, which fixed a boundary so much more liberal than had been foreshadowed by the protocol of the 16th of November, might have been carried into execution at once, had all the contracting powers been really in earnest. It embodied the views of Sir Stratford Canning, whose intimate acquaintance with the conditions of the problem seemed to guarantee its success; and it was warmly supported by France. But Russia had no desire to see the Greek question settled before she herself was in a position to wring terms out of the *Sultan*, and would have preferred to postpone the whole matter until she could make peace. The diplomatic pedantry, or the short-sighted policy, of Lord Aberdeen, played into the hands of the Russians. He consented, indeed, in order to keep on good terms with France, to sign the protocol; but he insisted at the same time on a diplomatic procedure which ended by postponing the whole question, until the result of her second campaign made Russia the sole judge.

> While Capodistrias was intriguing, while Sultan Mahmoud was fuming with rage, and while the population of Greece was perishing from misery, the English Foreign Secretary insisted on reserving to each of the Allied Courts the right of weighing separately the objections which the indignant *Sultan* might make to the proposed arrangements.—Finlay, ii.

Under these circumstances the judgment passed by Metternich on the work of the Allies was neither unjust nor untrue. He saw that the protocol was less concerned with the welfare of the Greeks than with the desire to arrange a *modus vivendi* for the concert, he said:

> The Triple Alliance can live on the protocol for a year; but the Alliance itself is impotent for good. It is only a combination of wiles against wiles.—Mendelssohn, ii.

In Greece itself the publication of the protocol was received with an outburst of indignation not inferior to that which had greeted the protocol of the 16th of November. To the Greeks it seemed that, all through the long and tortuous processes of the diplomatic negotiations, which had now reached another stage, they themselves had been regarded merely as pawns in the game of statecraft, to be moved hither and thither as the players pleased, and without regard to their own desires or aspirations. After all that they had done and endured, they were to be cheated of the freedom for which alone they had fought and suffered!

For what was this 'autonomy' worth that year by year had to acknowledge a degrading dependence; which merely substituted for the blood tax which the *rayah* had paid to the Ottoman, a lump sum paid yearly for the right of the nation to exist? The Hydriots and Spezziots had been 'autonomous' before the war. Had they fought and bled for eight years merely to be 'autonomous' at the end? The wild hillsmen of the Maina declared loudly that they would only pay tribute, as from time immemorial they had paid it, at the point of their swords. What, too, of the islands which had suffered so much in the cause of liberty, and were now to be left to languish under the yoke of the Turk? What of Samos, of Crete, above all, of Chios? Was this rent and mutilated fragment, arbitrarily cut off from the Hellenic body by the cynical selfishness of Europe, all that was to be left of the great Panhellenic ideal which had been so enthusiastically proclaimed by the constitution of Troezene?

Upon Capodistrias, too, as in a sense the representative of the powers, fell some reflection of this hostile criticism. He had indeed himself, though he had at the outset refused to subscribe to the wide claims of the Constitution of Troezene, consented to receive the protocol only under protest. He had, he said, under the terms of the constitution, no right to accept it on his own authority. Pending the meeting of the National Assembly, however, he would consent to do so. His experience of diplomacy and of the nature of protocols had probably taught him that, with the Russo-Turkish war still undecided, the protocol was worth little more than the paper on which it was written, and that its acceptance at the present moment, with the reservation of the ultimate right of the Assembly to decide, would in no wise compromise the eventual settlement of the question.

Capodistrias had, indeed, no intention of submitting to the terms of the protocol. On the question of the Ottoman *suzerainty* he was prepared to keep an open mind; but he resented the article which deprived the Greeks of the right to elect their own prince. In spite of the suggestion he had thrown out to the commission at Poros, that the crown should be offered to Prince Leopold of Coburg, he had never surrendered the hope that he himself might ultimately be the ruler selected; and this was the end to which all his efforts were directed, and to which the re-establishment of order and prosperity in Greece were means. It seemed to him intolerable that, after he had borne all the burden and heat of the day, and had turned the ungoverned wilderness which he had found into a strong and well-ordered state, at the eleventh hour another should step in and enjoy all the fruits of his toil. His prospects of being selected by the powers were remote. If the choice were left to the Greek nation itself, his popularity among the mass of the people and the measures he had taken to assure his influence would probably be sufficient to secure his appointment.

On the 18th of May the British resident requested the President, as the Ottoman Government had agreed to an armistice, to cease hostilities on his part, and to withdraw within the limits assigned by the protocol of the 16th of November. Capodistrias refused, on the plea that this had never been officially notified to him; and, at the same time, he formally protested against that article of the protocol of the 22nd of March, which deprived the Greeks of all voice in the selection of their sovereign. To the representative of Prince Leopold, who had been sent to make inquiries, he stated emphatically that the candidature of no prince would be acceptable to the Greek people under the terms of the protocol of the 22nd of March, which excluded the islands of Samos and Crete from the Hellenic State. He added furthermore that the acceptance of the Orthodox religion would be regarded as an absolutely essential condition of the acceptance of any ruler by the Greeks. This was the first of a long series of difficulties and objections raised by Capodistrias, by which he at length persuaded Prince Leopold to resign his candidature.

Capodistrias was now at the height of his power. He had succeeded, by one means or another, in bringing the whole administrative machinery of Greece into immediate dependence on his own will; and, under the shadowy forms of a constitutional republic, he was in fact an absolute monarch. His popularity among the mass of the people was as yet unimpaired; and though there was great discontent among certain sections of the political classes, any signs of this constitutional opposition were ruthlessly suppressed. Even the most private criticisms passed on the President were treated as treason against the State; and private letters were opened and examined by order of the government, their contents being used as evidence of disaffection against the existing order. (A priest named Pharmakidi was imprisoned for no other offence than having, in a confidential letter to a friend, dared to comment adversely on some measures of the President).

While, by such tyrannical means as these, Capodistrias had been able to establish an undisputed authority in all the affairs of Greece, he had succeeded also in maintaining his reputation throughout Europe unimpaired. He had throughout been careful to give the impression that his arbitrary measures were but temporary expedients, unhappily necessitated by the disturbed state of Greece, and that, as soon as the government had been placed on a firm foundation, and some degree of order and prosperity restored to the country, the liberties secured by the constitution, and which he had sworn to respect, would be once more conceded. With this explanation the Liberals of Europe were fain to be satisfied; and the support of the Philhellenes was still ungrudgingly bestowed. The European Governments, too, were now no longer backward in their support; and the President was relieved from the financial embarrassments which had hampered his operations on his first arrival.

The subsidies from Russia alone amounted, by the beginning of the year 1831, to over 3,000,000 *francs*, besides large consignments of munitions of war. Charles X. subscribed 250,000 *francs* a month for the '*Vendée du Christianisme*.' England, after a great many refusals, at last also sent a contribution of 500,000 *francs*. Finally, the Genevese banker Eynardt forwarded 700,000 *francs* as the beginning of a new loan. With these resources, for the expenditure of which he was responsible to no one, with his personal popularity, and his unshaken hold on the organisation of the government, the position of the President seemed unassailable. 'Greece,' said Metternich, 'is Capodistrias.'

When, on his arrival, Capodistrias had caused the suspension of the Constitution of Troezene, he had promised to summon a meeting of the National Assembly without undue delay. April had been the date originally fixed; but the President had, on one pretext and another, managed to postpone the Congress for more than a year. Now, however, the presentation of the protocols, and the international relations of Greece, made it necessary for him at last to carry out his promise, and summon a meeting of the representatives of the nation. He had indeed no fear as to the result.

The old communal liberties had been destroyed; the votes of the electors, for all purposes, were directed by the prefects appointed by the central government; and, to make assurance doubly sure, he now caused the Panhellenium to pass a law placing the electoral colleges absolutely under the heel of the administration. Not content with this, he undertook, in the month of March, an extended tour through the country, to influence the electors by his personal presence. The peasantry were just beginning to feel the return of prosperity after the exhaustion of the war, and 'Pappa Johannes' was greeted everywhere with the greatest enthusiasm. The result was the return of an assembly blindly devoted to his interests.

On the 23rd of July, Capodistrias, in a Russian uniform and his breast covered with orders, opened the new Congress, which met in the ruins of the ancient theatre of Argos.

Signs of opposition were, indeed, not wanting; but in the Congress itself no criticism of the President's policy could make itself heard. Kolokotrones, ever a notable supporter of Capodistrias, had ridden down from the mountains at the head of an armed band; and Niketas, the 'Turk-eater,' was present with a force nominally deputed to protect the Congress, really to overawe it in the interests of the President.

An address of confidence in the President was moved. Grivas and one or two other critical spirits desired to raise objections; but they could not succeed in making themselves heard. Kolokotrones leaped up, as soon as the tendency of their remarks became apparent, he cried:

> We want no European tomfoolery here! No babble! Let those who are in favour of the address stand up!

As he enforced his arguments by drawing his *yataghan*, and his followers were the more numerous, there was nothing to urge in reply, and the address of confidence in the President was passed without a dissentient voice! A government which could command so effective a closure had little to fear from factious opposition. There were violent scenes more than once. At one time Kolokotrones and Grivas were with difficulty kept from crossing. words. But, in the end, the resolutions passed by the Assembly were entirely in accord with the policy of the government; which was the less surprising since, as a matter of fact, they had all been drawn up by Capodistrias himself.

He had not indeed obtained his nomination to the presidency for life, as that would have been of little value without the previous consent of the powers, but he had obtained an Act of the Assembly declaring that the decisions of the Conference of London should not be held to be binding on Greece, without the ratification of the Greek legislature. He was, moreover, in negotiating the settlement of the Greek question with the powers, given a free hand in the matter of the *suzerainty* and the tribute.

On the 19th of August the Congress was dissolved; and the position of Capodistrias seemed more firmly assured than ever. But the constitutional opposition which had been so long suppressed was beginning to make headway. The decisions of an assembly so notoriously packed could carry no moral weight; it was known that it had merely registered the decrees of the President; and the discontented spirits expressed their sense of the situation by saying sarcastically 'John poured out; John drank!'

A new senate had been created by the assembly, of which the constitution overthrew all the democratic principles enunciated by former congresses. Sixty names were presented to the President, and out of these he selected twenty-one, adding six more on his own nomination. It was in connection with this that he experienced the first signs of the coming storm. Miaoulis, Konduriottes, and Mavrocordatos, to whom he offered places, refused, and formed the nucleus of an influential opposition.

CHAPTER 20

Anglo-Austrian Entente

The weary struggle was now dragging to its termination. Both sides had long been exhausted; the fiery enthusiasm of the revolt was quenched, and the stubborn opposition of the oppressors broken. For the Greeks there remained but the task of clearing continental Hellas of the last remnants of the Ottoman occupation.

Capodistrias, who had expressed himself dissatisfied with both Hypsilanti and General Church, at this juncture 'astonished the world by making his brother Agostino a general,' (Finlay, ii. Mendelssohn, ii.), and sending him, though he was little better than a fool, to take over the supreme direction of all civil and military matters in Western Hellas. In the absence of any qualifications for this position, fortune came to his assistance.

A wily Greek named Paparrigopulos, who had studied a rude diplomacy in the school of Ali Pasha, had for some time been at work undermining the morale of the Turkish garrisons of Lepanto, Missolonghi, and Anatoliko; and, when Count Agostino appeared off these cities, he easily succeeded in persuading them to surrender. The garrison of Lepanto capitulated on the 30th of April; and Missolonghi and Anatoliko were evacuated on the 14th of May. Agostino, who conducted the operations of the land forces from the secure vantage ground of the quarterdeck of the *Hellas*, gained all the credit of these successes, which were really due to the insidious propaganda of Paparrigopulos. (Mendelssohn, ii.).

A last expiring effort was made by the Turks in Eastern Hellas before hostilities ceased. A body of Albanians under Aslan Bey marched from Zeituni by way of Thermopylae, Levadia, and Thebes. Hypsilanti's troops were seized with a sudden panic, and scattered to all the four winds. Aslan advanced without opposition to Athens, left a select garrison in the Acropolis, and, collecting such Turks as were still scattered over the country, began his return march. Meanwhile, however, Hypsilanti's troops had assembled again as quickly as they had dispersed, and when Aslan reached the Pass of Petra, he found his retreat cut off by a superior Greek force. Unable to fight his way through, he was compelled, on September 25, 1829, to conclude a capitulation, by which the Turks engaged to evacuate all Eastern Hellas, except the Acropolis and the fort of Karababa on the Euripus. This was the last engagement of the War of Liberation. It fell, therefore, to Prince Demetrius Hypsilanti to conclude the war, which his brother had begun, eight years before, on the banks of the Pruth.

It was, however, by the victory of a mightier combatant that the fate of Greece had, meanwhile, been decided. The war, which for two summers had been waged between the Russians and Turks in the Balkan peninsula, had come to a sudden and dramatic end. It had from the first been a war of surprises, the Ottomans revealing unsuspected strength, and the Russians unsuspected weakness. And now by sheer force of assurance, the weaker forced the stronger to submit! General Diebitsch stood with about 13,000 men at Adrianople, in the heart of an enemy's country, threatened in the rear by the unconquered armies of the *grand vizier* and the Pasha of Skutari, and, in front, faced by the mighty city of Constantinople, which contained at least a hundred thousand men capable of bearing arms. Yet he conquered, where he ought to have capitulated. Though his scanty troops were decimated by disease, and he had no hope of reinforcements, he succeeded, by the boldness of his movements, in exaggerating the idea of his strength, and, finally, terrified the Ottoman Government into submission. (Fyffe. Modern Europe, i. Mendelssohn, ii.).

On the 14th of September the Peace of Adrianople was signed. Its terms largely increased the influence of Russia in the East, and especially in the Danubian principalities, which were rendered by its provisions practically independent of the Ottoman Government, and therefore all the more open to Russian interference. Besides certain provisions dealing with Russian trade rights and the free navigation of the Bosphorus, the treaty also included the acceptance by the Porte of the principles of the London Protocol of the 22nd of March, dealing with the affairs of Greece. (Prokesch, Appendix, x.).

Thus, owing to the procrastinating policy of the other members of the Alliance, Russia was able to pose before the world as the sole guarantor of the independence of Greece, and take to herself all the credit which she would otherwise have had to share with her allies.

The news of the conclusion of the Peace of Adrianople was received in Greece with the liveliest demonstrations of joy. Capodistrias, who believed that now he would reap the reward of his obedience to the mandate which the *Czar* had given to him at the meeting at Czarscoëselo, publicly announced the peace, and ordered *Te Deums* to be sung in the churches. When, however, the terms of the treaty became known, the delight of the Greeks was turned into disgust, and Capodistrias felt that he had been betrayed by the power which he had served so faithfully. Russia, from which they had expected so much, had after all only obtained for them the terms of the protocol of the 22nd of March, which they had already rejected with indignation and scorn.

Capodistrias also experienced a bitter disillusion. His own claims had been forgotten. Of the presidency for life, which was the least reward he might have expected for his faithful service to the cause of Russia, there was no mention; he was, after all, to be ousted in favour of some German princeling. The treaty, moreover, gave a serious blow to his popularity in Greece. He had all along been regarded as the representative of Russia, the guarantee and surety of the *Czar's* goodwill; and this had not a little contributed to strengthen his position. The disappointment and dismay of the Greeks now inevitably turned against him, as in some measure responsible for the dashing of their hopes; and from this period the opposition to his government, hitherto timid and depressed, gained in intensity and boldness.

If the Peace of Adrianople had made a bad impression on the Greeks, the news of it fell into the midst of the conference of the Powers with the disturbing force of a bomb. Serious as the effects of the Russian success undoubtedly were, they were exaggerated out of all proportion by the alarms of the statesmen of the Alliance. Not only had Russia outwitted and overreached her allies by settling the Greek question without their co-operation, but the whole edifice of the Ottoman Power, which it had been the policy especially of England to prop up, as a barrier against Russian ambition, was in danger of collapsing nay, had collapsed.

The Duke of Wellington declared that Turkey was not dying, but dead. (Report of Prince Esterhazy. Prokesch, Appendix, x.). He deplored that the conference had ever departed from the protocol of the 16th of November, and inquired what new independent power could be created to replace the Ottoman Empire as a barrier against

Muscovite aggression. Lord Aberdeen suggested raising the Porte up again, and propping it in place by means of a European guarantee; and it was even seriously proposed to establish a Greek Empire, with Constantinople as its capital. (Mendelssohn, ii.).

Metternich watched with cynical satisfaction the development of the storm within the councils of the Alliance. He regarded the present crisis as the direct result of the weak and hesitating policy which England in particular had throughout pursued; and he now asked the British Cabinet sarcastically whether in future 'Great Britain intended to follow an English or a Liberal policy.' (*Ibid*. ii). For his own part he did not believe in the collapse of Turkey, which had only been beaten because it believed itself to be so. Neither did he think that Russia had, for the present, any desire to destroy the Ottoman Power; and he was certain that she would never wish to see it replaced by a free and powerful Hellas. He now proposed to reopen negotiations on the basis of the maintenance of Turkey, and the creation of an independent Greek State.

The whole question was once more plunged back into the diplomatic kettle. Within the conference itself, which continued its sittings in London, there was a complete rearrangement of interests and parties.

On the 11th and 12th of October a cordial *entente* between the English and Austrian Cabinets had been arrived at; and the policy of the majority of the powers was henceforward directed to counteracting the preponderance obtained by Russia.

Wellington now recognised, what Metternich had insisted on so long, that Greece must be erected into an independent State; for, the Porte being caught inextricably in the toils of Russia, to create a vassal principality in the Levant would only be to open the way for the extension of Russian influence in the Mediterranean.

On the other hand, as long as there remained any hope of maintaining the Ottoman Empire, the Tory statesman would do nothing to raise up a power which might conceivably become a new source of danger to its existence. If, therefore, Greece was to be independent, its limits must be so curtailed that it could under no circumstances prove a menace to Turkey. (Mendelssohn, ii.). He did not see that a strong Hellas would have been the surest of all barriers against the advance of Russia, and the settlement, therefore, which of all others Russia would most have dreaded.

The views of the English Cabinet were embodied in a new protocol, which was signed at London, on behalf of the Powers, on February 3, 1830. By the terms of this protocol Greece was to be erected into an independent State, and its frontiers were fixed to run from the mouth of the river Aspropotamos to Mount Artolina, and thence, over the comb of the range of Oxia and Oeta, to the mouth of the Spercheios. Euboea and the neighbouring islands were to be Greek, as also Skyros and the Cyclades. Prince Leopold of Coburg was proposed as the ruler of the newly-constituted State, but with the title, not of king, but of 'sovereign prince.' (Holland).

Except the guarantee of complete independence, so grudgingly conceded, this settlement had nothing to recommend it to the acceptance of the Hellenes. Apart from the confinement of the new State within limits which would have made effective government impossible, and which rendered the gift of independence a hollow mockery, the lines of the frontier had been so drawn as to appear almost purposely offensive to Greek national feeling. Attica and Boeotia, where the population was mainly Albanian, were to be included in the new State, while Acarnania and Ætolia, which were inhabited by a Greek-speaking race, were to remain Turkish! Strategically, too, the proposed frontier was impossible; for it left in the hands of the Turks 'the barrier which nature pointed out'; that rugged mountain range which, from the Gulf of Arta to that of Volo, runs 'like a backbone behind Greece.' (Palmerston. Hansard, xxii.).

On the 8th of April the protocol of the 3rd of February was officially notified to Count Capodistrias. At the same time, he was directed by the powers to proclaim an armistice, and to order the withdrawal of the Greek troops within the borders assigned by the protocol. Capodistrias veiled his own refusal by taking refuge behind the forms of the Constitution, and answered that, though he would accept the protocol, he had, in fact, no right to do so until it had been laid before the National Assembly. (Mendelssohn, ii.). The Senate, in the hands of which the Powers of the Assembly were vested, when it was itself not sitting, but which really represented only the views of the President, thereupon presented a memorandum refusing to accept the protocol.

In face of the indignant opposition of the Greek Nation (for in this matter Capodistrias undoubtedly had the people on his side) it would have been a work of great difficulty to have enforced this latest settlement of the Hellenic question. As it was, it remained a dead letter, not only owing to the refusal of the Greeks to accept it, but because the serious occurrences in other parts of Europe during the year distracted the attention of the powers, for the time, from the affairs of Greece.

Unpopular as the protocol of the 3rd of February was, it contained, however, one provision which was highly acceptable to the Greeks, that, namely, which designated their future ruler. In the matter of the appointment of a prince, Capodistrias had been playing a dark and diplomatic game. There seems little doubt that he was himself ambitious of becoming the ruler of Hellas; and the ambition would have been perfectly justified. He seemed, however, quite incapable of using open and straightforward means for the attainment of an object, when underhand and crooked methods could be employed.

He had publicly proclaimed his anxiety for the speedy appointment of a king; in his private memoranda to the powers and to the ambassadors he had frequently expressed the same opinion; and he had himself proposed the name of Prince Leopold to the conference of ambassadors at Poros. Yet now that the appointment seemed about to be realised, he did everything, short of open protest and resistance, to make it impossible.

The Opposition had long been casting about for some effective means of embarrassing the government; and the popular enthusiasm aroused by the nomination of their new prince appeared to them to offer an opportunity which was not to be neglected. The President and the Senate had, it was true, rejected the protocol, but the President and Senate in no way represented the public opinion of Greece. The limitation of the frontiers was doubtless lamentable; yet their arrangement could not be regarded as final, and the question would not be compromised by accepting those benefits which the protocol undoubtedly did confer. The presence of the new ruler was ardently longed for by the country, groaning under the despotic sway of Capodistrias.

In short, it was decided by the members of the disaffected Opposition to counteract the action of the President and Senate by working up a popular demonstration of welcome to Prince Leopold; and to this end addresses were circulated for signature in all parts of the country, bidding welcome to the prince, and asking him not to delay in coming to a nation which was eagerly expecting him. The addresses were extensively signed; for Capodistrias's public utterances on the subject had led the people to believe that he himself was anxious for the arrival of the prince.

But Capodistrias was angered by what he regarded as a scarcely veiled attack upon himself, and alarmed at the number and importance of the signatories; for these included not only Mavrocordatos, Zaimis, Miaoulis, Petrobey, and numberless primates of the Morea and Hydra, but even Sissinis, the President, and several members of the Senate, who thus stultified their own previous action. He did not, indeed, dare to forbid the forwarding of addresses to the candidate approved by the powers; but he issued orders that these were not to be sent direct, but to be submitted first to the inspection of the government. Moreover, he let it be plainly known that those who signed would only do so at the risk of incurring his displeasure; and if they chanced to be government officials they were dismissed, on the plea that, in signing, they had been guilty of an act of insubordination. (Mendelssohn, ii.).

While, by these means, Capodistrias tried to stem the tide of enthusiasm for Prince Leopold in Greece, he was also occupied in attempting to shake the prince's own resolution to accept the crown. To Baron Stockmar, Leopold's representative, who had come to Greece to make inquiries, he had already given a vivid picture of the magnitude of the task the prince proposed to undertake. In the communications he now had with Leopold himself, he cunningly combined earnest entreaties for his speedy arrival, with alarming accounts of the difficulties he would experience when he did arrive: of the utter exhaustion of the country, the general corruption and insubordination, and, above all, the absolute lack of money. He impressed upon him the advisability, nay, the necessity, for joining the Orthodox Church; he asked whether he would be prepared to unite with the people in arranging a Constitution, in accordance with the decrees of the Congress of Argos, and whether he would consent to be bound by the decisions of that Assembly.

There has been some controversy as to what ultimately induced Leopold to resign the trust which had been solemnly conferred upon him, at his own solicitation, by the Powers of Europe. The death of George IV., and the shadowy prospect of a possible regency in England during the minority of Queen Victoria, can hardly be judged a sufficient motive, though they were considered so by many at the time. (So Prokesch-Osten, ii.). It is more probable that the intrigues and innuendoes of Capodistrias were successful, and that Leopold was disgusted by the prospect which his acceptance of the Greek crown had opened before him.

The policy of the President in suppressing the addresses of welcome had also borne fruit, and the prince was more than doubtful as to the nature of the reception that awaited him on the part of the Greek Nation. On the 21st of May, accordingly, he formally handed in his resignation to the representatives of the powers, stating as his reason the extreme unwillingness of the Greeks to accept the protocol of the 3rd of February.

By the Hellenes the news of his resignation was received with a grief that was akin to despair; (Mendelssohn, ii.), in the diplomatic world it excited a ferment of anger and disgust, which found loud expression. Lord Aberdeen, in the House of Lords, made a statement which was construed into an attack on the prince, and an arraignment of his motives in resigning the crown. (Hansard, xxiv.). Earl Grey, and other friends of Prince Leopold, took up the cudgels on his behalf; and, on the part of the Whigs, the affair was made the occasion for an elaborate attack on the whole Tory policy with regard to Greece.

A letter was read from General Church condemning utterly the frontier fixed by the protocol; and Lord Palmerston said that he could see no reason why Crete and the islands should not have been included, so as to make Greece a really powerful State. (Prokesch, ii. Cf. Hansard, xxii. For the whole question of Leopold's resignation, see also Mendelssohn, ii.).

The resignation of Prince Leopold, and the crisis which almost immediately followed in the affairs of Europe, put a stop to any strenuous endeavour to give effect to the protocol of the 3rd of February. It was at best but a weak attempt at compromise, and as such could never have satisfied anyone, or been more than a temporary settlement of the questions it affected to solve. The conception of an independent Greece, strong enough to form the nucleus of a State which should embrace all the Hellenes, and form an effective barrier against the aggressions of the Slav races in the East, would have been worthy of a strong cabinet. It was an act of political folly, born of vacillating and divided counsels, to endeavour to create an independent Greece too weak to maintain its independence, and foredoomed to fall under whatever influences should chance to be paramount in the East.

While the ultimate fate of the new State was thus still left undecided, the Porte had been quietly proceeding with the settlements necessitated by the new conditions of its existence. The first of these dealt with the future of Crete. On June 6, 1830, a firman was issued granting several new rights to the Cretan *rayahs*. (Prokesch-Osten, ii.). In future the annual poll-tax was to be collected by their own bishops and captains, who were themselves to be exempt from it, as also were all merchants trading in their own ships.

Free navigation of the Black Sea and of the Ægean was conceded, as well as the right of the Cretans to sail under their own flag. There were to be in future no extraordinary burdens levied, and the inhabitants were to elect their own local officials. These, and certain minor reforms, seemed to assure the Cretans a fair measure of liberty. To Samos also was conceded the right of dealing direct with the Porte through its own elected representatives, instead of, as heretofore, through the *Capitan Pasha*.

The prospect of these islands becoming contented under the Ottoman rule did not suit the purposes of the Greeks; and emissaries were accordingly sent who succeeded in persuading the Cretans and Samians to refuse all concessions. Soon afterwards, the Ottoman Government, weary of the turbulent island, sold Crete to Mehemet Ali for 25,000,000 *piastres*. Upon this, Grabusa, which, since the destruction of the pirate stronghold, had been held by the allied fleets, was handed over to the Egyptians. Large numbers of fugitives were brought by the war-ships of the allies, and by Kanaris, to Greece, where they formed an additional drain on the slender resources of the government. Such, for the time being, was the fate of Crete.

On the mainland everything remained as yet undecided. The revolution of July, with all the vast and pregnant issues which it raised, distracted the attention of the European Cabinets from the affairs of Greece. The London Conference, indeed, still continued to devote an occasional thought to the question, and on the 1st of July a protocol was issued confirming that of the 3rd of February, and appointing commissioners for the delimitation of the boundary. Very little, however, was done. The Turks demanded 300,000 Spanish *dollars* as compensation, before they would evacuate Attica and Boeotia; and the Greek Government had no money with which to meet the demand. Failing the payment of this sum, the Ottomans, in the summer of 1830, systematically devastated the country, and it was reckoned that half the olive trees in Attica were destroyed.

At last the 22nd of January was fixed on as the term for the evacuation to be carried out; but this proceeded, even then, very slowly. There were a thousand questions of compensation, and the like, to be settled; and the unhappy Mussulmans were naturally reluctant to leave their homes and their beloved country. A touching incident is told, which may serve to illustrate this aspect of the war and its results. A Turk, who was starting on his sad journey, turned once more to gaze for the last time on the Piraeus. Overcome with emotion, prostrated himself, and kissed the ground from which he and his fathers had drawn their life, he cried:

Sweetest fatherland! I am leaving you, and shall never see you again!—Mendelssohn, ii.

CHAPTER 21

Intervention of the Russian Admiral

The revolution of July, which hurled Charles X. from the throne of France, and established the popular monarchy of Louis Philippe, reacted in more ways than one upon the fortunes of Greece. Not only did it produce a rearrangement of the relations of the powers, the liberal Government of France drawing away from Russia and attaching itself more closely to the policy of England, but this first victory of the revolution stirred into activity all those forces of discontent which the policy of Metternich and the Holy Alliance had, for fifteen years, succeeded in repressing. Beside the vast and dangerous issues raised by these movements, the affairs of Greece sank into comparative insignificance.

During the autumn of 1830, England and France were fully occupied with the revolution in Belgium; and, towards the end of the year, the insurrection of the Poles claimed the whole attention of Russia. In the absorption of these more pressing interests Greece was, for the time being, forgotten; and Capodistrias was left to pursue his policy, unhampered by the interference of the powers.

The revolution had, however, another effect upon the affairs of the Hellenes. The old republican cry of 'Liberty! Equality! Fraternity' raised once more, amid the rattle of musketry, from the barricades of Paris, had penetrated to Greece, and awakened echoes among its islands and mountains. The opposition to Capodistrias, the 'Russian pro-consul,' as he had begun to be termed, gained fresh vigour, and was inspired by a new enthusiasm. To the mass of the peasantry indeed, at any rate in the Morea, where the word *Suntagma* (Constitution) was rapidly becoming synonymous with rapine and bloodshed, the personal rule of Capodistrias was not unwelcome. But to that large class of Greeks who had imbibed some degree of European culture, and still more to those independent island communities which had enjoyed, under the Ottoman rule, far more liberty than they were allowed by the prefects of the President of free Greece, the repressive and irresponsible government of Capodistrias became day by day more odious.

Under the influence of the French uprising a burst of 'republican babble' (Prokesch-Osten), broke forth among the more ardent spirits of the Opposition, and a hundred wild schemes were mooted. It was even proposed to invite the veteran Lafayette, 'the conqueror of two worlds' as he had once loved to be called, 'the fool of men and circumstances' as Napoleon had named him, to assume the presidency of Greece. In Paris the venerable Korais, to whom Hellas owed so much, supported this idea, which, however, of course, evaporated in talk. More powerful and more permanent were the results of the literary efforts which now began to be made by the Opposition, in order to influence public opinion against the existing regime in Greece.

By the terms of the Greek Constitution the complete liberty of the press had been secured. Taking advantage of this, a young Greek named Polyzoides, who had lately returned from Paris, imbued with the spirit of the revolution, started a newspaper, the *Apollo*, which was to represent the views of Opposition, and set up his office and press, in the first instance, in Nauplia, under the very eyes of the government. This was too much for the official mind of the Capodistrian administration. Constitution or no constitution, this impious criticism of the government must be stopped.

The issue of the very first number was followed by a police raid on the premises of the paper; the whole edition was confiscated, and the machinery and plant taken possession of by the government. Polyzoides urged in vain that in Greece, by the terms of the constitution, the press was free. The government replied that, though the constitution did not forbid attacks on officials, neither did it authorise them. Driven from Nauplia, Polyzoides removed the headquarters of his paper to Hydra, where it flourished under the protection of the Hydriot communal government, which refused all the President's demands for its suppression.

Capodistrias, true to the traditions of his Russian schooling, was not taught wisdom by this failure, and continued his efforts to curb the journalistic opposition. He protested, indeed, that he had no intention of interfering with the liberty of the press; but liberty was not licence, and he reserved to the government the right of deciding when the bounds between the two had been overstepped! The popular poet Alexander Soutsos, in one of his satires, gave voice to the public feeling aroused by this policy:

> *My friend, the press is free—for him who spares the crowd*
> *Of government officials and their friends,*
> *Nor criticises ministerial means and ends.*
> *—The press is free, my friend, but writing's not allowed.*
>
> — Mendelssohn, ii

This short-sighted action of the President produced the usual results. The violence and the circulation of the Opposition newspapers grew with the efforts of the authorities to suppress them; and a journal which, left alone, might have perished for lack of readers, expanded into an influence and a power.

The gathering forces of opposition and discontent found a centre and rallying place in the island of Hydra. From the very outset the haughty rejection of the advances of the Hydriots by Capodistrias, which has already been mentioned, had prejudiced the proud islanders against his government; and nothing that he had done since had tended to reconcile them to it. Accustomed to complete autonomy under the mild *suzerainty* of the *sultans*, they had seen their liberties curtailed by the action of Capodistrias, and their free communal constitution turned into a mere machine for registering the decrees of the government prefects. In common with Ægina, Spezzia, and Poros, they had writhed under the capricious and irresponsible tyranny of Viaro Capodistrias.

If this was Liberty, they might well begrudge the cost at which it had been purchased. Their once flourishing island was on the verge of ruin; their wharves deserted, their vessels rotting in the port. The self-chosen fate which bound them to a government whose chief was trying to stave off national bankruptcy by a ruinous fiscal policy threatened to destroy the last remnants of their prosperity. Already many of their merchants had transferred their business to islands which still enjoyed the blessings of Turkish rule; and the rest threatened to follow. These were the results of the immense sacrifices which the Hydriots had made for the cause of Greece, and for which, so far from receiving any compensation, they had received not even recognition.

The government was in their debt for losses and damage they had sustained in the national service, and they presented a claim for fifteen million *francs*. Capodistrias, after some prevarication, finally offered six millions in full satisfaction of the demand. The Hydriots refused in wrath, and their breach with the government was final. (Mendelssohn, ii.).

Hydra now became the focus of a huge conspiracy, which soon extended all over the archipelago, and which had for its end the establishment of a constitutional government. (Prokesch, ii.). The important island of Syra, which was, at this period, the main source of the national revenues, early gave in its adherence to the movement, and it was followed by most of the other island communities. The *Apollo,* under the vigorous editorship of Polyzoides, became the mouthpiece of the agitation; and its columns were filled with addresses, from all parts of the archipelago, clamouring for a free constitution. The mainland and the Morea as yet held aloof, and even sent the President petitions in an opposite sense. It seemed as though Hellas were about to be rent into two halves, with the waters of the Ægean, on which her liberties had been cradled, flowing as a barrier between them.

Within the councils of the Triple Alliance also a cleavage now became apparent; and, while Capodistrias could always reckon upon the support of Russia, the liberal Western Powers showed a scarcely veiled sympathy for the Opposition. The Hydriots had demanded the right to elect a new Demogerontia, or communal council; and Capodistrias had replied that they might elect whom they pleased, but that he would recognise only those who obeyed his government. Their growing hostility he proposed to meet with coercive measures; and he proceeded to sound the representatives of the powers, with a view to discovering how far he could reckon upon their support. To his questions the French minister replied by suggesting insidiously the occupation of Nauplia by French troops.

Mr. Dawkins, the English resident, answered that he failed to see that the demand of the Opposition for the assembling of the Congress was ill-timed, or that the Congress in itself would be harmful in the present state of the country. The Russian representative on the other hand told the President that he should 'stamp on the head of the viper of revolution' at once, and promised him the active sympathy of Russia if he should take this course. (Mendelssohn, ii.). Capodistrias followed the advice which appealed most to his own prejudices and convictions. He took up the only weapon which lay immediately to hand; he refused to issue to the Hydriots their ships' papers, without which they were liable to be treated as pirates; and, at the same time, he applied to the admirals of the three Powers to support him, by preventing the Hydriot ships from keeping the sea without their legal warranty.

Admiral Ricord, who commanded the Russian squadron, at once acceded to this request. The French and English admirals on the other hand said that they had no authority to prevent the Hydriot vessels from sailing, Hydra now took up an attitude of open hostility to the government, and the whole party of Opposition concentrated itself on the island. The Council of Demogeronts, or communal elders, which had been entirely in the interests of Capodistrias, was dissolved, and the government commissary fled. Mavrocordatos had already arrived in the island to give the support of his presence to the movement; and now active preparations were pushed forward for summoning a National Convention to Hydra, where, in the meantime, a 'Constitutional Committee' was established, consisting of seven members, and including such well-known names as Konduriottes and Miaoulis.

Matters were now rapidly reaching a crisis. The defection of Syra especially had been a severe blow to Capodistrias; and he recognised the necessity for taking vigorous measures to restore this and the other islands to their allegiance. The national fleet of Greece, including the fine frigate *Hellas*, and the steamer *Karteria*, lay in the harbour of Poros, where also the arsenal was established, and Capodistrias now sent orders for this to be made ready for sea, with a view to coercing the refractory islands. But the Hydriots had realised this danger, and determined to anticipate it.

On the 26th of July, by order of the Hydriot Government, Admiral Miaoulis sailed, with only some fifty men, to Poros, and, with the help of the inhabitants, seized the arsenal and the fleet. Kanaris, the hero of Chios, was on board the corvette *Spezzia*, and Miaoulis tried to win him over to the constitutional cause. But the sturdy old seaman, who believed heart and soul in the divine mission of Russia, true to his sense of duty, refused the hand that was held out to him, and was placed for a short time under arrest.

When the news of the exploit of Miaoulis reached Capodistrias, he was furious. Three days before, yielding to the representations of the English and French residents, he had promised to summon the National Assembly in October, or earlier if possible. This *coup d'état* of the Hydriots was all that he had got by his weakness. In his dealings with these rebels at any rate there should be no consideration shown, and the insult to the majesty of government should be wiped out in blood. On the Greeks, however, he could no longer reckon; and he turned for assistance to the representatives of the powers. By an unfortunate mischance, the English frigate, commanded by Captain Lyons, had sailed for the Gulf of Athens that very morning; and the French resident, M. de Rouen, was also absent. This gave Capodistrias an opening of which he was not slow to avail himself.

The crisis called for immediate action; and he appealed to the Russian admiral to compel the Hydriots to evacuate Poros, and surrender the fleet. Admiral Ricord, a bluff seaman, ready to do anything that seemed to serve the interests of his master the *Czar*, was easily persuaded by the ex-minister of Russia. Without waiting for his colleagues, he sailed for Poros, and summoned Miaoulis to surrender the fleet, and return to Hydra. The intrepid Hydriot replied that he owed obedience only to the government of Hydra, that he would yield, if at all, only to the united commands of the three powers, and that, if the Russian admiral attacked him, he would oppose force to force.

In any case, however, sooner than let the national fleet fall again into the hands of the government, he would himself destroy it. For the present the Russian did not venture to proceed to extremes; and contented himself with watching the outlets of the harbour, so as to prevent Miaoulis carrying off the fleet. A considerable force had also meanwhile been sent, under Niketas, to attack the island from the land side, where it was only separated from the Peloponnese by a narrow channel.

At the end of the month the English frigate, with Captain Lyons on board, returned; and with the French frigate, under Captain Lalande, proceeded to join the Russian admiral before Poros. It was impossible for them, under the circumstances, to dissociate themselves entirely from the action of their colleague; and they now combined with him to demand the withdrawal of Miaoulis. They had, however, no authority to use force; and, when the Hydriot admiral refused to obey, they returned to Nauplia to ask for instructions, having first obtained a promise from both Miaoulis and Admiral Ricord that neither of them would take action during their absence.

To the residents of the Western Powers it seemed that, however technically wrong the action of Miaoulis may have been, morally he was in the right; they were jealous, moreover, of the attitude of Russia in the matter; and they refused to have anything to do with measures of coercion. Ultimately a compromise was agreed upon. The Hydriot admiral was to be summoned, in the name of the Triple Alliance, to surrender the property of the State; but Capodistrias, on his side, was to announce a general amnesty, and to promise once more to convene the National Assembly. With these instructions, Captains Lalande and Lyons sailed on the 12th of August for Poros.

Meanwhile, however, Capodistrias had sent a letter overland by a swift messenger, explaining the state of affairs to the Russian admiral, and bidding him strike while there was yet time. (Mendelssohn, ii.). The Russian was nothing loth to obey. The inhabitants of Poros, intimidated by the hostile attitude of the Russians, had already concluded a convention with him, by which they agreed to surrender the town and the arsenal. But, before this happened, it had come to a fight between him and the Hydriot admiral.

The Russians, while nominally inactive, had blockaded both ends of the narrow strait which divides Poros from the mainland, and in which the Greek fleet lay. A Hydriot brig, which was bringing provisions for the admiral, was fired upon by the Russians, who were thereupon themselves attacked by the Greek ships, and by the small fort which commanded the narrow entrance to the channel. In the course of this battle the *Spezzia* was dismasted, and, with a Hydriot brig, ultimately fell into the hands of the Russians.

Miaoulis now threatened, if the Admiral Ricord did not cease hostilities, to carry out his purpose of destroying the Greek vessels that still remained in his hands; and the Russian, who knew the Hydriot's resolute character, upon this thought it best to refrain from further hostilities. The letter of the President, however, now seemed to him an authorisation to proceed; and, on the 13th, he began moving his ships in, with a view to taking up a position for battle. The sharp eye of Miaoulis, accustomed, from the experience of years of naval warfare, to note the slightest signs of an enemy's intentions, immediately discovered the object of this manoeuvre.

As the Russian ships sailed toward their new quarters, two explosions were heard, and over the brow of the island great columns of smoke ascended. Admiral Miaoulis had carried out his threat, and rather than suffer them to be used to coerce the freedom of the islands, had blown up with his own hands the magnificent frigate *Hellas* and the corvette *Hydra*. He himself escaped with his men, in the ships' boats, to Poros, and thence to Hydra.

On the same day the troops of Niketas and Kallergis entered the town of Poros, and, though this had capitulated freely, it was treated as a hostile city taken by storm. For hours the unhappy town was given over to the cruelty and lust of the brutal mercenaries, who, when they at last desisted from outrage and robbery, returned to Nauplia laden with booty. Though they had not struck a blow in honest fighting, their zeal was rewarded by a public proclamation, in which Capodistrias hailed them as the saviours of their country.

The affair of Poros was decisive as to the relations of the representatives of the powers among themselves and towards the President. The action of the Russian admiral was naturally resented by the other members of the Triple Alliance; and even the Russian resident had, for form's sake, to reprimand the admiral for exceeding his instructions. But the antagonistic interests of the three 'allies' were now clearly defined; and while the Opposition felt that they could reckon upon the support of France and England, Capodistrias threw off all disguise, and openly avowed his dependence upon the goodwill and the assistance of Russia. The French officers of the Greek regular troops, who had expressed their disgust at the devastation of Poros, were dismissed, and their places filled by Russians.

The Greek fleet, too, being now destroyed, Capodistrias did not hesitate to appeal for aid to the Russian admiral, and even proposed that Russian officers should be placed on board such Hellenic ships as still remained. At the request of the President, Admiral Ricord now sailed to blockade Hydra and Syra; and the French and English frigates followed to prevent hostilities. For their part, the Greek islanders, who ever since the treaty of Kainardji in 1774 had been accustomed to sail under the Russian flag, now tore this down, and hoisted the revolutionary tricolour.

Capodistrias now announced his intention of summoning, *pour des raisons majeures*, the National Assembly for the 13th of September, and at once began to move heaven and earth to secure a pliant majority. The Congress of Argos had, as a matter of fact, been merely prorogued; but the President feared a possible change in the opinions of the representatives who had before been so amenable to his will; and to guard against this, he now announced that the electoral colleges might either choose the same deputies as before, or proceed to the election of new ones. At the same time, he took care that all the machinery of corruption and intimidation was in good working order; while, with the idea of stirring up public feeling against the Opposition, he flooded the country with pamphlets denouncing the action of the Hydriots in destroying the national fleet.

The representatives of Hydra, and of those districts which acknowledged the Constitutional Commission, were to be excluded from the new Congress. The Commission replied by summoning on their own account a National Assembly to meet at Hydra; and the Hydriot vessels sailed from island to island, and along the coast, to invite representatives to attend.

To this activity the Russian admiral, at the request of Capodistrias, endeavoured to put a stop. Three Hydriot brigs which, in the course of canvassing for the Assembly, had entered the Gulf of Coron, were attacked by the Russians; and their crews, seeing no chance of escape, ran them ashore and set fire to them, while they themselves took refuge with the French garrison in Kalamata.

Capodistrias now tried to recover some of his vanishing popularity by dismissing some of the most hated instruments of his oppressive rule; and his brother Viaro, and the astute chief of police, Gennatas, were deprived of their offices. But this came too late to influence public opinion favourably, and merely cost the President, at a critical time, the services of two devoted and trustworthy servants. Whatever good effect it might have produced was swept away in the storm of ill-will which broke forth when he once more announced the postponement of the Congress. To those who had hoped against hope that the President would exchange his personal for a constitutional regime, this seemed the final confession that he was afraid to meet the representatives of the nation, and that he had set his face permanently against the establishment of liberty in Greece. The wilder spirits began now to look back into the classic ages for a parallel, and to talk of the virtue of tyrannicide.

Chapter 22

The Approach of the Crisis

Though all things seemed to point to the approaching collapse of the rule of Capodistrias, the catastrophe was hastened not so much by his contempt for constitutional liberty, as by his endeavour to crush out the savage instincts inherited by a tribe of wild hillsmen from centuries of barbarism.

Petrobey Mavromichales, popularly known as the King of the Maina, had been one of the first chiefs to raise the standard of revolt in the Morea. A man of dignified and venerable presence, the father of nine stalwart sons, and the absolute ruler of a brave and warlike tribe, the position of Petrobey seemed to raise him high above the brigand chiefs by whom he was for the most part surrounded, and to point him out as the natural leader of the Greek revolt. But his mild and genial character, and his lack of political intuition, had early pushed him into the background, and compelled him to give place to men who, like Kolokotrones, were of a fiercer and more masterful disposition. For the rest, his objects in rising against the Turks were probably no more disinterested than theirs.

But few of the Greek leaders ever rose to the idea of a patriotism to which all personal interests were subordinate; and, for the most part, they desired to end the dominion of the Ottoman *pashas* only that they themselves might reign as *pashas* in their stead. To this rule Petrobey was no exception. When, therefore, it began to appear that the sole outcome of all the ten years' struggle was to be a highly centralised despotism worked in the interests of Russia, the old chief was naturally but ill-content.

At first, indeed, Capodistrias had been at pains to conciliate him. He was made a member of the Senate, and his demands for money were from time to time listened to. But Petrobey's ideas of feudal magnificence and patriarchal generosity made him a lavish spender; and Capodistrias at length wearied of the 'eternal petitioner,' as he called him. The insubordination and restlessness of the Mainotes moreover offended the President's sense of administrative order, and for these he held the old chief largely responsible. He began, therefore, to treat Petrobey with increasing coldness, and to oust him more and more from the counsels of the government.

The character of the Mainotes was scarcely such as to appeal to a believer in a cut-and-dried system of government; and perhaps, in the eyes of any modern ruler, despotic or democratic, their picturesqueness would not compensate for their obvious deficiencies as citizens of a civilised State. They had, indeed, their own code of morality, which they enforced with ruthless severity; but it was hardly such as could have been included in the statute book of Hellas.

★★★★★★

Death was the penalty for seduction; but, under certain circumstances, the seducer might be allowed to leave the country, in order to make money sufficient to enable him to marry the girl. If he failed to return at the time appointed, the girl was put to death.

★★★★★★

They were taught to reverence women and old men, to obey their chief, to honour their parents, to keep their word, to show courage in battle, to rob without being found out, and, above all, never to forget an injury. Blood feuds were handed down from generation to generation; they were transmitted by will, by adoption, by marriage even, the man who married a woman 'having blood' undertaking the duty of revenge. Murder was even employed as a legal instrument; and Capodistrias was shown a bill, signed by persons still living, in which the debtor, in case of non-payment, gave the creditor the right to assassinate him or two of his relations.

To the mind of the President, trained in the rigid discipline of the Russian administrative system, the existence of this turbulent State within the State seemed at once a scandal and a menace; and he determined to take measures for its reform. The readiest road to this seemed to be to overthrow the paramount influence of the family of the Mavromichales; and to this end Capodistrias proceeded to encourage those local chieftains who had from of old been their bitter rivals. At the same time, he instructed his prefect Genovallis to do all in his power to curb their unruliness. The immediate result of this policy was that, at Eastertide in the year 1830, Djami Mavromichales, the brother of Petrobey, headed a rising of the Maina against the prefect.

Capodistrias thereupon had recourse to the arts of Machiavellian diplomacy. He summoned Petrobey's son George to an interview, and treated the young man with such distinction and kindness that he persuaded him to proceed to the Maina, and to induce his uncle Djami to come to Nauplia, for the purpose of discussing his grievances with the President. Once within the walls of Nauplia, however, Djami was arrested, tried on an old charge of murder, and imprisoned in the fortress of Itsh-kalé, where he remained for eighteen months. The rest of the members of his family were, at the same time, placed under police supervision, and forbidden to leave the town.

In January 1831, however, 'Katzakos' Mavromichales, Djami's son, succeeded in making his escape, fled to the Maina, and there spread the news that the President was compassing the ruin of the Mavromichales. He was soon joined by his Uncle Constantine, and between them they succeeded in arousing the fury of their wild clansmen. The Mainotes flew to arms, and threatened, if the government refused to liberate their chiefs, that 5,000 'Spartans' would march upon Nauplia.

When the news of the rising in the Maina reached his ears, Petrobey asked Capodistrias to allow him to go and make an attempt to stay the excitement. The President refused; and thereupon Petrobey also fled, sailed in an English vessel to Zante, and proceeded to cross thence to the Maina. The weather, however, was stormy; and the old chief was driven by a contrary wind into Katakolo on the coast of Elis, where he was arrested by Kanaris, who had been sent in pursuit, and carried back to Nauplia. He was now tried for treason, by a special commission (as being a senator and peer of Greece), was found guilty, and imprisoned in his turn in the fortress of Itsh-kalé.

The news of the chieftain's arrest was sent to the Maina; and his brother Constantine was persuaded, by the promise of his personal freedom being respected, to proceed to Nauplia for the purpose of opening negotiations. No sooner, however, did he reach the capital than he and his nephew George were likewise placed under police supervision, and forbidden to leave the town.

After some lapse of time, the venerable mother of Petrobey, an old lady eighty-six years of age, appealed to the Russian admiral to intercede with the President for the release of her son; and Admiral Ricord was moved to undertake the charge, nothing doubting that his personal influence with Capodistrias would enable him to bring about a settlement. The President, in fact, so far yielded as to promise to release Petrobey, on condition of his acknowledging his errors; and with this decision the Russian admiral proceeded to interview the old chieftain. At first the proud old man refused to consider the question of an apology; but, at last, worn out with eight months' imprisonment, and longing for a breath of the free air of the mountains, he reluctantly allowed himself to be persuaded.

His submission was to take place at an interview with Capodistrias, which was fixed for five o'clock on the afternoon of October 8, 1831. Unfortunately, the President had that very morning received a copy of the London *Courier*, containing a violent tirade against his person and a scathing criticism of his policy. Weary and overwrought with the labours and anxieties of his office, his mind seemed, at this last insult, to lose its balance; and, jaded and angry, when Petrobey arrived under guard at the time appointed, he refused to see him.

When this message was delivered to him, the old chieftain was petrified with rage and mortification. Was it for *this* that he, the Bey of the Maina, had consented to demean himself by asking pardon of a Corfiot upstart? Was he, a Mavromichales, forty-nine of whose kinsmen had fallen in warfare with the Turk, to plead in vain for pardon in the ante-chamber of a man who had never struck a blow for Greece? Speechless with anger, the proud old man was led back through the streets to his prison. On the way he passed in front of the house occupied by his son George and his brother Constantine. Here a sudden thought struck him. He paused, and called out 'Ho there, children!'

At the sound of his voice the two hurried to the window, and, leaning out, asked him how he fared. The old man only pointed to his guards, said, in a voice choked with passion, 'You see how I fare!' and passed on. But the Mavromichales had understood. The code of the Maina allowed them, under the circumstances, only one course of action. Their chief, and the head of their family, had received a wrong, and this must be wiped out in blood.

The resolution to assassinate the President was, indeed, not a new one. The Mavromichales had already received wrongs enough at his hands to abundantly justify this act in their eyes; and they had long since, by the connivance of their guards, provided themselves with weapons for the purpose. They now determined no longer to delay their action.

On Sunday morning, the 9th of October, Capodistrias rose, as usual, at five o'clock, and, after devoting an hour to work, proceeded, accompanied by his one-armed servant, Kokonis, and a soldier named Leondas, to the Church of St. Spiridion to hear mass. On the way he was passed by Constantine and George Mavromichales, who saluted him hurriedly, and hastened on to the church. This was already full of worshippers, and the two Mainotes took up a position, one on each side of the door through which the President would have to pass. Capodistrias had been warned from several quarters that his life was in danger, but he had refused to take any precautions, he said:

> Providence watches over the President of Greece. They will reverence my white hairs!

When, however, he saw the two Mavromichales, he hesitated for an instant, for he knew the customs of the Maina. The hesitation was but momentary, and the next minute he had passed up the steps of the church. The Mavromichales waited till he had passed them; then Constantine fired a pistol, loaded with a double charge, at his head; and, as he staggered and fell, George plunged a dagger into his heart. The two murderers then turned and fled. Capodistrias fell without a cry and without a groan; his servant, Kokonis, caught him with the stump of his arm, and laid him gently on the ground; then, leaving the body of his master, rushed after the assassins. A shot which he fired at Constantine took effect; but, after a stumble, he managed to continue his flight, though with difficulty.

Meanwhile the sound of the scuffle and the pistol shots had disturbed the worshippers in the church, who now poured out, and, with an excited crowd that had collected, joined in the pursuit. Constantine, who had been wounded in the leg, was speedily overtaken, dragged to the ground with curses and imprecations, and torn and mauled by the infuriated mob. Yet his wild courage did not desert him, he cried:

> Don't dishonour me, boys! Better light a candle at the church door! Ho! Is there no *palikari* here will end me with a pistol-ball? (The candle is lighted at the church door when anyone dies).

He had not to wait long. (Mendelssohn, ii.).

Meanwhile George had taken refuge in the French consulate, which was speedily surrounded by a howling mob clamouring for his blood. On learning what had happened, the French resident could not refuse to deliver him up to the proper authorities, especially in view of the threatening attitude of the crowd; and he was presently marched off to Itsh-kalé under the guard of a strong body of soldiers. He was tried by court-martial, and condemned to be shot.

George Mavromichales, handsome, brave, winning, and of an open and generous disposition, had been a general favourite; and when he was led out to execution, the crowd of spectators were strangely divided between sympathy for himself and hatred of his crime. He showed no trace of fear, and faced his death with a serene courage worthy of a nobler cause. He expressed and felt no regret for a deed which was fully justified by the code of conduct under which he had been reared. Turning to the crowd, just before the fatal volley was fired, he cried out, 'Freedom! Unity! Love!' a strange political testament for one who died to expiate a crime, inspired by the wild law of retaliation which he had inherited from an age of tyranny and barbarism.

The light in which the deed was regarded by the mass of the common people was sufficiently shown by the rage of the populace at the time, and which certainly was not due to any artificial stimulation. Among the liberal Opposition, however, always somewhat too ready to justify ill-doing by an appeal to classical precedents, the two Mavromichales were hailed as martyrs in the cause of freedom. Journalists wrote and poets sang of the modern Harmodios and Aristogeiton, who had rid the world of a new Pisistratus; and the students of Ægina, in imitation of the Athenians of old, went about singing the ancient ode:

In myrtle spray I'll wreathe my blade,
Like those two friends in freedom's cause,
Who low in blood the tyrant laid,
And gave to Athens equal laws.

But was Capodistrias a tyrant? His motives and his policy have been variously judged, according as the standpoint of his critics has varied; but by the mass of opinion his government has been condemned. It was condemned indeed by its failure, for it could have been justified only by success. If his iron-bound system of bureaucracy could have secured order for a time to the distracted country, this might have been cheaply bought at the cost of a temporary sacrifice of liberty. As it was, liberty was sacrificed, without order being secured; and, this being so, the unconstitutional dealings of Capodistrias may be stigmatised, in the language of Talleyrand, as worse than a crime as a mistake; for where methods confessedly dishonest, but defended on the ground of expediency, fail, it may be permitted to assert that honesty would have been the best policy.

Baron von Prokesch-Osten indeed, writing from the point of view of the *entourage* of Prince Metternich, considers the policy of the President the only one possible under the then existing conditions, and ascribes its failure to the factious opposition of greedy adventurers, unprincipled agitators, radical windbags, *et hoc genus omne*, aided and abetted by the unscrupulous machinations of the English and French residents.

But this is only to say that Capodistrias failed, as Metternich failed, because he had not sufficient sympathetic imagination to grasp all the conditions of the problem he was called upon to solve, and persisted in leaving out of his political calculations that important, and fatal, factor of 'sentiment.'

Yet, though the methods of Capodistrias were tyrannous, this is not to say that he was a 'tyrant;' for the true tyrant is as selfish in his ends as he is unscrupulous in his means. Capodistrias doubtless had ambitions, and legitimate ambitions; he aspired to rule his country; and he laboured to this end. But, for all that, it was for Greece that he toiled as much as for himself, or more; and if he desired to rule his country, it was for her good. To his love for Greece he had sacrificed, long since, his splendid position in the councils of Russia; to this, when he was called to the presidency, he surrendered his time, his health, his pleasures, and all that he possessed.

On his arrival, the Assembly had proposed to vote him an income out of the national funds; but this Capodistrias had refused; and, so far from receiving a penny from the revenues of Greece, he devoted the whole of his slender fortune to the attempt to eke out the poverty of the national treasury. His personal habits were worthy of the elder Cato. He rose early, and worked the whole day in his bureau, the sole furniture of which was a square sofa and a plain writing-table. For the pleasures and amusements which 'tyrants' usually allow themselves, he cared nothing; and he used to remark that his extreme temperance in youth had left him an old age 'like winter, cold but healthy.'

The simplicity of his dress was, indeed, a rock of offence to the Greeks, who love gorgeous attire; and only during his progresses through the country did he ultimately always wear a uniform; because he had been told that, on the first occasion of his visiting the rural districts, the peasants had prostrated themselves before the out-rider, under the impression that that splendid person must be the President.

Count John Capodistrias, in short, was a man whose talent for government, though great, fell very short of genius, as his moral character, though high, yet did not attain to the highest virtue; and Fate, or, as he would have preferred to say, Providence, had placed him in a position where a greater and a nobler man might well have failed.

Chapter 23

Civil War

Murder cannot under any circumstances be considered an effective method of democratic reform, because the heated political atmosphere which it engenders is not favourable to the growth of free institutions. The appetite for slaughter, moreover, grows with indulgence; and, as likely as not, the party, or the man, that appeals to the sword will in the end perish by the sword. To this rule the assassination of Count Capodistrias was no exception. To the hundred causes of faction and bitterness which already distracted the unhappy country was now added this blood-feud between the parties; all hope of an orderly and constitutional rule was for the time at an end; and, in place of the liberty they had expected, the Liberals saw Hellas given over to all the miseries of an unbridled anarchy.

As soon as the assassination of the President became known, the Senate had assembled, and had appointed a provisional committee of three members to carry on the government. The three selected were Count Agostino Capodistrias, Kolokotrones, and Kolettes. Though the Senate had no constitutional right to take this step, the Residents of the Powers had thought it best, in the absence of any other authority, to support their action, and to recognise the provisional government thus established, until the National Assembly could be called together and a legal administration appointed.

Agostino Capodistrias had already, during his brother's lifetime, posed as his heir and successor; and now that he was really thrust into the place of the murdered President, he attempted to ape his policy. He possessed, however, not a tithe of the ability which had not saved his brother from ruin; and arbitrary, ignorant, vain, and incompetent, he could not hope to succeed, where a stronger and a better man had failed. Kolettes, already meditating a stroke for the supreme power, now threw himself into opposition, and made Agostino's pro-Russian policy especially the object of his attacks.

The National Assembly was summoned to meet at Argos on the 19th of December. The national crisis arising from the death of Capodistrias might have been used to make, at any rate, some attempt to heal the divisions in the State. Kolettes, supported by the English and French residents, urged that the representatives who had been summoned to the Congress at Hydra should be invited to attend at Argos; but to this both Agostino and Kolokotrones strenuously objected, and the opportunity for healing the breach was lost. When the Assembly ultimately met at Argos, it was discovered that the majority of the deputies were devoted to the Capodistrian party; and in the division on the future constitution of the government, a hundred and forty-six of these voted for the exclusion of Kolokotrones and Kolettes from the provisional committee, and the appointment of Agostino Capodistrias as sole President.

The growing jealousy of the Moreots for the Rumeliots now broke out into open feud. Many of the chieftains had descended to the Assembly, as usual, surrounded by crowds of followers; and Argos was full of armed men. Already, on the afternoon of the 21st, there had been a skirmish in the streets, between Grivas and the Suliot Djavellas; and the greater number of the Capodistrian majority in the Congress had fled in alarm to Nauplia. On the 23rd there was a regular battle between about twelve hundred Rumeliots and the troops of the government, in which the former, who had insufficient ammunition and no artillery, were beaten, and compelled to withdraw from the town.

Kolettes, ousted from the government, now determined to throw in his lot with the Rumeliots; and, followed by about sixty of the deputies and several of the more important leaders, he proceeded to the Isthmus. At Megara the Rumeliots had gathered their strength, and here it was determined to set up a provisional government in opposition to that at Nauplia; while at the same time negotiations were opened with the Hydriots. Kolettes himself, Zaimis, and Konduriottes, were elected to form the governing committee; and Mavrocordatos, who had come over from Hydra, was made State secretary. Greece was once more rent in twain, and threatened anew with the horrors of civil war.

The powers had now begun, after a long interval, to concern themselves again with the affairs of Greece. On the 26th of September the conference had met once more in London, and had issued a protocol, the Whigs being now in power, conceding the frontier from Arta to Volo; and, at the same time, ordering the residents to support the government, and aid it in repressing the unruliness of the Hydriots. This protocol, arriving after the death of the President, most of whose demands it conceded, well illustrates the cumbrousness of the attempt to regulate the affairs of Greece from a committee-room in London. Events were moving fast in Hellas, and by the time a second protocol had been sent to correct the first, it, too, was out of date.

There were now two governments face to face, and the problem was too complicated to allow of its being solved by recognising one and regarding the other as simply revolutionary and unauthorised. Sir Stratford Canning, who had arrived at Nauplia, on his way to Constantinople, in the midst of the crisis, tried to overcome the difficulty by arranging a reconciliation. Supported by the Russian and French residents, he handed a memorandum to Count Agostino suggesting the proclamation of an amnesty, and the summoning of a new Assembly, to which the representatives both at Hydra and Megara should be admitted.

But Agostino was infatuated, and would yield nothing. He believed that, with the aid of Kolokotrones, Niketas, and the other Moreot chieftains of his party, he could hold his own against Kolettes and his Rumeliots, and he would be content with nothing short of their absolute submission. Canning and the residents now began to suspect that the justice of the case lay on the side of the Opposition rather than on that of the government, and they sent despatches to London in this sense. (Prokesch, ii.)

Meanwhile, however, on the 24th of February, there arrived another protocol of the London Conference, dated January the 7th, which confirmed the orders contained in the first, and ordered the representatives of the Powers to recognise the government established by the Congress of Argos. This the residents, in spite of their better judgment, were now compelled to do; and Capodistrias, fortified by their support, issued a proclamation promising an amnesty to all those who should submit. (*Ibid*, Appendix, xii.). The Hydriots, who, in common with the Assembly at Megara, had taken up an attitude of uncompromising hostility to the Government of Agostino, were thereupon threatened by the admirals with severe consequences if they refused to accept the amnesty. But threats and promises were alike unavailing.

Even the news, which reached Nauplia on the 11th of March, of the election of the young Prince Otho, second son of King Ludwig of Bavaria, as King of Greece, which it was hoped would put a stop to the civil strife, had but little effect. What effect it did have was rather contrary to that which had been expected; for each party was anxious to be in possession on the new king's arrival, so as to have the greater claim on any favours he might have to bestow, and they redoubled their efforts to oust their rivals. To the notification of the election of the king, the Assembly at Megara replied that, king or no king, they would not lay down their arms until Count Agostino Capodistrias had quitted the country; and, to give force to their representations, they proceeded to acts of open hostility.

After occupying Lepanto, they laid siege to the castle of Salona, which was held for the Capodistrians by Mamouris, attacked Metaxas in Delphi, and plundered Arachova. Once more the dogs of war were unleashed, to raven and slay over the devoted country. The miserable peasants, who had just begun to recover somewhat from their ten years' agony, cursed the name of Liberty, which had meant for them nothing but wrong and suffering, and the cry of 'Constitution,' which they had learned to associate only with robbery and violence; and they prayed for the speedy arrival of the foreign king, with his alien troops, to save them from the misrule of their own self-constituted leaders.

The forces of the contending parties were unequally matched; and, since it was to come to a trial of strength, it became apparent that Kolettes was likely to get the upper hand. Against the five thousand men whom he could bring into the field, Agostino could rely upon no more than some two thousand. In view of the emptiness of the treasury, it was impossible for him to rely on the venal loyalty of such chiefs as the Suliot Djavellas. Zaimis had not yet declared himself; and on his decision depended the allegiance of Achaia and Arcadia. The forces of the government were, moreover, distracted by the necessity for dealing with troubles in the south of the Morea; for the Mainotes had attacked and taken Monemvasia, and the Messenians had called in the French to their aid against the exactions of Kolokotrones.

Distrusted and distrustful, the government seemed incapable, in this crisis of their affairs, of giving either help or advice. As though to proclaim their impotence to all the world, they could think of no better plan for reducing the Mainotes to obedience than releasing the Mavromichales, upon their promising, for the tenth time, to call their turbulent tribesmen to order. The Assembly at Nauplia, occupied, amid wars and rumours of wars, in debating the future constitution, fell into absolute contempt.

Meanwhile the time was approaching for the arrival of the new king; and as yet, among all this turmoil of conflicting factions, there was no one to represent his authority. As he was under age, the question of the regency was a serious and pressing one, demanding immediate settlement. Under the present circumstances of the country the best and safest plan would undoubtedly have been to have appointed a committee of regency, fairly representative of all parties; but the hostile factions each aimed at undivided power, and preferred plunging the country into war to surrendering one shred of the spoils of office. The deputies at Nauplia gave the signal for the definite outbreak of hostilities by electing Agostino Capodistrias Regent of the Realm.

By the Rumeliot party this was taken to mean that, even after the arrival of Otho, Agostino would, as regent, still hold the reins of power; and Kolettes, determined to prevent this at all hazards, decided at once to invade the Morea, and to compel Capodistrias to resign. On the 6th of April he crossed the Isthmus, at the head of a force which the government troops were powerless to resist.

On the next day he entered Argos, where he issued a proclamation, in which he said that his only object was to escort back those deputies who, in December, had been intimidated into flight by the Capodistrians. On the 8th he advanced in triumph to Nauplia. Here, however, he met with a check; for the representatives of the powers had landed troops, and occupied the gates of the town; and they now met Kolettes with a demand for an armistice of a few hours, in order that the position might be discussed. Kolettes thereupon took up his quarters in the suburb of Pronia.

By a fortunate chance a protocol of the London Conference, dated the 7th of March, and embodying the recommendations of Canning's memorandum of the 28th of December, had arrived the day before, in the very nick of time. The forces of the Alliance were now ordered to intervene to keep the peace, and negotiations were to be opened on the basis of the recommendations made by Canning in his memorandum, the resulting government to be supported by force of arms.

The residents now declared for a mixed government, which should be fairly representative of all parties, and proceeded to lay this decision before Count Agostino Capodistrias, who, seeing that, under these circumstances, he could neither resist the will of the powers nor obtain any real share in a government of which Kolettes would be the moving power, resigned, and the next day left the country, carrying with him the body of his brother.

The Senate now once more stepped into the breach, and, after negotiating with the residents, appointed a governing committee. In this, Kolettes was included; but, as the remaining four members were either openly or secretly hostile to him, he insisted on the impossibility of carrying on the government under these circumstances, and enforced his views by the very practical argument of summoning the remainder of his troops to join him at Pronia. The residents, recognising the soundness of his objections, and anxious to avoid the battle which now seemed imminent between the hostile factions, prevailed on the Senate to reconstitute the committee, which was ultimately composed of seven members, of whom four were partisans of Kolettes.

Kolettes had now attained the object for which he had plotted and schemed so long, and was, in the eyes of all, the virtual ruler of Hellas. Originally physician to Ali Pasha, he had learned in the corrupt court of Janina all the meaner arts of political activity. He was cunning and plausible, and a solemn and reticent demeanour had given him, among the volatile Greeks, a reputation for wisdom which was not altogether founded on fact. At the outset of his career at the helm of state, he was confronted with difficulties which would have made a wiser man despair.

He soon discovered that the Senate, the majority of which were Capodistrians, though they had conceded his demands as to the personnel of the committee, had so ordered it that it was, for his purposes, practically powerless. Decrees had to be signed by all the members; they were invalid if any three protested against them; and no business could be transacted unless five members were present. As three of its members were known to be hostile to him, it is obvious that this arrangement left him absolutely powerless, and in fact rendered the Committee itself a farce.

Under these circumstances it is not surprising that the new government was scarcely more effective than the old. It had in opposition to it all the supporters of the fallen party, a majority of the Senate, many of the most powerful of the Moreot chiefs, including Kolokotrones, Niketas, and Rhangos, and a large number of the wealthy primates, who feared for their property, menaced now by the wild bands of mercenaries who had raised Kolettes to power. Besides all these, the squadrons under Kanaris and Andruzzos were hostile; and, last but not least, the English and Russian residents, jealous of the influence acquired over Kolettes by the French, began to favour the opposite party.

The very instruments of his power were now turning to Kolettes' destruction. The most immediately pressing question was how to rid himself of the soldiers whom he had brought into the Morea, and who, to the number of seven or eight thousand, were living at free quarters upon the unhappy population. Every day that they remained increased the bitterness of the hostility of the Moreots to his rule; and yet, in the absence of any money to discharge the arrears of their pay, it was impossible to induce them to recross the Isthmus. In Patras, and in Nauplia itself, there were signs of open insurrection; and, in his extremity, Kolettes had been compelled to call in the French to his aid.

On the 20th of May, twelve hundred men, under General Corbet, marched into Nauplia, and occupied the castles of Itsh-Kalé and Palamidi. At Patras, however, they had been anticipated. The Suliot Djavellas entered the town before the French detachment could reach it, roused the inhabitants by telling them that the government had sold them to the foreigners, and prepared to hold the place against all comers. The French, finding that their occupation would be opposed, did not attempt to take the town; and a force which Kolettes subsequently sent against it fraternised with the troops of Djavellas, who remained in possession of Patras till the arrival of King Otho.

A new National Assembly was now summoned for the 30th of April, in spite of the opposition of the powers, who thought that it would have been better to have postponed its meeting, in view of the approaching arrival of the king. Deputies, elected or self-chosen, streamed from all sides to the appointed place. It was like the heaping together of highly inflammable materials for a conflagration. The suppressed anger of the fallen party was fed by an increasing suspicion of the encroachments of the French, which the government seemed to favour; and the growing hatred of the Peloponnesians for the Rumeliots would alone have been sufficient to feed the flames of civil war. This was not long delayed.

Kolokotrones, refusing to have anything to do with the Congress, held himself, like a modern Achilles, moodily aloof in the stronghold of Karytaena. Kolettes, mistrusting his attitude, sent Grivas, with his Rumeliot bands, from Argos into the districts of Leondari and Phanari in the interior of the Morea. Kolokotrones well understood that this move was directed against himself. The bands of Grivas, largely composed of Mussulman Albanians, were the most ruthless and bloodthirsty of all the hordes of mercenaries by which the country was overrun; and, when they occupied Tripolitza, from all Arcadia rose up a wail of terror and despair. Kolokotrones, with characteristic promptness, now issued a proclamation to the Hellenes, declaring the government to be the enemies of the country, the Assembly unconstitutional, and war against them both just and necessary.

At the same time he summoned the Peloponnesians to arms, to aid him in expelling the hordes of Grivas. His appeal met with a ready and immediate response; and the Moreot captains crowded to his banner, to help in the expulsion of the hated Rumeliots. Gennaios Kolokotrones marched on Tripolitza, while Niketas raised the Messenians, and did battle with the hillsmen of the Maina. Kolettes endeavoured to take measures to suppress the revolt; but, at this crisis, Zaimis and the other Capodistrian members of the Committee of Government withdrew, and the executive was thereby deprived of all constitutional powers. All was now complete anarchy. The Assembly at Argos began the work of verifying its powers, while the Senate denounced it as illegal and unconstitutional.

The executive, paralysed and impotent, depended entirely on the precarious support of the mercenary bands, who upheld it only as an excuse for plundering the Morea. The government, as a last expiring act of protest, issued a ban against Kolokotrones, signed by four only of its members. The answer was a raid of Kallergis, with his horsemen, into the plain of Argos; and the Assembly, in alarm for its safety, once more fled, and took refuge within the walls of Nauplia.

At this juncture arrived the news of a weighty decision of the conference in London, which promised to be a final settlement of the Greek question. The crown had, as already mentioned, been offered to Prince Otho, the second son of King Ludwig of Bavaria, whose youth (he was scarcely seventeen) was considered an advantage, as it would enable him to adapt himself more readily to the conditions of the country he was called upon to govern. In accepting for his son, the King of Bavaria had insisted on certain important modifications of the former protocols, and most of his demands had been conceded.

The extension of the frontier beyond the line of Arta—Volo, fixed by the protocol of the 26th of September was, indeed, refused, as was also the suggestion to include the island of Crete in the new kingdom. But Otho was to be King, not 'Sovereign Prince' of Greece; and an adequate loan was guaranteed, to enable the new government to start unhampered by want of funds. The united squadrons of the powers, and the French troops, were also placed at the disposal of the regency, for the maintenance of order. (Prokesch, Appendix, xii.).

This treaty was signed on the 7th of May, and the news of it reached Greece just as the Assembly was escaping from Argos to Nauplia. The representatives of the powers besought the government to dissolve the Congress, which, under present circumstances, could do nothing but harm. But the government was neither willing nor able to comply, and the Assembly, asserting that its session was necessary in order to confirm the election of the new king, refused to dissolve. Denied admittance to Nauplia by the French troops, it occupied a house in the suburb of Pronia, where it carried on a precarious existence, discussing the constitution and preparing an address to King Otho.

Here, on the 22nd of August, Grisiotis, with his mercenaries, fell upon it, clamouring for arrears of pay; and, when it became clear that they had no money with which to meet his demands, he scattered the deputies to all the four winds, carrying off Notaras, the President, and several of the wealthier members, to his camp at Argos, whence they were only released on paying a ransom of 110,000 *piastres*.

On the 18th of August Demetrius Hypsilanti, who had been a member of the governing committee, died; and as this still further weakened the position of the administration, Mavrocordatos, Tricoupis, and one or two others, attempted to effect a reconciliation of parties, but without success. The civil war continued with daily increasing fury; and day by day the power of Kolokotrones grew. All the Morea was on his side; and Grivas was hard pressed in Tripolitza. In the south, the Mainotes had gone on a plundering expedition on their own account, and Niketas was endeavouring to reduce them to order. In the north, Kallergis was fighting the Rumeliots.

In Corinth Karatassos had established himself; and Djavellas still held Patras and the surrounding country. The flames of war had crossed the Gulf of Corinth, and the *Armatoli* of Gardikiotis Grivas had attacked and captured Missolonghi; while, in East Hellas, both parties had united, and were marching on the Isthmus for an invasion of the Peloponnese. Nauplia, alone in all Greece, was in the enjoyment of the blessings of peace, under the protection of the French garrison.

In the midst of all this tumult, on the 15th of August, Sir Stratford Canning arrived from Constantinople, bringing the confirmation by the Porte of the treaty agreed upon by the powers in London. The Ottoman Government had accepted the extension of the frontier, and had agreed to evacuate the ceded districts before the end of December, on condition of the compensation due being paid before that time. Certain minor questions raised by the evacuation, and dealing with the future relations of the two nations, were at the same time arranged; and the representatives of the powers now declared the object of the Treaty of London attained, and the Greek question settled for ever. (Prokesch, ii.).

THE BISHOP OF OLD PATRAS GERMANOS BLESSES
THE FLAG OF REVOLUTION

Chapter 24

Conclusion

The arrival of the new king might now be daily expected. Some final details had been arranged by the London Conference; and, at the end of August, King Ludwig had replied to the addresses of loyalty and welcome sent by the Committee of Regency and the Senate. An embassy, consisting of Admiral Miaoulis, Constantine Botzares, and Dimitrios Paploutas, was now despatched to Munich, to do homage to the new ruler, on behalf of the Hellenic nation.

The prospect of the speedy arrival of the king, however, did nothing to put a stop to the civil contest; on the contrary, the parties fought with all the greater violence in their effort to oust each other while there was yet time. Kolokotrones was everywhere victorious. He had driven Grivas and his Rumeliots out of Tripolitza; and these now cut their way back over the Isthmus, and finally joined Gardikiotis Grivas in Missolonghi. Kallergis had again advanced on the capital; and Kolokotrones now had an interview with Admirals Ricord and Hotham in Nauplia, in which he demanded the reconstruction of the government.

Conferences and intrigues followed, in which Kolettes was supported by the French, while the party of Kolokotrones had the sympathy of the Russians and English. In the end, Kolettes was left nominally in possession, sharing the government with two colleagues. But his rule was in fact confined to the town of Nauplia. Outside the walls Kolokotrones governed the whole of Greece; and the Morea at least was regularly apportioned among his captains. As though to put the finishing touch to the spectacle of utter impotence presented by the nominal government in Nauplia, the Committee of Regency quarrelled with the Senate, and the latter fled to Astros.

The year 1832 had been the most miserable of all the war; the

Greeks had suffered more from the cruelty and rapine of their own countrymen than in all the Ottoman invasions, more even than they had endured at the hands of the armies of Ibrahim; and now, at the end of the year, the country was utterly exhausted, and both parties were wearied out with the suicidal strife. The high-sounding principles proclaimed in the constitutions of Troezene, Astros, and Epidaurus had been forgotten, drowned in the din of war and lost amid the clamour of party cries. Of the elaborate administrative edifice erected by Capodistrias, but broken wrecks and fragments remained. The courts of law were closed, the Senate scattered.

In Nauplia, the Secretaries of State carried on the shadow of a government, in order to make it possible to speak of Greece; for of a united Hellas there was otherwise no sign. North of the Isthmus the country was comparatively free from local tyrants; and the communes governed themselves, in the absence of any superior authority, with good success. South of the Isthmus, Kolokotrones gradually freed the Morea from every oppression but his own, and governed, after a patriarchal fashion, with the aid of his captains, and of such of the Capodistrian officials as were left. Only in the extreme south, the Mainotes, true to their character to the last, were still in arms, and carrying on war against Kolokotrones on the one side, and the admirals of the allied fleets on the other.

Active preparations were now being made in Nauplia for the reception of the new king. He was to be accompanied by some Bavarian troops, to guard his person, and form the nucleus of a disciplined army. To make room for these in the capital, three companies of French troops were transferred to Argos, which was at that time in the hands of the forces of Kolokotrones and Grisiotis. The appearance of the French was the signal for suspicious murmurs on the part of the wild *Armatoli*; and from words it soon came to deeds. The French were attacked in the streets of the town, and a regular battle ensued, in which the Greeks lost many killed and wounded; and several executions followed. This was the last blood shed in the War of Liberation.

On the 28th of January, the watchmen on the hills about Navarino reported that a large squadron of men-of-war, of which the leading ship flew the ensign of Hellas, was passing along the coast; and the news at once spread like wild-fire that the king was coming at last. The next day, amid the thunder of artillery and the joyful shouts of the people, the fleet entered the harbour of Nauplia, and the first King of the Hellenes disembarked upon the shores of Greece.

The landing of the Bavarian king forms a convenient epoch for bringing the narrative of the Greek War of Independence to a close. Not that King Otho proved an effective *deus ex machina,* to unravel the tangled plot of the Hellenic drama; nor that by his arrival the Greek question had, as the diplomatists of the conference had fondly imagined, been settled for ever; but it was the formal end of the struggle against the Turkish domination; and it opened a new phase in the history not only of Greece but of Europe, in the commonwealth of which a new Christian Kingdom was now included. How pregnant this last fact was with dangerous issues for the future, the history of the last sixty years, and especially the events of the present time, have proved.

It may be doubted, indeed, whether the peril would have been so great to European peace, had the powers been less timid in their handling of the question of Hellenic independence. It is, however, the essential weakness of every concert that, even when its mutual jealousies allow it to achieve anything at all, it can never effect more than a compromise. Now, in politics, compromise is the seed of all evils. A one-sided settlement, even when unjust, will in the end be better for the world; for, though one party to the arrangement may be dissatisfied, the other will be content; whereas, in case of a compromise, both sides will be discontented, and the chances are that the question at issue, instead of being settled, will only be postponed. In the case of the revolt of the Greeks against the Ottoman Empire, the truth of this is especially obvious, and has been proved only too clearly by the subsequent development of the Levantine question.

Yet Metternich alone, of all the statesmen of the concert, realised it clearly at the time, and was, from the very outset, opposed to any form of compromise. As long as he had any hope of carrying the Cabinets of Europe with him, he insisted on the absolute right of the Ottoman Government to crush a rebellion of its own subjects; yet in the end, though he could not be suspected of possessing a shred of Philhellenic sentiment, it was he who first proposed the establishment of a strong and independent Hellenic State. In this change of attitude there was no inconsistency. It was merely the objection of a keen and far-seeing statesman to those half measures which are the expedients of weakness and timidity.

The peace of Europe he saw could be best maintained by adopting one of two alternatives: by crushing or by conciliating Hellenic sentiment. He believed that the policy of crushing was safer than that of conciliation; but as soon as he saw that the conditions of the problem rendered the former impossible, he recognised the latter as the only alternative. Just, however, as the speed of a fleet is that of its slowest vessel, so the policy of a concert is that of its most short-sighted member; and, in the settlement of the Greek question, it was England that acted as a drag upon the counsels of Europe. Had Canning lived, it is possible that, utterly antagonistic as the views and aims of the two statesmen really were, he might ultimately have united with Metternich in creating a powerful Greece.

With Turkey tied hand and foot in the power of Russia, this would indeed have seemed the obvious policy for England, as for Austria, to pursue. But the tradition of friendship for the Ottoman Empire was too strong for the Tory statesmen into whose hands the fate of Hellas had been in the first instance committed. They had inherited from Canning a policy which they loathed; and pledged as they were to bestow some measure of liberty upon Greece, they doled this out with a niggard hand. They seemed to hope that, if they reduced the concessions to Greece to the lowest possible point, Turkey might, after all, consent to overlook this unfriendly action on the part of a friendly power.

But '*no man loves one the better for giving him the bastinado, though with never so little a cudge*l,' (Burleigh's *Advice to Queen Elizabeth, &c.* Fourth collection of Somers' *Tracts*, i.), and possibly even hates one the worse, if the beating be accompanied by expressions of affection and esteem. To the Ottoman Government the attitude of Great Britain, even before the Battle of Navarino, was frankly incomprehensible. While Lord Strangford, at Constantinople, was protesting the goodwill of England towards the Porte, English volunteers and English gold were being poured into Greece, to aid the rebellious *rayahs*; and that the British Government had no power to prevent this, the Turks refused to believe. Navarino, of course, confirmed the Porte in its rooted distrust of English professions. The open hostility of Russia it could appreciate; but the hypocrisy of a power which illustrated its friendship by slaughtering, in time of peace, six thousand of the true believers, passed all understanding.

England, in fact, through her anxiety to maintain Turkey as a barrier against Muscovite aggression, played straight into the hands of Russia; and it should have been clear that if such a barrier was to be erected, it was certainly not to be found in a power which viewed Great Britain with well-grounded distrust, and had, since the Peace of Adrianople, surrendered itself to Russian influence. What Russia dreaded, and resisted with all her power, was not the preservation of an empire which was bound, sooner or later, to break up, but the erection on its ruins of independent Christian States strong enough to resist her own advance, and especially the creation of a Hellas sufficiently powerful to stem the rising tide of Slavonic influence.

If, then, it was essential for England to resist the establishment of Russia as a power in the Mediterranean, this could best have been effected by doing what Russia most dreaded, and founding a Greek State on a basis so strong that there would have been no danger of its becoming a mere appanage of more powerful neighbours. Broadly speaking, this was the only possible policy worthy of the name; for it was the only policy which the English people would, in the long run, tolerate. But the conditions under which English statesmen work make a really strong and consistent foreign policy almost impossible. Wellington had been hampered by the Philhellenic legacies of Canning; Palmerston was hampered by the Turcophile tradition of the Tories.

In opposition, he had advocated the inclusion of Crete in the Hellenic kingdom, a course which would have obviated many future troubles; in office, he could effect no more than the extension of the frontier to the line of Arta-Volo. The Greece thus created was strong, but not strong enough to make her contented; and '*what the mixture of strength and discontent engenders needs no syllogism to prove.*' (Lord Burleigh's *Advice to Queen Elisabeth, &c.* Fourth collection of Somers' *Tracts*, i.). Whilst the Philhellenic policy of the British Government had thus succeeded only in achieving either too much or too little, the pro-Turkish policy into which it speedily relapsed could never be rendered really effective, because it was in constant danger of being hampered by the outspokenness of English public opinion, which is not in sympathy with Turkish methods of government.

The net result, then, of sixty years of British diplomacy in the near East is that, at the present moment, every vestige of influence which England ever possessed at Constantinople has vanished; and Greece, which might have been a bulwark of British power in the Mediterranean, lies crushed and bleeding beneath the heel of the Turk. How far this latter fact is due to the action of English statesmen, and how far to the vanity and impatience of the Greeks themselves, may be left for the future to decide. To the author it seems probable that the cautious diplomacy of Lord Salisbury was directed to the creation of that

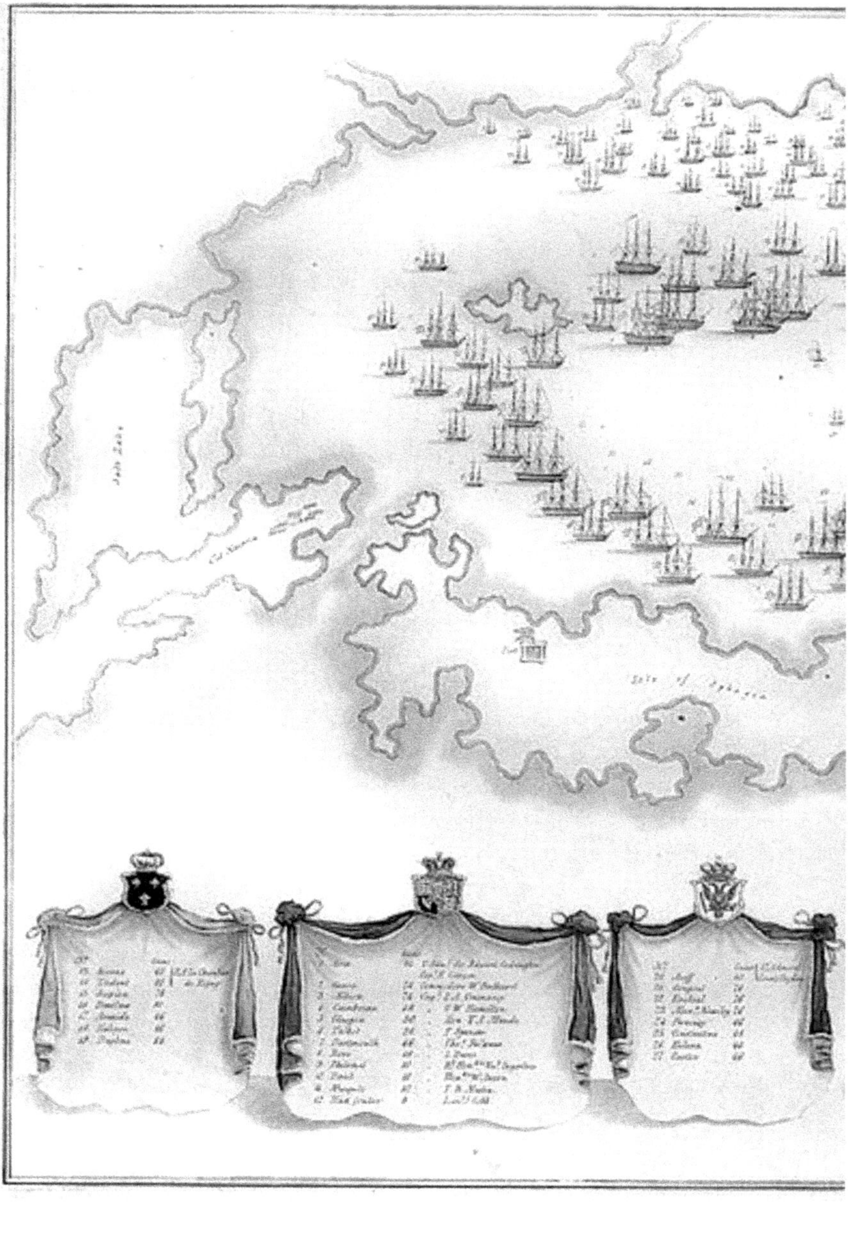

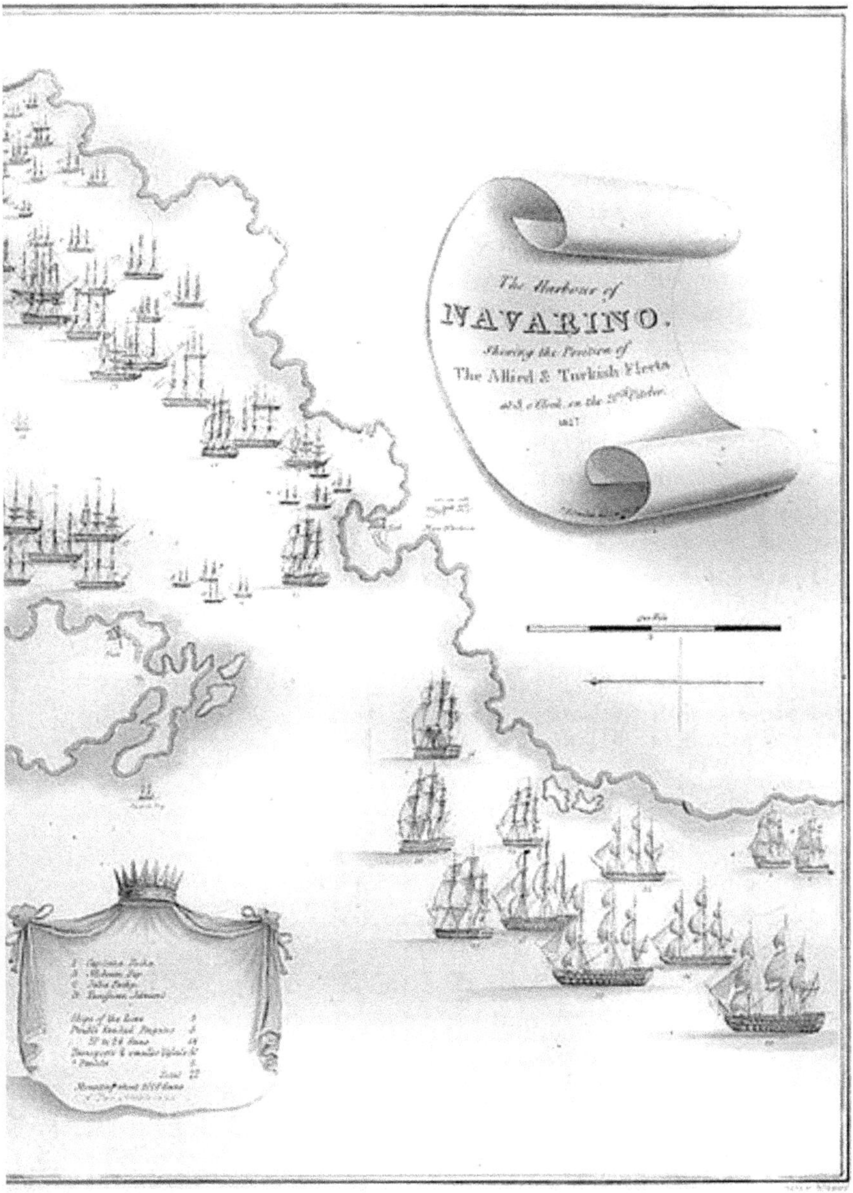
The Harbour of
NAVARINO.
Shewing the Position of
The Allied & Turkish Fleets
1827

greater Greece which the precipitate action of the Greeks themselves, and in no slight degree also the ill-judged agitation of Philhellenes in England and elsewhere, has rendered impossible for at least a generation to come.

★★★★★★

I do not think this opinion inconsistent with a sincere sympathy with the original struggle of the Greeks for freedom, or even with their desire for further expansion. But, from the point of view of European sentiment, there is all the difference in the world between the love of liberty and the desire of territorial aggrandisement. A war under taken merely to substitute 'union' for 'autonomy' in Crete could have been justified only by success. As it was, the action of the Greeks seems to have been worse than a crime a folly.

★★★★★★

To the constitution of a nation, however, more is needed than an extension of territory and the guarantee of the Powers; and it has been questioned whether the character of the Greeks is such as to warrant their being entrusted with any extended dominion. It is pointed out that, as a nation, they are bankrupt, and, as a people, though possessing many attractive qualities, factious, unstable, and dishonest. Yet, though all this may be said of them, and, indeed, appears only too clearly in the history of the War of Independence, that war, and the one which has just been concluded, prove that the Greeks are capable of making great sacrifices for the sake of a national ideal; and it is possible that, with a wider field on which to work, their conceptions of duty and patriotism would likewise expand.

To maintain that the Greeks are, as a race, incapable of establishing and maintaining a powerful State, is to ignore the teaching of a long, if comparatively neglected, period of history. The Byzantine Empire was a Greek State; and, hopelessly corrupt as it doubtless too often proved itself at the centre, it nevertheless preserved civilisation and the remains of ancient culture for a thousand years against the flood of barbarism which, from the north and east, threatened to overwhelm them.

We are what suns and winds and waters make us;

....and the Greeks of today are very much what their fathers were before them. There never was an age when Greece was peopled by a race of heroes and philosophers, or when her counsels were governed solely by the purest patriotism. The Athenian crowd which listened to the masterpieces of Æschylus or Sophocles was as fickle, as superstitious, and as cruel as the Athenian crowd of today. The sun of the ancient culture of Hellas is set, and we see but the after-glow which lights up the highest and purest peaks; while over all that was low, and sordid, and commonplace, the night of oblivion has fallen. It is not for us, then, to judge the modern Greek as unworthy of our sympathy, because he seems cast in a less heroic mould than those from whom he boasts his descent. Our attitude may well be that of Lord Byron, of whom Colonel Napier said:

> All (the Philhellenes) came, expecting to find the Peloponnesus filled with Plutarch's men, and all returned, thinking the inhabitants of Newgate more moral. Lord Byron judged them fairly; he knew that half-civilised men are full of vices, and that great allowance must be made for emancipated slaves. He, therefore, proceeded, bridle in hand, not thinking them good, but hoping to make them better.

The conditions have changed, for Hellas, since then, has enjoyed half a century of freedom; yet we should do well to regard its people with a like charitable judgment, and a like hope. For assuredly the future of the East lies not with the Turks, who, in spite of their high qualities and personal worth, are fettered by a system which seems incapable of reform, but with those despised and often degraded Christian peoples, who yet possess, in their religion, if not in their race, the potentiality of progress and improvement.

Navarino
By Herbert Russell

The immediate causes which led to the Battle of Navarin, or Navarino, are of a romantic and dramatic character. On the 6th of July. 1826—the Greeks having risen in revolt against the oppression of the Turks in 1820—a treaty had been signed in London on the part of Great Britain, France, and Russia, having for its object the pacification of the Levant by intervention between Turkey and Greece. Through the indiscretion of some unknown official the treaty found its way to the *Times*, which published it in its issue of July 12th, 1826—six days after its signature. It thus became fully known to all concerned before the official instructions which it rendered necessary could be delivered. As a result, Sir Edward Codrington, the British admiral in the Mediterranean, found himself in a situation of perplexity, and was directed to consult with the French and Russian admirals, and arrange a plan of action with them.

The instructions of the three admirals in question definitely required an armistice between Turkey and Greece, and limited the period for its acceptance to one month. If the result of negotiations should be—as was, of course, anticipated—acceptance by Greece and rejection by Turkey, the admirals were instructed to enter into friendly relations with the former country-, and unite their fleets to prevent all Turkish or Egyptian reinforcements or warlike stores from being transported for employment against the Greeks. Each of the allied admirals had particular instructions to take care, if possible, that any measures they might adopt in restraining the Ottoman Navy should not wear the aspect of open hostilities. They were directed to endeavour to carry their arguments rather by a display of force than by the employment of it. This, briefly, is a review of the situation whose climax was the Battle of Navarino.

Sir Edward Codrington, the British admiral in the Levant, as we have already said, found himself in a situation of perplexity on the publication of the treaty. The French squadron was at Milo, and the Russians had not yet arrived. But with that instant resolution which has always been such a fine characteristic of the British naval officer's spirit. Sir Edward determined to take the initiative, and with three sail of the line he placed himself before Hydra to oppose, "when all other means are exhausted, by cannon shot" the whole of the Turkish and Egyptian fleet. The "general order," which he issued to all his captains on September 8th, 1827, well illustrates the policy which the English commander-in-chief resolved to adopt. He writes from on board the *Asia*:

> You are aware, that a treaty has been signed between England, France, and Russia for the pacification of Greece. A declaration of the decision of the powers has been presented to the Porte, and a similar declaration has been presented to the Greeks. The armistice proposed to each, in these declarations, has been acceded to by the Greeks, whilst it has been refused by the Turks. It becomes, therefore, the duty of the allied naval forces to enter, in the first place, on friendly relations with the Greeks; and, next, to intercept every supply of men, arms, etc., destined against Greece, and coming either from Turkey or Africa in general. The last measure is that which requires the greatest caution, and, above all, a complete understanding as to the operations of the allied naval forces. Most particular care is to be taken that the measures adopted against the Ottoman Navy do not degenerate into hostilities.
>
> The formal intention of the powers is to interfere as conciliators, and to establish, in fact, at sea the armistice which the Porte would not concede as a right. Every hostile proceeding would be at variance with the pacific ground which they have chosen to take, and the display of forces which they have assembled is destined to cause that wish to be respected; but they must not be put into use, unless the Turks persist in forcing the passages which they have intercepted. All possible means should be tried, in the first instance, to prevent the necessity of proceeding to extremities; but the prevention of supplies, as before mentioned, is to be enforced, if necessary, and when all other means are exhausted, by cannon shot.

In giving you this instruction as to the duty which I am directed to perform, my intention is to make you acquainted thoroughly with the object of our government, that you may not be taken by surprise as to whatever measures I may find it necessary to adopt. You will still look to me for further instructions as to the carrying any such measures into effect.

On September 11th Sir Edward Codrington, with the *Genoa* and *Albion*, arrived off Navarino, and beheld the whole of the expedition from Alexandria at anchor in the harbour, where it had arrived two days previously. The English squadron hovered off this place for above a week, awaiting the coming of the allies. On the 19th September Sir Edward Codrington notified the admiral commanding the Ottoman force in the port of Navarino that he would be prevented—by extreme measures, if necessary—from attacking the Greeks. Notwithstanding, on the 21st a division of the Turkish expedition got under way, and came out of the harbour. Their intentions were clear, and the British ships cleared for action. What the issue of this incident might have been it is difficult to say, had not the sails of a strange squadron appeared upon the horizon to windward whilst the English and Turks were still manoeuvring near the land. The vessels turned out to be the French fleet, under Admiral de Rigny, and whatever might have been the intentions of the commander of the Ottoman expedition, it retired back into the harbour immediately the strangers were near enough for the French colours to be visible.

By the arrival of Admiral de Rigny at Navarino, not only was Sir Edward Codrington's force largely augmented, but he was relieved of his isolated and critical responsibility by the certainty of a joint action in whatever steps might now be taken. The Russian squadron had not yet appeared; but the British and French admirals at once commenced proceedings by interviewing Ibrahim Pacha, the commander of the Turkish forces at Navarino, and clearly impressing upon him the determination of the allied Courts to carry out the spirit of the treaty, and the necessity imposed on them (the admirals) to enforce the armistice referred to in their instructions. The interview was a long one. Ibrahim said that the admirals must be aware he was a soldier like themselves, and that it was as imperative for him to obey orders as for them; that his instructions were to attack Hydra, and that he must put them into execution, it being for him merely to act and not to negotiate.

The admirals replied that they quite sympathised with the feelings of a brave man under such circumstances, and that they congratulated him upon having a force opposed to him which it was impossible to resist. They reminded him that if he put to sea in defiance of their amicable warning they must carry their instructions into execution, and that if he resisted by force the total destruction of his fleet must follow, which, they added archly and significantly, was an act of madness the Grand Seignior could not applaud. Amidst a profusion of Oriental compliments, French politeness, and British bluntness was this interview between the warlike Turk and the allied admirals carried on; and, although in conclusion Ibrahim pledged his word of honour to observe the armistice, yet the actual result of the long palaver was to leave things very much in the same situation in which they had been before.

Admiral Codrington's description of Ibrahim, contained in a letter written by him to his sister Jane shortly after the interview referred to, is particularly interesting. After a very graphic description of the Turkish camp and of Ibrahim's tent, he proceeds:—

> They first began with the ceremony of introduction, which, as there were a good many of us on either side, was proportionally long. . . . At length, however, I got settled, and began to look around me again. . . . This tent also was open, and from his sofa he looked down over the whole harbour, and really the sight was beautiful, covered as it was by the ships and boats of all sorts continually passing to and fro. His tent was *outside* the walls of Navarin; and, indeed, what force he had with him appeared to be outside of the town. Altogether, I thought he had chosen the coolest and most convenient place to pitch his tent in that could be found.
>
> But to return thither. He is a man of about forty years old, not at all good-looking, but with heavy features, very much marked with the smallpox, and as fat as a porpoise. Though I had no opportunity of seeing his height—as he was on his sofa, lying down or sitting the whole time—I should not think him more than five feet seven inches. He was, *for a pacha,* plainly dressed, I think, particularly as his followers and officers were covered with gold and embroidery; and, for a Turk, I think his manners were very good indeed. The conversation first began about the weather, and such common-place things; for I learnt (from the interpreter) he does not talk of business till *after coffee.*

Ibrahim proved treacherous. He disregarded his own word of hon-

ZANTE

our to accept the armistice, and there followed a long series of negotiations, in which the attitude of the allied admirals gradually grew more threatening and that of the Ottoman leader proportionately defiant. On the 2nd of October, in the midst of a heavy thunderstorm, the Turkish fleet boldly put to sea. This was a direct breach of the parole which had been passed, and the Honourable Captain Spencer, in the *Talbot*, was instructed to inform the Turkish admiral that he would not be permitted to proceed, and that if he allowed a single gun to be fired at the English flag the whole of his fleet would be destroyed.

This message speedily caused the Turks to bring their ships to the wind, and the second in command, Halhil Bey, came on board the *Asia*. He admitted that he had been present at Sir Edward Codrington's interview with Ibrahim Pacha, when the latter bound himself in honour not to send any of his fleet out of the port, but pretended to believe that it had been sanctioned for a Turkish squadron to go to Patras. The British admiral bluntly informed Halhil that, having broken their faith with him, he would not trust them henceforth, and that if they did not put about and return to Navarino he would make them. This message was accompanied by the *Asia* firing a gun and filling her main-topsail; on which the Turkish fleet, by a signal from their admiral, swung their yards afresh and stood back towards the harbour.

This little incident confirmed Sir Edward Codrington in his intention of summarily enforcing the treaty he had been despatched to uphold. Admiral de Rigny, on his part, showed no less a degree of determination to maintain the pledge which his nation had conjointly given to the Greeks. Down to this period, however, the Russians had not appeared upon the scene; but on the 15th of October their squadron, under Count Heiden, joined the French and British fleets off Zante. Sir Edward Codrington, from seniority of rank, was commander-in-chief of the combined fleet. On the 18th of October the three admirals held a conference for the purpose of concerting the measures of effecting the object specified in the Treaty of London—namely, an armistice *de facto* between the Turks and Greeks. They considered that:

> Ibrahim Pacha having violated the engagement he entered into with the admirals on September 25th for a provisional suspension of arms, by causing his fleet to come out and proceed towards another point in the Morea; that since the return of the fleet, owing to meeting Admiral Codrington near Patras, the *pacha's* troops had carried on a warfare more destructive

and exterminating than before, killing women and children, burning habitations, etc., for completing the devastation of the country; and that all endeavours to put a stop to these atrocities by persuasion and conciliation, by representations to the Turkish chiefs, and advice given to Mehemet Ali have been treated as mockeries, though they could have been stopped by a word: Therefore the admirals found that there remained to them only three modes of action :—

1st. The continuing throughout the whole of the winter a blockade—difficult, expensive, and perhaps useless, since a storm might disperse the squadrons, and afford to Ibrahim the facility of conveying his destroying army to different parts of the Morea and the islands;

2nd. The uniting the allied squadrons in Navarin itself, and securing by this permanent presence the inaction of the Ottoman fleets, but which mode alone leads to no termination, since the Porte persists in not changing its system;

3rd. The proceeding to take a position with the squadrons in Navarin, in order to renew to Ibrahim propositions which, entering into the spirit of the Treaty, were evidently to the advantage of the Porte itself.

Having taken these three modes into consideration, the admirals unanimously agreed that the last method was best calculated, without bloodshed, but simply by the imposing presence of the squadrons, to produce the desired end. Sir Edward Codrington had a considerable difficulty to contend with in the jealousy which existed between the Russian and French admirals, and it called for no small exercise of tact on his part to maintain harmony in the combined fleet. The allied force was as follows:—

English: Three line-of-battle ships, four frigates, four brigs, one cutter.

French: Three line-of-battle ships, one double-banked frigate, one frigate, two cutters.

Russian: Four line-of-battle ships, four frigates.

In all twenty-four ships of war. The Ottoman force was as follows:

Three line-of-battle ships, four double-banked frigates, thirteen frigates, thirty corvettes, twenty-eight brigs, six fire brigs, five schooners, forty-one transports.

In all, one hundred and thirty sail of vessels. The Turks had in addition to this imposing force an army of 35,000 Egyptian troops in the Morea, of whom 4,000 were on board the transports.

On the 19th of October Admiral Codrington issued his instructions to his colleagues as to the manner in which the combined fleet was to be disposed on entering the port of Navarino. The order runs:

> It appears, that the Egyptian ships in which the French officers are embarked are those most to the south-east. It is, therefore, my wish that his excellency Rear-Admiral Chevalier de Rigny should place his squadron abreast of them. As the next in succession appears to be a ship of the line with a flag at the main, I propose placing the *Asia* abreast of her, with the *Genoa* and *Albion* next to the *Asia*; and I wish that His Excellency Rear-Admiral Count Heiden will have the goodness to place his squadron next in succession to the British ships of the line.
>
> The Russian frigates in this case can occupy the Turkish ship next in succession to the Russian ships of the line; the English frigates forming alongside such Turkish vessels as may be on the western side of the harbour abreast of the British ships of the line; and the French frigates forming in the same manner, so as to occupy the Turkish frigates, etc. abreast of the French ships of the line. If time permits, before any hostility is committed by the Turkish fleet, the ships are to moor with springs on the ring of each anchor. No gun is to be fired from the combined fleet without a signal being made for that purpose, unless shot be fired from any of the Turkish ships, in which case the ships so firing are to be destroyed immediately.
>
> The corvettes and brigs are, under the direction of Captain Fellows, of the *Dartmouth*, to remove the fire vessels into such a position as will prevent their being able to injure any of the combined fleet. In case of a regular battle ensuing, and creating any of that confusion which must necessarily arise out of it, it is to be observed that, in the words of Lord Nelson, '*no captain can do very wrong who places his ship alongside that of an enemy.*'—Edward Codrington, Vice-Admiral."

★★★★★★

Note:—It was known that a number of French officers were in the enemy's ships, and to these Admiral de Rigny addressed a letter of warning.

★★★★★★

The combined fleet made an attempt to stand into Navarino on the 19th of October, but the wind was too light and the current too strong to enable them to effect their purpose. On the following day, however, at about two o'clock in the afternoon, the allied squadrons passed the batteries at the entrance to the harbour to take up their anchorage. The Turkish ships lay moored in the form of a great crescent, with springs upon their cables, the large ones presenting their broadsides towards the centre, and the smaller craft filling up the intervals between them. The allied fleet was formed in the order of sailing in two columns, the British and French forming the starboard or weather line, and the Russian the lee column.

Sir Edward Codrington, in the *Asia*, led in, closely followed by the *Genoa* and *Albion*, and anchored in succession close alongside a line-of-battle ship flying the flag of the *Capitana Bey*, another ship of the line, and one of the large double-banked frigates, each thus having her proper opponent in the front line of the enemy's fleet. The four ships to windward, which formed a portion of the Egyptian squadron, were allotted to Admiral de Rigny's vessels; and those to leeward, in the bight or hollow of the crescent, were to mark the stations of the whole Russian squadron, the ships of their line covering those of the English line, and being followed by the frigates of their division.

Admiral Codrington had been very express in his instructions that no gun should be fired until some act of open hostility was committed by the Turks, and this order was strictly carried out. The three English ships were permitted to pass the batteries, and proceeded to moor in their respective stations with great celerity. But upon the *Dartmouth* sending a boat to one of the six fire vessels lying near the entrance to the harbour. Lieutenant Fitzroy and several seamen in her were killed by a volley of musketry. This immediately produced a responsive fire of musketry from the *Dartmouth* and likewise from *La Syrène*, the flagship of the French admiral, followed almost at once by the discharge of a broadside gun from one of the Egyptian ships, and in a breath almost the action became general.

The *Asia* was ranged alongside the ship of the *Capitana Bey*, and equally close to that of Moharem Bey, the commander of the Egyptian squadron. As neither of these ships opened upon the British flagship, notwithstanding the action was raging briskly to windward, Sir Edward Codrington withheld his fire. No interchange of hostilities between the vessels took place, therefore, for a considerable while after the *Asia* had returned the first volley of the *Capitana*; and, indeed, it was evidently the intention of the enemy to try and avoid a regular battle, for Moharem sent a message that he would not fire at all. Sir Edward Codrington, equally willing to avert bloodshed, sent the British pilot, Peter Mitchell, who also acted as interpreter, to Moharem with a message to the effect that it was no desire of his to proceed to extreme measures. As the boat went alongside, a discharge of musketry from the Egyptian ship killed Mitchell, and at the same time she opened fire upon the *Asia*. Upon this Admiral Codrington opened his broadside in real earnest, and so furious was this fire from his ship that in a very little while the ship of the *Capitana Bey* and that of Moharem were reduced to total wrecks, and went drifting away to leeward.

The French and Russian squadrons played their part gallantly and well. Sir Edward wrote to the Duke of Clarence:

> The conduct of my brother admirals, Count Heiden and the Chevalier de Rigny, throughout was admirable and highly exemplary.

In the British division the Genoa and Albion took their stations with magnificent precision, and maintained a most destructive fire throughout the contest. The *Glasgow*, *Cambrian*, and *Talbot* followed the example set by the intrepid Frenchman who commanded the *Armide*, which effectually destroyed the leading frigate of the enemy's line and silenced the batteries ashore. Captain Fellows, in the *Dartmouth*, succeeded in frustrating the designs of the fireships stationed near the mouth of the harbour, and preserved the *Syrène* from being burnt. The battle was maintained with unabated fury for above four hours, and owing to the crowded formation of the Ottoman fleet, and the close quarters at which the allied ships engaged them, the havoc and bloodshed were prodigious.

As the Turkish vessels were one after another disabled, their crews set them on fire and deserted them, and the lurid scene was rendered infinitely more terrible and weird by the flaming ships and incessant explosions among the huddled and shattered craft. The resistance of the enemy then began to sensibly slacken. By the time that night had closed down upon the scene, the Turkish fleet was so crippled as to cease any longer to be a menace to the violation of the Treaty.

Sir Edward. Codrington wrote:

> When I found that the boasted Ottoman's word of honour was made a sacrifice to wanton, savage destruction, and that a base

Battle of NAVARINO.

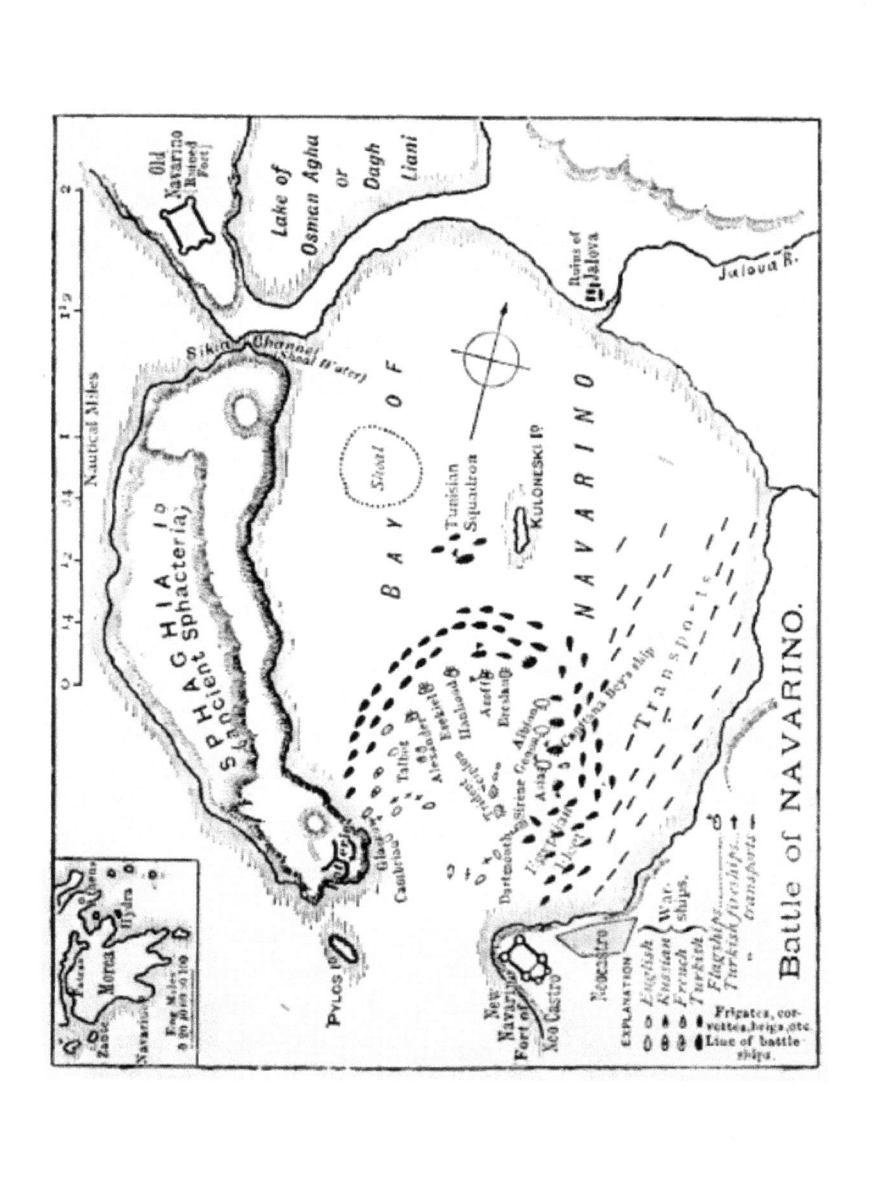

advantage was taken or our reliance upon Ibrahim's good faith, I own I felt a desire to punish the offenders.

And most terribly punished they were. Never did British arms bear part in a more complete and decisive victory. When the dusk of the Oriental evening, obscured into a pall-like gloom by the dense banks of smoke, descended over the terrific spectacle, the enemy's cannonade had grown feeble and scattered, and presently ceased altogether. Their vessels continued to blaze and to explode. Out of the proud fleet which in the noontide of that day had floated serenely upon the blue waters of Navarin harbour sixty ships were totally destroyed, and the remainder driven ashore in a shattered condition, with the exception of the *Leone*, four corvettes, six brigs, and four schooners, which remained afloat after the battle.

The carnage was frightful. According to the statistics furnished by Monsieur Letellier, the French instructor to the Egyptian Navy, to Commander Richards, of the *Pelorus*. the enemy's losses amounted to 3,000 killed and 1,109 wounded. The defeat, indeed, practically amounted to annihilation. At ten o'clock on the night of the battle, Sir Edward Codrington was writing an account of the victory to his wife:

> Well, my dear, the Turks have fought, and fought well too, and we have annihilated their fleet. We have lost poor Smith, Captain Bell, R.M., and many good men.... I am entirely unhurt, but the *Asia* is quite a wreck, having had her full allowance of the work.

The admiral, however, had a succession of marvellous escapes, and, indeed, almost seems to have borne a charmed life throughout the battle. Mr. Lewis, the boatswain of the *Asia,* while speaking to him early in the action, was struck dead. Mr. Smith, the master, was also shot down whilst talking with him. Sir Edward was a tall man, and in his uniform must have made a conspicuous figure upon the *Asia's* deck. Instead of his cocked hat he wore a round hat, which afforded better shade to his eyes; this was pierced in two places by bullet-holes. His coat-sleeve, which chanced to be rather loose, had two bullet-holes in it just above the wrist. A ball struck the watch in his fob and shivered it, but left him uninjured.

Tahir Pacha afterwards admitted to Mr. Kerigan, on board the *Blonde*, that he himself posted a company of riflemen to aim at the British admiral and shoot him if they could.

The combined fleets quitted the harbour of Navarino on the 25th

THE BATTLE WAS MAINTAINED WITH UNABATED FURY FOR ABOVE FOUR HOURS

of October, having tarried awhile, unmolested, to repair damages. They were suffered to depart by the Turks without the firing of a single shot, although it had been quite expected that the batteries would open upon them as they passed the harbour mouth. On the 3rd of November they arrived at Malta. Here they spent some considerable time in refitting. For his services Sir Edward Codrington received the Grand Cross of the Bath; the King of France conferred upon him the Grand Cross of the Military Order of St. Louis; and the Emperor Nicholas of Russia, in an autograph letter, bestowed upon him the rare honour of wearing the second class of the Military Order of St. George.

Navarino was fought without any declaration of war, and the news of hostilities created great surprise in England. Many questions were asked in Parliament as to whether the British commander-in-chief had done wisely to treat the Turks as enemies, and there was much vacillation displayed by the weak government—Lord Goderich's—then in power. In the following June Sir Edward Codrington received a letter of recall from Lord Aberdeen, dated at the Foreign Office, London, May, 1828. It was a most elaborate document of twenty paragraphs, embodying a number of charges of misconception and actual disobedience of his instructions, and concluded:

> His Majesty's Government have found themselves under the necessity of requesting the Lord High Admiral to relieve you in the command of the squadron in the Mediterranean.

He left Malta for England on September 11th, amid the hearty regret of his companions-in-arms, and arrived home in the *Warspite* on the 7th of October, 1828. A revulsion of public feeling had meanwhile taken place during the interval—indignation at his recall and general reprobation of the injustice with which he had been treated. The Duke of Wellington's ministry was now in office. His Grace summoned Sir Edward to an interview, but seems to have behaved in a very cavilling manner. The pride and sense of honour of the fine old naval officer were deeply injured by the treatment he was receiving from a country to whose annals he had just added fresh laurels. His resentment of the injustice done him is well illustrated by the following anecdote:—

About a year after he had been recalled, Sir Edward Codrington was present at a party given by Prince Leopold, when the Duke of Wellington came up to him and said: "I have made arrangements by which I am enabled to offer you a pension of £800 for your life."

The admiral's answer was ready, and immediate: "I am obliged to your Grace, but I do not feel myself in a position to accept it. . . . I cannot receive such a thing myself while my poor fellows who fought under me at Navarin have had no head-money, and have not even been repaid for their clothes which were destroyed in the battle."

The duke: remonstrated, said there was no precedent for head-money, and insisted that, as the pension was bestowed by the king. Sir Edward could not refuse it. But refuse it he did, stoutly and resolutely.

Shortly afterwards one of the duke's political friends inquired: "What are you going to do with Codrington?"

"Do with him!" answered the duke, "what are you to do with a man who won't take a pension?"

But time rights most things; and Sir Edward Codrington lived to see full honour accorded to him. and those who had fought under him at the Battle of Navarino.

ALSO FROM LEONAUR
AVAILABLE IN SOFTCOVER OR HARDCOVER WITH DUST JACKET

THE FALL OF THE MOGHUL EMPIRE OF HINDUSTAN by H. G. Keene—By the beginning of the nineteenth century, as British and Indian armies under Lake and Wellesley dominated the scene, a little over half a century of conflict brought the Moghul Empire to its knees.

LADY SALE'S AFGHANISTAN by Florentia Sale—An Indomitable Victorian Lady's Account of the Retreat from Kabul During the First Afghan War.

THE CAMPAIGN OF MAGENTA AND SOLFERINO 1859 by Harold Carmichael Wylly—The Decisive Conflict for the Unification of Italy.

FRENCH'S CAVALRY CAMPAIGN by J. G. Maydon—A Special Correspondent's View of British Army Mounted Troops During the Boer War.

CAVALRY AT WATERLOO by Sir Evelyn Wood—British Mounted Troops During the Campaign of 1815.

THE SUBALTERN by George Robert Gleig—The Experiences of an Officer of the 85th Light Infantry During the Peninsular War.

NAPOLEON AT BAY, 1814 by F. Loraine Petre—The Campaigns to the Fall of the First Empire.

NAPOLEON AND THE CAMPAIGN OF 1806 by Colonel Vachée—The Napoleonic Method of Organisation and Command to the Battles of Jena & Auerstädt.

THE COMPLETE ADVENTURES IN THE CONNAUGHT RANGERS by William Grattan—The 88th Regiment during the Napoleonic Wars by a Serving Officer.

BUGLER AND OFFICER OF THE RIFLES by William Green & Harry Smith—With the 95th (Rifles) during the Peninsular & Waterloo Campaigns of the Napoleonic Wars.

NAPOLEONIC WAR STORIES by Sir Arthur Quiller-Couch—Tales of soldiers, spies, battles & sieges from the Peninsular & Waterloo campaingns.

CAPTAIN OF THE 95TH (RIFLES) by Jonathan Leach—An officer of Wellington's sharpshooters during the Peninsular, South of France and Waterloo campaigns of the Napoleonic wars.

RIFLEMAN COSTELLO by Edward Costello—The adventures of a soldier of the 95th (Rifles) in the Peninsular & Waterloo Campaigns of the Napoleonic wars.

AVAILABLE ONLINE AT **www.leonaur.com**
AND FROM ALL GOOD BOOK STORES

ALSO FROM LEONAUR
AVAILABLE IN SOFTCOVER OR HARDCOVER WITH DUST JACKET

ZULU: 1879 by *D.C.F. Moodie & the Leonaur Editors*—The Anglo-Zulu War of 1879 from contemporary sources: First Hand Accounts, Interviews, Dispatches, Official Documents & Newspaper Reports.

THE RED DRAGOON by *W.J. Adams*—With the 7th Dragoon Guards in the Cape of Good Hope against the Boers & the Kaffir tribes during the 'war of the axe' 1843-48'.

THE RECOLLECTIONS OF SKINNER OF SKINNER'S HORSE by *James Skinner*—James Skinner and his 'Yellow Boys' Irregular cavalry in the wars of India between the British, Mahratta, Rajput, Mogul, Sikh & Pindarree Forces.

A CAVALRY OFFICER DURING THE SEPOY REVOLT by *A. R. D. Mackenzie*—Experiences with the 3rd Bengal Light Cavalry, the Guides and Sikh Irregular Cavalry from the outbreak to Delhi and Lucknow.

A NORFOLK SOLDIER IN THE FIRST SIKH WAR by *J W Baldwin*—Experiences of a private of H.M. 9th Regiment of Foot in the battles for the Punjab, India 1845-6.

TOMMY ATKINS' WAR STORIES: 14 FIRST HAND ACCOUNTS—Fourteen first hand accounts from the ranks of the British Army during Queen Victoria's Empire.

THE WATERLOO LETTERS by *H. T. Siborne*—Accounts of the Battle by British Officers for its Foremost Historian.

NEY: GENERAL OF CAVALRY VOLUME 1—1769-1799 by *Antoine Bulos*—The Early Career of a Marshal of the First Empire.

NEY: MARSHAL OF FRANCE VOLUME 2—1799-1805 by *Antoine Bulos*—The Early Career of a Marshal of the First Empire.

AIDE-DE-CAMP TO NAPOLEON by *Philippe-Paul de Ségur*—For anyone interested in the Napoleonic Wars this book, written by one who was intimate with the strategies and machinations of the Emperor, will be essential reading.

TWILIGHT OF EMPIRE by *Sir Thomas Ussher & Sir George Cockburn*—Two accounts of Napoleon's Journeys in Exile to Elba and St. Helena: Narrative of Events by Sir Thomas Ussher & Napoleon's Last Voyage: Extract of a diary by Sir George Cockburn.

PRIVATE WHEELER by *William Wheeler*—The letters of a soldier of the 51st Light Infantry during the Peninsular War & at Waterloo.

AVAILABLE ONLINE AT **www.leonaur.com**
AND FROM ALL GOOD BOOK STORES